CW00537549

ROYAL HISTORICAL SOCIETY

STUDIES IN HISTORY 63

GUNPOWDER, GOVERNMENT AND WAR
IN THE MID-EIGHTEENTH CENTURY

GUNPOWDER, GOVERNMENT AND WAR IN THE MID-EIGHTEENTH CENTURY

Jenny West

THE ROYAL HISTORICAL SOCIETY
THE BOYDELL PRESS

First published 1991

A Royal Historical Society publication
Published by The Boydell Press
an imprint of Boydell & Brewer Ltd
PO Box 9, Woodbridge, Suffolk IP12 3DF, UK
and of Boydell & Brewer Inc.
PO Box 41026, Rochester, NY 14604, USA

ISBN 0 86193 221 8

ISSN 0269-2244

British Library Cataloguing-in-Publication Data
West, Jenny
Gunpowder, government and war in the
mid-eighteenth century. – (Royal Historical
Society studies in history)
I. Title   II. Series
623.409
ISBN 0–86193–221–8

Library of Congress Cataloging-in-Publication Data
West, Jenny.
Gunpowder, government, and war in the mid-eighteenth century /
Jenny West.
p.   cm. – (Royal Historical Society studies in history,
ISSN 0269-2244 ; no. 63)
Includes bibliographical references and index.
ISBN 0–86193–221–8 (hardback : alk. paper)
1. Great Britain – Armed Forces – Ordnance and ordnance stores –
History – 18th century.   2. Gunpowder industry – Great Britain –
History – 18th century.   3. Great Britain.   Board of Ordnance –
History – 18th century.   4. Seven Years War, 1756–1763 –
Equipment and supplies.   I. Title.   II. Series.
UF555.G7W47   1991
355.8'2526'094109033–dc20   91–21124

Printed in Great Britain by
Woolnough Bookbinding Ltd, Irthlingborough, Northants

TO MY FAMILY

Contents

The Society records its gratitude to the following whose generosity made possible the initiation of this series: The British Academy; The Pilgrim Trust; The Twenty-Seven Foundation; The United States Embassy's Bicentennial funds; The Wolfson Trust; several private donors.

Publication of this volume was aided by a further grant from the Isobel Thornley Bequest.

Tables

Abbreviations

BL	British Library
CCA	Canterbury Cathedral Archives
CSPD	Calendar of State Papers Domestic
ERO	Essex Record Office
GL	Guildhall Library
GLRO	Greater London Record Office
GMR	Guildford Muniment Room
IHR	Institute of Historical Research
KAO	Kent Archives Office
LUL	Library of the University of London
PRO	Public Record Office
SH	Syon House
SRO	Surrey Record Office
VCH	Victoria County History

Where the '&' connects names of gunpowder makers this indicates a partnership between the two.

Preface

This book has its origins in a long standing interest in watermills and their varied industries, and specifically the gunpowder mills of Surrey's Hogsmill River. From this it was apparent that little recognition had been given to the strong links between powder mills, government, war, and London trade. I was fortunate to have the opportunity to undertake research on the subject for a Ph.D thesis at the Institute of Historical Research of London University, supported by an award from the Social Science Research Council (now the ESRC).

Watermills in south east England produced gunpowder for the government department of the Ordnance Office for the needs of the armed forces, for such trade as coal and metalliferous mining, the North American fur, and African slave trades, and for hunting. For no period has there been a detailed study of supply to the government and the competition from private trade.

There are many advantages to a study concentrating on the mid-eighteenth century. It was a period of sharp contrasts between war and peace; between high demand for gunpowder and unemployment; and between the demands of the armed forces and of merchants. There was a central period of war unprecedented in its severity, geographical extent, and consequent demand for ordnance stores. The powder makers experienced the greatest pressure on their abilities to date, yet were still dependent on a level of knowledge little changed for centuries. Considerable organisational, scientific, and technological discoveries and changes were at least a quarter of a century away. Finally, and of major importance, extant documentary sources concerning the trade, supply, and distribution of gunpowder, central government, and particularly the Ordnance Office and Privy Council, are richer and more complete than for any other period.

Many people have helped in the preparation of this book. In particular, I should like to thank Professor F.M.L.Thompson, Director of the Institute of Historical Research, for supervision of the doctoral research and continued interest; Dr John Chartres and Dr Peter Earle, who examined the thesis, for their constructive comments and particularly those resulting in the new, additional first chapter; Dr Earle for commenting on certain chapters of the revised manuscript; Dr Ian Roy, for reading a substantial part of the manuscript in connection with the Ordnance Office and the armed forces, and drawing my attention to two important documentary sources; and Dr Peter Edwards, whose infectious enthusiasm for research was significant in the original idea. I am indebted to a number of people who kindly read and commented on certain other parts of the manuscript: Glenys and Alan Crocker, Keith Fairclough, Tony Hayter, Kenneth Major, and Arthur Percival; and also to Keith Fairclough and Stephen Porter for their valued discussion throughout. On historical sources, particular acknowledgement is due to His Grace the Duke of Northumberland for permitting study of papers at Syon House, an important source in the study of individual mills; to the staff of the Institute of Historical Research, and those of the Public Record Office, particularly at Kew where the major part of my research was undertaken. In addition, I would like to acknowledge the staff of the British Library, Goldsmith's Library of the University of London Library, the Greater London Record Office, Guildford Muniment Room, Guildhall Library, and the County Record Offices of Essex, Kent, and Surrey. I am also greatly indebted to Christine Linehan, Executive Editor of the Royal Historical Society Studies in History, for invaluable professional guidance. Finally, I thank my family for unending support, and especially my husband Richard for his readiness to discuss the subject at any hour and for reading the completed manuscript.

Jenny West   1991

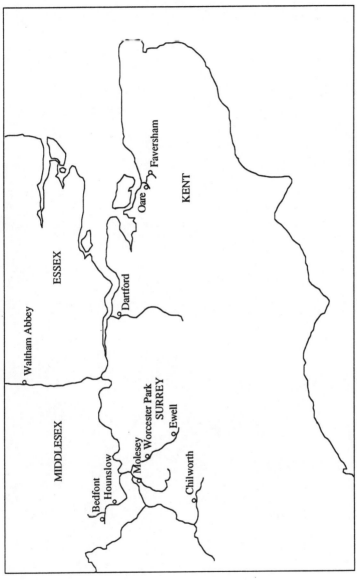

Sites of the Gunpowder Mills Supplying the Ordnance Office in the Mid-Eighteenth Century

Introduction

'Though a simple mixture, no substance has ever probably given rise to so extensive a literature or to so much death and destruction.'[1]

Hogg's statement is simple yet provocative. As a chemical substance gunpowder has been much studied, and as a material of war its destructive powers are indisputable; but to consider the subject exhausted would be to ignore the opportunity of studying certain important and neglected aspects of British history. Few, if any, industries have been more important to the government in its supply of the armed forces and few more important to the nation as a whole for defence, and for overseas trade. Watermills in England, continually in use from the Roman period for corn milling, and eventually for such additional industries as cotton, paper, timber, iron, wool cloth, dyeing, and seed crushing, were also employed from the mid-sixteenth century for crushing and mixing the raw materials which constituted gunpowder. This latter role is less well known.

From the mid-sixteenth century, when the first gunpowder mill was recorded in England, to the second half of the eighteenth century the mills which supplied the Crown for the Army and Navy were usually located in one specific area of England, the South East. This had the advantage of proximity to London. Unlike most other industries this had to take place well away from habitation due to the continual risk of explosion and fire. Initially, the monopoly of supply to the Crown was held by gunpowder makers in Surrey but after the monopoly ceased in 1641 the area of supply gradually extended into Kent, Middlesex, and Essex.[2] There was one major exception to the predominance of the South East; this occurred during the Civil War when Royalist forces were compelled to rely on mills in Oxford on the Rivers Isis and Cherwell, those in certain areas of Gloucestershire and Worcestershire, and those of Bristol after that city's capture.[3] There is no record of contracts between the government and the comparatively few mid-eighteenth century powder mills located elsewhere in such areas as

[1] O. F. G. Hogg, *Artillery: its origin, heyday and decline* (1970), p. 122.
[2] Giuseppi cites a mill at Rotherhithe in 1555: M. S. Giuseppi, 'Industries: Gunpowder', *Victoria County History of Surrey* (1905), ii, p. 310.
[3] Ian Roy (ed.), 'The Royalist Ordnance Papers 1642–1646', *Oxfordshire Record Society*, 43 (1964), 29, 37.

Battle, Woolley, and Thelwall, in the counties of Sussex, Somerset, and Cheshire respectively.

It is clear that gunpowder brought dramatic increase in the range and complexity of warfare but whether in so doing it caused change in certain aspects of state structure is debatable. In his discussion of technological development between 1500 and 1750 Hall states that this greater complexity of warfare stimulated both growth in the power of the state, and enforcement of stern discipline and training within its armed forces.[4] Further, while asserting that the consolidation of power under bureaucratic monarchies occurred with the help of many other factors, Batchelder and Freudenberger do, nevertheless, consider that the introduction of gunpowder was a 'significant factor in shifting military and political power from the nobility to the crown in European states'.[5] In contrast is Hale's view of the influence of gunpowder on civilisation. He disputes the notion that 'gunpowder blasted feudalism at the behest of the centralised state', and regards such claims as attractive but 'the complex development of the feudal into the centralized state began before cannon became effective and can be explained without reference to firearms'.[6]

Although prior to the reign of Henry VIII there had been wide use of cannon there had not been a corresponding increase in firearms because of the unshakeable faith of the English in their 'justly famous long-bow'.[7] Powder requirements had therefore been limited and certainly not equal to those on the Continent. Until then such requirements were obtained from domestic workshops but the quantities were insignificant and the plant for producing them primitive.[8] This was supplemented by powder supplies from the Continent. Most of the saltpetre required for domestic manufacture had also been purchased on the Continent after importation from India and Persia although, for a limited period in 1577, some was purchased by England direct from Morocco.[9] However, under Henry and subsequently Elizabeth there was a determination to gain increased independence in such supplies. Assisted by information from the Continent, this was achieved by the application of water power to gunpowder manufacture and by the domestic production of saltpetre, the main constituent. The first

[4] A. R. Hall, 'Military Technology', in Charles Singer, E. J. Holmyard, A. R. Hall, Trevor I. Williams (eds.), A History of Technology (Oxford 1957), iii, 348.
[5] Ronald W. Batchelder and Herman Freudenberger, 'On the Rational Origins of the Modern Centralised State', Explorations in Economic History, 20 (1983), 1.
[6] J. R. Hale, Renaissance War Studies (1983), pp. 389–90.
[7] E. W. Bovill, 'Queen Elizabeth's Gunpowder', Mariners' Mirror, 33 (1947), 182.
[8] J. U. Nef, 'The Progress of Technology and the Growth of Large Scale Industry in Great Britain 1540–1640', Economic History Review, 1st series 5 (1934), 6.
[9] Bovill, 'Queen Elizabeth's Gunpowder', 181.

recorded watermill for the purpose in England was constructed at Rotherhithe in Surrey in 1555, with the first recorded contracts for supplying the Crown evident a few years later; the manufacture of saltpetre by simulating the natural conditions for its formation commenced in about 1560.[10] The number of gunpowder mills, all privately owned, gradually increased in number although from the early seventeenth century they no longer depended entirely on the unsatisfactory domestic production of saltpetre; by now there was a regular supply of natural petre direct from India via the East India Company.

The need for gunpowder, arms and ordnance increased further in the century to follow. Roy considers that although the requirements of seventeenth century armies were still relatively unsophisticated gunpowder had, by the Civil War, forced the archer's retirement. Large, destructive cannon were present at sieges, and a train of field artillery of varying sizes accompanied most marching armies. 'Each nation-state of Europe hoped to become self-sufficient in these essentials, and developed, so far as it was able, its own armaments and munitions industries: the first based largely on the supply of iron, the second on that of gunpowder. Caroline England was no exception.'[11]

Hale however considers that firearms had little effect on the fortunes of campaigns as a whole or on the balance of political power, and that: 'Gunpowder, in short, revolutionised the conduct but not the outcome of wars.' Once really effective firearms were owned by all powers neither side had a significant advantage.[12] Nevertheless, the sigificance of gunpowder to one side or the other should not be underestimated. Once dependent for this revolutionised conduct of war on a substance which could not be stored indefinitely and therefore stockpiled, it was only that side which had the ability to ensure a continued and plentiful supply of adequate standard in the field for its arms and artillery which had the true advantage. If that should fail the weaponry, however sophisticated it had become, was absolutely powerless.

The literature on gunpowder, its properties, use and influence, is considerable. Among studies which include the early history of incendiary substances and origin of gunpowder are those of Needham, Partington, and Hogg.[13] Between 1628 and 1742 the properties, preparation, and testing of gunpowder were described by such writers on artillery as Norton, Venn, and Robins, and later more general histories

---

10 Giuseppi, VCH Surrey, pp. 307, 310.
11 Roy, 'Royalist Ordnance Papers', 7.
12 Hale, Renaissance War Studies, p. 391.
13 Hogg, Artillery; Joseph Needham, 'The Guns of Khaifeng-fu', Times Literary Supplement (11 January 1980), 39–42; J. R. Partington, A History of Greek Fire and Gunpowder (Cambridge 1960).

on the subject were provided by Hart, Hime, and Brayley Hodgetts.[14] Papers read to the Royal Society as part of the surge of scientific interest in the properties and action of fired gunpowder from 1775 were those of Hutton, Thompson, and Ingenhousz.[15] Published at about the same time were the statements on the improved organisation in the industry by Congreve, and by Coleman.[16] Reference to supply is also made in the main works on the administration of the Ordnance Office; these are by Ashley on the Tudor period, Roy on the Royalist and Lewis on the Parliamentarian supplies in the Civil War, Tomlinson on the later Stuart period, and Hogg on the Office's entire period. Of these, Roy and Tomlinson provide the most detailed information on gunpowder and gunpowder makers.[17] Pertaining to one county in particular is Giuseppi's detailed study of gunpowder in Surrey, the county which initially dominated national supply.[18] The works of Giuseppi, Roy, and Tomlinson form essential background to any study of gunpowder supply to the government.

Not only has there been no detailed study for any period of the manufacture and supply of gunpowder for the Ordnance Office or of the demand for purposes of private trade, but no study either of its distribution for the needs of the armed forces, or of the sharp variations in demand between peace and war. Such variations were more evident than for other munitions due to the substance's uncertain storage life.

---

[14] Robert Norton, *The Gunner, showing the whole Practise of Artillerie* (1628); Thomas Venn, *Military and Maritime Discipline* (1672); Benjamin Robins, *New Principles of Gunnery* (1742; new (edn) with notes by Charles Hutton 1805); William Henry Hart, *A Short Account of the Early Manufacture of Gunpowder in England* (1855); Henry W. L. Hime, *Gunpowder and Ammunition* (1904); E. A. Brayley Hodgetts (ed.), *The Rise and Progress of the British Explosives Industry* (1909).

[15] Charles Hutton, 'The Force of Fired Gunpowder and the initial Velocities of Cannon Balls', *Philosophical Transactions of the Royal Society*, 68 (1778), 50–85; Benjamin Thompson, 'New Experiments on gunpowder' *Philosophical Transactions of the Royal Society*, 71 (1781), 229–328; John Ingenhousz, 'Account of a new kind of inflammable air or gas a new theory on gunpowder', *Philosophical Transactions of the Royal Society*, 69 (1779), 376–418.

[16] William Congreve, *A Statement of facts relating to the savings which have arisen from manufacturing gunpowder at the Royal Powder Mills and of Improvements made in its strength and durability since 1783* (1811); R. Coleman, 'The Manufacture and constituent Parts of Gunpowder', *Philosophical Magazine*, 9 (1801), 355–65.

[17] R. Ashley, 'The organisation and administration of the Tudor office of ordnance' (Unpublished B. Litt. thesis, University of Oxford 1973); D. E. Lewis, 'The Office of Ordnance and the parliamentarian land forces 1642–8' (Unpublished Ph.D. thesis, Loughborough University of Technology 1976); Roy, 'Royalist Ordnance Papers'; H. C. Tomlinson, *Guns and Government* (1979); O. F. G. Hogg, *The Royal Arsenal* (2 vols., Oxford 1963).

[18] Tomlinson, *Guns and Government*; Giuseppi, *VCH Surrey*.

In attempting to fill this historical gap the period 1740–70 was chosen. There are three main reasons for this. Firstly, it covers greatly contrasting periods of war and peace – the central one of which was the Seven Years War, from 1756 to 1763 undoubtedly the most severe to date and therefore more demanding of men and armaments of any then known. Secondly, it demonstrates unprecedented problems for, and responses from, the Ordnance Office. These concerned not only higher demand than ever before, combined with failure of the powder makers to respond, but also implementation for the first time of legislation to limit private trade, and the purchase of the first powder mills ever in this country to be administered by the State. Thirdly, extant central government sources pertaining to the subject are richer than for any period prior to the nineteenth century. There is no evidence that such sources have been studied for this purpose previously. For the period 1754–63 in particular, records of Ordnance Office, Admiralty, Privy Council, Treasury, and Chancery are all complete pertaining to such subjects as government contracts, quantities and quality of powder from each of the mills, distribution to the armed forces in many parts of the world, the sale of Faversham mills, and the private export trade. Although extant business records of individual powder makers are lacking, central government records and the many documentary sources pertaining specifically to both men and mills provide much information on manufacture in south east England at this time.

The book is divided into four main sections. The first is concerned with the origins and development of both gunpowder and the Ordnance Office, the contrast in the nature of demand for powder between the War of the Austrian Succession and the period of peace of 1749–54 and, most important, supply during the Seven Years War and the year of escalating conflict preceding it. The period of peace demonstrates severe problems for the gunpowder makers. They had no government employment, due to the inability of the Ordnance Office to agree contracts prematurely for a substance which could not be stored indefinitely. They were therefore entirely dependent on private trade. This was an industry subject not only to more severe fluctuations in demand and less adaptability to other uses than most, but to risk of fire and explosion in buildings which were difficult or impossible to insure.[19] The sudden increase in international conflict in 1755 and the extensive war which followed brought an unprecedented demand for ordnance stores, particularly gunpowder. However war brought not only long awaited government contracts but an equal rise in demand

[19] WO 47/46 p. 8, 1 July 1755; 'Memorial of the Gunpowder Merchants to the Lords of the Treasury', November 1818, *House of Commons Sessional Papers*, 17 (1819), p. 2.

from private trade. The implications and problems for both makers and Ordnance Office are examined in detail. Problems of supply increased as war progressed. The Ordnance Office was largely unsuccessful in its several attempts to increase stock; these included the introduction of legislation to limit trade and the purchase of Faversham mills.

The second section examines the distribution of gunpowder to military and naval bases at home and overseas and all shipments of ordnance, powder, and other stores to the Army in the field; this concerned North America from 1755 and Germany from the date of the first dispatch of troops in 1758. Particular emphasis is placed on the dispatch of artillery trains to North America, for in terms of quantity and of geography this was on a scale never before experienced. Included are the important administrative links between the various departments of government and the immense problems concerning distance from North America with transportation, communication, and estimation of ordnance requirements for combat in unfamiliar terrain.

The third section studies the significant problem of the private trade in gunpowder, the main competitor to the government. Attention is given to the prohibitive legislation, its lack of effect because of the importance of such trade to the nation, and links between trade, government, and influential bodies and individuals in the City of London. Presented for the first time are details of all private licence applications during the Seven Years War for coastal and overseas shipment of powder. Due to this rich source, not recorded by the Privy Council for any previous war, it is possible to trace the nature of the private trade in gunpowder in more detail for this period than for any other before it.

Section Four concerns Faversham mills and also mid-eighteenth century problems of gunpowder manufacture in general. Among the nine privately owned mills supplying the government until 1759 those at Faversham were then purchased by the Crown with the aim of increasing government stock and lessening dependence on other mills. The purchase itself was marked by confusion and error because of the complexity of the land holding and lack of efficiency in all the government departments involved. Ordnance administration at the mills at this time produced no more successful results than elsewhere, as shown by comparisons between supply from this and other mills, and between the influence of private and crown ownership. Extant administrative records of Faversham under government control highlight the many difficulties of the period. Finally, detail of mid-eighteenth century problems in manufacture have been identified not only from contemporary comment but also from evidence from the latter part of the century concerning scientific and technological advances and greatly improved industrial organisation.

PART ONE
THE ORDNANCE OFFICE AND GUNPOWDER SUPPLY

1

Origins and Development

Gunpowder is a combination of saltpetre, charcoal, and sulphur, most commonly in the proportions of seventy-five, fifteen, and ten per cent respectively. Saltpetre (potassium nitrate) was mainly imported from India and sulphur mainly from Italy. Wood for charcoal was felled in the woodlands of south east England. Gunpowder burns brightly on ignition, is explosive if fired in a suitable container, acts as a propellant for shot in an appropriate weapon, and was the only explosive in use for cannon and firearms in general until the high explosives of the mid-nineteenth century. Until the fifteenth century the powder in use was serpentine, a loose dusty mixture of the three constituents which could easily separate during transportation. On ignition this mixture was characterised by slow irregular combustion. The introduction of the procedure of corning or graining of the powder by which the mixture was formed into separate grains made the product more stable and handling easier, and provided more rapid combustion when fired. Until the mid-sixteenth century the mixing of the ingredients in England was usually by hand with pestle and mortar. Thereafter, the main power source was animal or water, or a combination of the two. In its simplicity and the ease with which it could be undertaken in secrecy milling by hand for small quantities would have continued alongside the more effective power sources. Until the early eighteenth century gunpowder was produced mainly by stamp mills but by the Seven Years War most mills supplying the Ordnance Office mixed and ground their raw materials by large millstones, each mill unit having a pair of heavy edge runner stones revolving on a horizontal bedstone.

The main use for gunpowder was for ordnance purposes for military and naval forces. Purchase and distribution to the armed forces in Britain were administered by the government department of the Ordnance Office until 1855 when the duties of this body were absorbed by the War Office.

Origins of gunpowder

Information on the exact date and location of the origin of gunpowder is inconclusive. Its invention has been dated variously between 1240 and 1320 and ascribed in turn to Chinese, Arabs, and Europeans. The subject is made more complex by variation in the terminology employed between the three stages in evolution: the earlier purely incendiary substances, such as Greek Fire of distilled petroleum or naphtha; the non-explosive, proto-gunpowder of saltpetre, sulphur, and a carbon source with only incendiary and deflagatory properties and, finally, true gunpowder with its explosive and propellant properties. Although the explosive stage was made possible by a higher nitrate content, achieved by about 1230 and employed in Chinese military campaigns, the substance did not reach the vital propellant phase until the period between approximately 1280 and 1320. Needham is among those who strongly favour China as the place of origin. Certainly it was there that the earlier substances were widely employed, but the wide use of the term 'gunpowder' should be viewed with care. Needham provides evidence of the use of true gunpowder in Chinese warfare by the late thirteenth century, made possible by the appearance of metal cannon of the period which enabled the full propellant force of this explosive to launch a projectile. On the other hand detailed research by such authors as Partington and Hogg on incendiary and explosive substances, and on artillery respectively, demonstrate more caution regarding the exact place of origin. Partington states that although it is probable that gunpowder was discovered in China, it is by no means definite, and Hogg considers that 'the precise origin remains obscure'.[1] It is probable that most early incendiary experimentation occurred in China but, aided by previous diffusion of knowledge, the discovery of a formula for true gunpowder in the thirteenth or early fourteenth century took place in more than one place at approximately the same time, or the necessary information spread very rapidly from one place to another.

[1] Needham, 'Guns of Khaifeng-fu', 39–41; Partington, *Greek Fire*, pp. 32, 78, 287–8; Hogg, *Artillery*, pp. 122–4; O. F. G. Hogg, *English Artillery, 1326–1716* (1963), 41–3.

8

Origins of the Ordnance Office and supply

From the fourteenth century the history of gunpowder was closely linked with that of artillery, the Great and Privy Wardrobes, and eventually the Ordnance Office which evolved from these. Gunpowder was stored at the Tower of London by 1333, was in use by the Navy by 1340, and by military forces approximately five years later.[2] The evolution of an ordnance system was gradual. Although warlike stores initially formed part of the Royal Wardrobe these had, by the mid-thirteenth century, become part of the Great Wardrobe which developed from it. This was, in turn, a distinct and financially independent institution by 1324 when it purchased and stored fighting supplies, by now housed separately from other possessions. A separate arsenal branch came to be located in the Tower, known as the Privy Wardrobe in the Tower, a wardrobe of arms financially independent of the Great Wardrobe by 1399. Munitions then ceased to be the direct responsibility of the monarch. It was from the Privy Wardrobe that the Ordnance Office was eventually born. By the beginning of the Tudor period the 'embryo of the future Ordnance Office had emerged from the depths of the King's Household'.[3] With Henry VIII's desire for increased national defence came expansion in ordnance administration and in 1543 the establishment of a definite ordnance staff. Although the Tower continued to be the main storehouse for most ordnance purposes during the Stuart period and stayed so for small arms, Woolwich later became the main centre for ordnance, and Greenwich the centre for proof and storage of powder. The magazine was moved to Purfleet in Essex after the Seven Years War, the last powder being received at Greenwich in 1768.[4]

Until 1716 the main function of the Ordnance Office was to provide ships of the Royal Navy with cannon, small arms, gunpowder, and ammunition, and with gunners to act as gun crews. It also provided the Army with ordnance stores and gunners for castles though with less emphasis than on the Navy.[5] From the early eighteenth century the Office was divided into two branches. The civil branch was concerned with supply, storage, maintenance, and issue of ordnance stores; it provided the armed forces with arms and ammunition while its land service responsibility was extended to include coastal defence and the establishment and maintenance of barracks and fortifications in Britain and her colonies. The military branch was concerned with the

2   Ashley, 'The Tudor office', p. 22; Partington, *Greek Fire*, pp. 108–9.
3   Tomlinson, *Guns and Government*, p. 3; Hogg, *Royal Arsenal*, i, pp. 10–11, 31.
4   WO 47/70, p. 167, 29 March 1768.
5   Hogg, *Artillery*, p. 161.

affairs of the Artillery and the Engineers. In 1755 the civil branch comprised the master general of the Ordnance and the five principal officers who formed the Board; these were the lieutenant general, the surveyor general, the clerk of the Ordnance, storekeeper, and clerk of deliveries. The master general was commander in chief of the Ordnance troops, a post sometimes combined with that of commander in chief of the Army as a whole, as with Ligonier during the Seven Years War. He was usually a prominent member of the Army, attended meetings of the Privy Council and acted as principal military adviser to the Crown. Responsibility for the daily management of the Office was that of his deputy, the lieutenant general, who was also usually of military importance and concerned particularly with the affairs of the Artillery. The surveyor general's duties included the ordering, inspection, and proof of all stores and a responsibility for the Engineers. There was also a treasurer, and a secretary to the master general. Each officer had his own clerks, numbering forty in all. Also on the staff were the storekeepers and their clerks at the eight outports and ten garrisons. At the Tower were fifteen members of staff including the storekeeper of saltpetre and two proofmasters in charge of proof of powder at Greenwich magazine.[6] Most of the staff were connected with the reception, storage, and distribution of gunpowder.

Initially, gunpowder was the responsibility of a craftsman at the Tower with a gunner's patent for making cannon and for manning them in action. In 1515 an additional independent maker was employed outside the Tower confines. By 1545 the number had increased to seven. The contribution of official makers at this time would not have been large for the main national stock was held in Antwerp and imported as required.[7] There were certain changes in manufacture in England in the mid-sixteenth century. These resulted from the need for increased national supply for the more effective weapons of the period and also from the need for greater national security and therefore less dependence on imported gunpowder and saltpetre. The changes, which were made possible by technical information originating on the Continent, concerned the application of water power to specialised manufacturing machinery, and of methods for the domestic production of saltpetre. Initially, powder makers were charged with producing their own saltpetre but saltpetre men were employed subsequently by commissioners of saltpetre and gunpowder acting on the Ordnance Office's behalf. In spite of many linked social and administrative problems

---

[6] WO 54/113 March quarter 1755; PRO 705. 1. 2 Defence and Supply: Board of Ordnance; the role of proofmasters is discussed by A. H. Mockridge, 'The proving of ordnance and propellants', *Journal of Royal Artillery*, 67 (1950), 82–8.
[7] Ashley, 'Tudor office', 66.

saltpetre was produced artificially between the mid-sixteenth, and mid-seventeenth centuries by mixing vegetable and animal refuse containing nitrogen with lime, earth and ashes. However, stock was inadequate and of poor quality. It was gradually replaced by direct supplies of natural saltpetre from India imported by the East India Company from the 1620s.[8] Apart from a short interval during this same period there is no indication that England was ever entirely independent in gunpowder supply.

Until 1620 contracts for the supply of gunpowder were arranged directly with the Crown but from then until 1641 these were supervised by the Lords of the Admiralty as commissioners on the Crown's behalf.[9] The monopoly of supply was held by various Surrey powder makers until the Civil War. There was simultaneous illicit production, including that by certain mills such as Bristol which later supplied the Royalist forces in the War. The Crown attempted to impose stricter measures against illicit powder making during the pre-war monopoly of Chilworth mills in Surrey but the increased demand for powder, the dislike of restrictive practice, and the growth of political opposition finally undermined royal control over supply; the monopoly was ended in 1641. For a short period there was freedom of supply when the Ordnance Office was served by mills in other areas such as those of Sewardstone on the River Lea in Essex.[10] This freedom was then curtailed by the Civil War. Initially, the Ordnance Office, the South, and East, and therefore Chilworth mills and its administration, and most existing powder stock came under the control of Parliament, although senior members of the Ordnance Office later defected to the King. The King ordered the destruction of Chilworth mills but they seem to have continued to supply Parliament, together with certain Essex mills.[11] The allegiance of the powder makers was governed more by geography than politics and with the Royalist Ordnance Office based in Oxford and separated from the pre-war contractors alternative powder mills were required. Newly built or adapted, these were centred mainly in

[8] Examples concerning saltpetre include *Calendar of State Papers Domestic 1623–1625*, pp. 25, 157, 419, K. N. Chaudhuri, *The Trading World of Asia and the English East India Company, 1660–1760* (Cambridge 1978), pp. 336–8.
[9] Giuseppi, *VCH Surrey*, pp. 314–15; *CSPD 1634–5*, pp. 511, 561, February, March 1634.
[10] Roy, 'Royalist Ordnance Papers', 10; Keith Fairclough, 'Early gunpowder production at Waltham', *Essex Journal*, 20 (1985) 11–12.
[11] Ian Roy, 'Royalist Ordnance Papers 1642–1646', *Oxfordshire Record Society*, 49 (1975), 506; Keith Fairclough, 'Temple Mills as an industrial site in the seventeenth century', and 'Mills and ferries along the Lower Lea', *Essex Archaeology and History*, forthcoming; for further history of Chilworth mills see Giuseppi; also Glenys Crocker, *Chilworth Gunpowder* (Guildford 1984)

Oxford with others in Worcestershire and Gloucestershire and, after its capture in 1643, in Bristol. Royalist Ordnance commissioners took over supervision of these mills from individual powder makers in 1644. Apart from some additional stock from the Continent these places were the main sources of Royalist supply until the end of the war.[12] During the Commonwealth period supply was from six mills in the South East and apart from the first few years after the Restoration and again between 1675 and 1682, when the monopoly system was reinstated, contracts were between the Ordnance Office and a number of mills. The number of makers under contract to the Office varied between sixteen in 1667, ten in 1705, eight in 1745, and ten in the Seven Years War, with mills situated not only in Surrey but also in Kent, Essex, and Middlesex.[13]

Gunpowder mills and makers

Apart from the Civil War period all watermills supplying gunpowder to the Crown between the sixteenth and eighteenth centuries were located in south east England. Until crown purchase of Faversham mills in 1759, the first such mills ever run by the State, all mills were privately run and supplied their powder under contract. Although the actual buildings may have decayed and required replacement the majority of eighteenth century gunpowder mills were at, or near, the sites of earlier mills involved in this or some other industry. Some powder mills had been constructed specifically for the purpose while others were for such purposes as corn milling and converted later. It was not unknown for one site to change function on several occasions and to include gunpowder making among these, as at Bedfont in Middlesex.[14]

Among references to sixteenth, and early seventeenth century mills are those at Bedfont, those near Faversham in Kent, and at Stratford in Essex, but the earliest and most significant area of manufacture prior to the Civil War was Surrey.[15] Among the first recorded mills was one at Rotherhithe in 1555; this supplied the Crown from approximately 1562. From 1589 the monopoly of supply was held by George Evelyn and his son John, and Richard Hill. Members of the Evelyn family ran

[12] Roy, 'Royalist Ordnance Papers', 43 (1964), 14, 28–30, 39.
[13] For mills of the later Stuart period see Tomlinson, *Guns and Government*, pp. 114–15.
[14] Phil Philo and John Mills, 'The Bedfont Gunpowder Mills', *The London Archaeologist*, 5 (1985), 97.
[15] Edward Hasted, *The History and Topographical Survey of the County of Kent* (Canterbury 1798), vi, p. 353; Glenys Crocker, *Gunpowder Mills Gazetteer* (1988), pp. 8, 16.

the powder mills at Long Ditton, Wotton and, later, at Godstone. They also held the respective manors. Hill probably ran the mill at Abinger where he was lord of the manor.[16] Precise dates and extent of business at the individual mills are uncertain but it appears that each was worked independently and the quantity required for contracts apportioned between them.[17] On Evelyn's retirement in 1599, at the same time as that of Hill, supply to the Crown was continued by John and another son, Robert. The royal patent was held for a ten-year period from 1607 in the name of the Earl of Worcester, by then the keeper of the Great Park of Nonsuch in which the Long Ditton mills were situated.[18] It is unclear exactly how long the Evelyns remained at Long Ditton and Wotton, and whether they ran the former for the Earl of Worcester at the same time as their mills at Godstone. The Wotton mills had ceased work by 1625.[19] Those at Godstone where the family had held the manor since the late sixteenth century appear to have been established by 1613, and possibly much earlier. These mills supplied the Crown until 1636. The monopoly was then held until its termination five years later at Chilworth mills. In spite of the previous monopoly of the Evelyns elsewhere gunpowder had been produced at Chilworth since 1625 by the East India Company. After the Civil War official supply was again centred in the South East but, as already stated, this then involved more mills over a wider area.

The South East was the dominant area of gunpowder production because it was to the industry's advantage to be near London. London was the location of the central offices of the Ordnance Board at the Tower and at Palace Yard, Westminster, and of the main magazine at Greenwich for the reception, storage, and proof of gunpowder for the armed forces. It was the centre of government, commerce, and trade, and of the importation of those raw materials crucial to production. Above all, it was within a comparatively short distance of the mills. Transport from the mills to Greenwich was entirely by water where respective Thames tributaries were navigable but by land as far as the Thames if not. In London the gunpowder makers under contract with the Ordnance Office had their own offices from which they could negotiate with the Board, attend the Board in person, and from which they could arrange finance, participate in other trades and, as with

[16] Giuseppi, VCH Surrey, pp. 310–12, 316; Owen Manning and William Bray, The History and Antiquities of the County of Surrey (3 vols. 1804–14), ii, pp. 326–7, iii, pp. 13, 15, 151; Crocker, Gazetteer, p. 18.
[17] Giuseppi, VCH Surrey, p. 312.
[18] CSPD 1603–10, p. 356; CSPD 1634–5, p. 513; John Dent, The Quest for Nonsuch (1962, 2nd edn 1970), p. 187; William Taylor purchased the Park in 1752 and ran the later mills at or near this site; see appendix 1, Gunpowder mills.
[19] Crocker, Gazetteer, p. 26.

certain men such as Walton and Chauncy, hold positions of prominence in commercial bodies in the City.

Concerning raw materials, London was the main port of entry for saltpetre imported by the East India Company, and for import and sale of sulphur. Although mills at a greater distance, as those near Bristol and Liverpool, had access to both of these materials imported via the outports, there was a definite disadvantage concerning saltpetre. That supplied to the government from the East Indies was distributed to the powder makers from storage at Rotherhithe only after the refraction or acceptable degree of impurity had been agreed between the Company and the Ordnance Board. That purchased at the outports would not necessarily have been of the same refraction. Although saltpetre required further purification before being mixed with sulphur and charcoal the initial condition could affect the degree of both the purification required and that actually achieved and, in turn, affect the final quality of the gunpowder. The full significance of this was not recognised until later in the century. For the third material, charcoal, the South East and particularly the Wealden area of Surrey, Kent, and Sussex was one of the nation's main areas of natural supplies of timber. Timber became increasingly scarce in Britain during the eighteenth century and the Weald was no exception but this area did, nevertheless, continue to be vital to supply. Even stocks for Waltham Abbey mills, purchased locally in Essex until the late eighteenth century, had to be sought south of the Thames thereafter.

The comparatively short distance between London and the mills was important, for ease of transportation of so bulky, potentially delicate and hazardous a product was essential with respect to time, cost, and safety. Not only might the gunpowder explode in transit but it was also highly susceptible to both damp, which could cause the grains to clog and become ineffective, and to damage due to violent movement which could break the grain. Once at Greenwich, from where it was dispatched to many parts of the world, it was the responsibility of the Office but during transportation to Greenwich from the mills it was entirely the responsibility of the makers. The less distance it had to cover the less risk of damage to the product, an advantage to both mills and Office. The comparatively short sailing routes were necessary not only for delivery of gunpowder from the mills but also for collection from Greenwich of that powder which had to be returned. The latter included all powder which had failed proof. Due to shortage of government storage space this needed to be collected as quickly as possible after the proof session, which took place within one and a few weeks after delivery. It also included unserviceable government stock which had deteriorated while in store or while on board naval ships. This returned powder was either for reworking at the mills under contract

14

ready to be received back into official store, or for outright purchase from the Office for the powder makers' own use.[20] Those mills furthest from the capital were situated only as far as Chilworth and Faversham, but Edward Pryce considered that even his Chilworth mills were 'at a great distance from London'.[21] Indeed, both of these mills experienced a number of delays in getting powder to Greenwich due to problems of transport. A further disadvantage of distance was that in coastal shipment to Greenwich it was likely that Customs officials would insist on a shipping licence subject to the prohibitive legislation of 1755. This could cause considerable delay, as experienced by Benjamin Pryce of Faversham who had to await special arrangements between the Ordnance Office and Customs officers in 1756 to avoid the need for licence.[22]

Of ten mills supplying the government during the Seven Years War eight were in operation at the start of hostilities, and those of Hounslow in Middlesex, and Chilworth in Surrey were added later. In 1759 Faversham mills in Kent, which had previously functioned privately, became crown property. All, except those of Hounslow and Chilworth, the latter possibly due to disrepair, had also supplied the government during the War of the Austrian Succession. All, except those of Hounslow, of Ewell in Surrey, and Dartford in Kent, had produced powder since the early eighteenth century, and those of Chilworth, Worcester Park, and Molesey in Surrey, Bedfont in Middlesex, Faversham in Kent, and Waltham Abbey in Essex, long before. Apart from a certain quantity of Dutch powder imported officially during the early part of the war government stock was, until 1759, supplied entirely by independent makers under contract. After that date it was prepared at both the private mills and those recently purchased by the Crown at Faversham.

In the majority of cases the business had been passed down through the family since the beginning of the century; this was either directly from father to son, husband to widow, to widow or trustee until a son was of age or indirectly by marriage of a daughter or widow to someone outside the family. Considering the precarious nature of this industry, with high demand in war and little in peace, it was necessary for those involved to have other commercial interests or substantial financial means or, alternatively, commercial or social positions of significance. The men or partnerships involved in the industry were of varied social backgrounds. Some held manorial estates in other parts of the country, and some were purchasing large areas of land in the vicinity of their

---

[20] See ch. 4; and appendix 2, table 4.
[21] WO 47/66, p. 172, 25 October 1765.
[22] WO 47/47, p. 502, 11 May 1756. For detail of legislation see ch. 7.

mills. Others were in City commerce as directors of City companies or trading in corn, linen, hemp, or iron cannon and shot. A few were involved in several of these simultaneously; for example, Chauncy of Oare mill who held the 1,340 acre Edgcote Manor in Northampton-shire, was a director of the East India Company, dealt in gunpowder and linen, and had commercial offices in the City.

Lack of extant business records makes it difficult to assess the extent to which money emanated from, or was invested in gunpowder mills as opposed to other endeavours. For the same reason it is impossible to judge to what degree certain bankruptcies, such as those of Grueber of Oare mills in 1743, Pryce of Chilworth in 1776, and Thomas Edsall of Dartford in 1778, were connected with gunpowder or with other aspects of their lives and, if the former, whether connected with government contracts or with private trade. All except those of Dart-ford and Chilworth mills conducted a private trade in gunpowder during the war, run from offices in the City or in close proximity to it.[23]

Although the Seven Years War was the most extensive yet, the number and location of mills supplying powder was approximately the same as in the preceding War of the Austrian Succession; yet the later war was to be very much more demanding of arms and gunpowder. Even before the declaration of war in May 1756 it was obvious not only that a considerable quantity of gunpowder was going to be needed but that there would be serious problems of supply. The situation was to a certain extent alleviated by the official importation of Dutch powder but this was only a temporary arrangement and difficulties in supply from British mills were to persist throughout the war. As the compara-tively small number of suppliers had no contractual time limit for delivery, the Office was entirely dependent on the makers' performance and unable to produce any effective penalty when that performance was inadequate. When agreeing contract with the two additional men during the war, at Hounslow and Chilworth, it still failed to stipulate that supply be solely for the government or to specify any penalty for poor performance.[24]

Supply to the government was limited by the fact that the mills were providing for a private trade whose needs were boosted as dramatically by the intensity of this war as were those of the Ordnance Office. This industry was further hampered in producing sufficient powder of the correct quality by the organisational and technological limitations of the day. No previous war had been as demanding as this. No such

[23] See appendix 1; and appendix 3, table 17; private trade also included powder supplied by the makers to the East India Company.
[24] WO 47/49, p. 634, 24 June 1757, Hounslow; WO 51/206 p. 57, 26 May 1759, Chilworth.

pressure had ever before been imposed upon the industry.[25] As the social and financial backgrounds of the makers were varied the marked increase in demand might affect men in very different ways. Their ability to satisfy this demand was, in turn, influenced by their ability to react quickly and effectively to the new situation. Much depended on the degree of experience, of available finance, the number of pairs of grindstones in action in the mills, the ability to keep these in good repair in both peace and war, the availability, size, and experience of the workforce, attention to detail in preparing and mixing raw materials, and the degree of supervision provided by the proprietor himself or someone in his stead.[26] The harder the machinery and horses were worked, the greater the need for repair or replacement and the greater the likelihood of fire or explosion. The more time an experienced proprietor or supervisor spent at the mills the more he was aware of the effect of such demands. The speed with which necessary repair or replacement could be undertaken depended on the person in charge being readily available to assess damage, to link with a millwright for repair, and to provide sufficient money to finance it. The more mill units within the complex the more chance there was of continuing production in the face of explosion or problems with machinery. The less the proprietor was involved in other endeavours, the more time he could give at the mills, yet the more he was involved in alternative and successful commercial undertakings the more financial ability he had to refurbish and extend his mill holdings, to solve with speed the problems caused by explosion, and to sustain him in peacetime when his mills could be employed for no other purpose.

Limitations and hazards

Why, in the face of such problems, did the Ordnance Board not seek additional gunpowder mills during the Seven Years War in order to boost its stock? This was primarily because only a few other mills were in evidence at this time. Only two of these, at Battle and Sedlescombe were in the South East; the others were near Bristol, and at Thelwall in Cheshire.[27] Those of Maidstone, Wandsworth, and Carshalton, the

[25] This is demonstrated by the unprecedented measures taken by the government, discussed in more detail in ch. 4.
[26] There are references in various sources to the number of water wheels or, alternatively, 'mills' at different mill sites; however, the terminology is not consistent and varies between 'numbers of wheels', 'pairs of wheels', and one or more 'pairs of stones'. It is therefore impossible to compare size with accuracy.
[27] Reference to earlier mills can be found in the following: Keith Fairclough, 'Early Gunpowder Production', 11; H. Blackman, 'The Story of the Old Gun-

latter two of which had supplied the government, are known to have been in existence during the two decades prior to the war but not functioning during it.[28] Those mills built soon after the war in the North East, were involved only with private trade, mainly with supplies for mines, and not until a later date were additional mills constructed to supply the government. There is no evidence that the Sussex proprietors considered the possibility of government contracts at this time or that the Bristol makers at Woolley mills sought contract before November 1761; nor is there any sign of the Board having had cause to even consider the need for any mill outside the South East prior to this war. The Sussex mills concentrated on producing fine sporting powder while Woolley mills near Bristol had been concerned until now solely with private trade and particularly that of the African slave trade. The mills at Thelwall had been constructed only recently when their Liverpool proprietors sought a contract at the beginning of 1762. However, when the proprietors of both these and Woolley mills sent powder samples to the Tower for trial these failed to meet the desired standard and all negotiations between proprietors and Ordnance Board eventually came to an end.[29] Considering that no such trials had been demanded of the Hounslow and Chilworth mills when they successfully sought contracts in 1757 and 1759 respectively, that a high proportion of powder from the current mills was substandard anyway, that the demand for gunpowder was now greater than ever before, and that the Office did not have sufficient stock to run the service as efficiently as it wished, it is apparent that there must have been other, additional reasons why the Board did not look for supplies elsewhere.

There were several factors at work. Firstly, the government had in 1759 taken the unprecedented step of purchasing Faversham mills, and obviously intended by this means to produce a more effective supply and to decrease gradually its dependence on the private mills. Secondly, it considered that a combination of the legislation intended to limit private trade and financial incentives for improved performance at the mills would eventually result in increased supply.[30] Thirdly, and of

powder Works at Battle', *Sussex Archaeological Collections*, 64 (1923), 114–15; B. J. Buchanan and M. T. Tucker 'The Manufacture of Gunpowder: a study of the documentary and physical evidence relating to the Woolley Powder Works near Bath', *Industrial Archaeology Review*, 5 (1981); Robin Atthill, 'The gunpowder mills of north Somerset', *The Countryman* (Autumn 1971), 134–9; only those of Woolley approached the government at this time.

[28] Giuseppi, *VCH Surrey*, p. 323; R. J. Spain, 'The Loose Watermills', *Archaeologia Cantiana*, 88 (1973), 182–3.

[29] This is referred to in ch. 4.

[30] See chs. 4 and 7.

considerable importance to mills and Office were the advantages of the proximity of the mills to London. Location would have featured prominently in the Board's eventual refusal of the proposals for contract from Bristol and Liverpool proprietors. The Board experienced enough problems in obtaining its powder from the mills of the South East at this time without increasing its difficulties by linking with those further afield. Problems during longer routes might have severely hampered not only those most directly involved but, in turn, the Office in its ability to refurbish stock quickly at a time when demand was at its highest. Gunpowder mills, like other water mills, were subject to difficulties through drought and lack of water power in summer and ice or flood in winter. Such problems, combined with those specifically applicable to powder mills, would all have been exaggerated if combined with distance from London and therefore difficulties in transportation and in communication with the Board.

Whether it would have considered negotiating with additional local mills had these been established at the time, or whether it would have preferred to concentrate on the other methods aimed at increasing supply is not known. The only sign of consideration of additional means of supply from mills already under contract was in the offer in 1758 of financial aid towards the addition of further units to existing mills. Only the Hounslow proprietors appear to have taken advantage of this offer, and then only to replace mill units lost by explosion.

The other question that should be asked is why, considering the comparatively low number of mills in so intensive a war, and recognising the continual demand for gunpowder and the potential financial gain to be made from two totally separate and demanding markets, did no one else in the South East attempt to establish themselves in this industry? Undoubtedly, this was primarily due to the risk of investing in so precarious an undertaking. There were profits to be made in wartime and, indeed, the continuation of certain businesses for several decades or longer in one family suggests that such commercial undertakings were not without some very worthwhile gain. However, there were numerous distinct disadvantages pertaining to the industry. Although in wartime there was high demand and therefore opportunity for long awaited prestigious contracts and chance for profit, meeting such a demand was by no means simple.

In theory, the greatest advantage in this situation would have been to invest in more buildings, machinery, and men to produce more powder. As already shown, there was reluctance to do this as no one accepted the Board's offer of 1758 to help finance construction of new, additional mill units within each complex to increase output. The risk was that war might end within a few months and peace last for ten years. There was no way of assessing in advance the onset, intensity, and duration of war and therefore what profits might or might not be made. In peacetime the government required only sufficient powder to replenish its basic stock for defence and training purposes and for this contracts were comparatively few and infrequent. These usually served only a certain number of its more favoured or longest serving powder makers and seldom fully occupied the workforce anyway.[31] At this time mills were heavily dependent on private trade, their one continuing market, although this could also decrease to a very low level as in the period 1750-5. The suppliers of guns on the other hand were more fortunate. There was always demand for large guns by merchants and Ordnance Office, the latter replenishing stock ready for future war. It could not do this with gunpowder. In addition, iron mills could always diversify when necessary to produce other iron products; powder mills had no such opportunity.

There were further problems for the industry in ascertaining how to produce powder which would pass government proof, and in determining why some stock passed proof and other did not. The subject was a complicated one, and the varying results and incidence of failure caused much distress, frustration and loss of time and profit.[32] This would have been a significant factor both in deciding whether to invest in such mills in the first place, and whether to pay more attention to government contracts or to private trade. Private trade was so much easier to satisfy. There had been suspicions about the accuracy and consistency of proof methods and results for over a century but the powder makers were powerless to do anything about the problem and the Office had, as yet, no obvious reason and certainly insufficient knowledge to attempt change. Both sides had to await the organisational, scientific, and technological improvements in the procedure at the end of the eighteenth century when proof became not only more accurate but consistently so.

Unlike other mills those producing powder were always faced with danger because of the continual risk of fire or explosion. Such occurrences could cause injury and death to workers and what could be serious or even irreparable damage to buildings and machinery. Not surprisingly, apart from the consequent delay in adding to its own stock, the Ordnance Office had no direct interest in the plight of powder makers who were thus indefinitely delayed, without payment, and forced to finance immediately the necessary repairs. Its own first

[31] The Dartford makers were considered comparatively reliable suppliers undoubtedly because they were more concerned with supply to the Office than to merchants. In contrast, Pryce of Chilworth, who experienced delays in transport and had to close his mills temporarily for repair after the war, was subsequently refused a peacetime contract.

[32] See ch. 10.

direct experience of the effect of explosion was in its management of Faversham mills from 1759.[33] Furthermore, because of the fire risk, such buildings had to be widely separated to minimise damage and spread of fire which meant more land had to be purchased or leased than for other mills, while the risks of production and transportation caused consternation among local residents. Moreover, such mills were extremely difficult if not impossible to insure. Of the many references to insurance of buildings held by the powder makers in the mid-eighteenth century none refers to the mills themselves. A few entries refer to buildings near the mills but usually exclude any loss from fire caused by the powder works.[34] This and other difficulties experienced by such men were demonstrated by the petition of powder makers to the Treasury at a later date. In 1818, in a complaint concerning sale by the government of old powder stock to an 'outsider', they stressed concern about the consequent damage to their mills 'the loss of which must wholly fall on ourselves, as it is a species of property no office will insure'. They referred also to the difficulty of lack of work in peacetime, the need to dismiss men as a result, the problem of having to find experienced workmen quickly in wartime and in a 'manufactory so full of hazard'.[35]

Because of the continual risk of fire and explosion gunpowder was a hazardous material not only to produce, but to store and transport. There were many instances of local inhabitants complaining about danger from mills in the vicinity. These concerned, among others, Faversham and Hounslow mills. From the early eighteenth century the quantity of powder which could be stored within a certain distance of London was restricted by legislation. For this reason magazines had to be constructed for storage further afield, as at Barking Creek.[36] The restriction of the quantity stored and transported at any one time was the subject of increasing legislation during the century, with additional restriction from 1772 on the amount which could be produced at any one time between one pair of mill stones, together with the need for licence for all involved in production.[37]

[33] For reference to explosions see ch. 9.
[34] GL Sun Insurance, 11936. 56, p. 562, No: 86503, 8 January 1740 concerning buildings near the mills at Dartford; another reference to insurance pertains to refining houses and offices at Waltham Abbey in 1767, ibid., 11936. 174, 243052, February 1767, (Dr Keith Fairclough, October 1990).
[35] 'Memorial of the Gunpowder Merchants', pp. 1–2.
[36] Syon House, Northumberland Papers, DXXII 5g (1) 1720; this involved the mills of Waltham Abbey, Molesey, East Bedfont, Faversham and, at the end of the century, Chilworth also.
[37] These include: 5 Geo. II c. 26, 1718; 11 Geo. II c. 23, 1724; 15 Geo. II c. 32, 1742; 22 Geo. II c. 38, 1749; 12 Geo. III c. 61, 1772, *Statutes at Large* (new edn), v–vii, xi.

Therefore, producing gunpowder for the the Army and Navy was no simple matter. The industry, centred in the South East, was fraught with difficulty for both government and mills, not least due to the extremes in demand between peace and war. One of the main reasons why more men did not come forward at this time of exceptionally high demand was the precarious nature of the industry and the risks involved. As a result, those involved were either connected with other trades, of prominent social standing, in positions of influence in City commerce, or a combination of these. The period 1740 to 1770 provides opportunity not only for comparison of gunpowder supply and demand between different wars, and between war and peace, but also for examining a period when problems between Ordnance Board and powder makers were, undoubtedly, at their greatest to date.

2

Gunpowder Supply
in War and Peace, 1740–55

The period 1740 to 1755 includes the War of the Austrian Succession, an intervening period of uncertain peace, and the year of escalating international conflict which preceded the Seven Years War. This provides an important basis for comparison in supply not only between two periods of war but also between the very varying demands of war and peace.

The War of the Austrian Succession, 1740–8

Between February 1740 and the peace negotiations at the end of 1748 nine men or partnerships received government contracts to supply gunpowder, six of whom continued throughout the war. Although comparatively few records survive on the daily activities of the Ordnance Office in the War of the Austrian Succession, the Ordnance bill books are complete concerning the quantity of gunpowder purchased, relevant payment, and identities of suppliers. These illustrate that in one particular aspect supply differed from that in the Seven Years War.[1]

The first contract of the period was with Robert Norman of Molesey in Surrey on 15 February 1740. This was followed in April by those with Pearse of Faversham in Kent (later Pearse & Stevens), Underhill of Bedfont in Middlesex, and Walton of Waltham Abbey in Essex and in December by those with Pyke & Edsall of Dartford in Kent and of Taylor of Worcester Park in Surrey. Grueber of Oare in Kent supplied only between 1741 and 1743, while contracts with Eade of Ewell in Surrey and with Chauncy & Vigne of Oare did not begin until the autumn of 1745. The main difference between this war and the next was that while in the Seven Years War most of the powder supplied was new stock prepared from fresh raw materials, in the War of the Austrian Succession twenty-two per cent of the total quantity delivered was of old unserviceable government stock which had been sent to the mills for 'repair' or reprocessing. The highest percentage of repaired

---

[1] WO 51/145–61, 163–71, 173–4, 179, February 1740 – December 1748.

powder was supplied by William Taylor of Worcester Park; of his entire total of 11,069 barrels, twenty-eight per cent had been sent from the Office to be reprocessed. Apart from 1757, when contracts were agreed for repairing a comparatively small quantity of old powder, all powder submitted during the Seven Years War was new. The only other unserviceable powder sent from Greenwich to the mills in this later period was that sold outright to the makers, most in 1755 the year preceding war.[2]

Gunpowder reprocessed at the mills at this time was official stock of questionable serviceability. Originating from naval ships returning to port or from long storage in any of the government magazines this was returned to the main magazine at Greenwich and resubjected to the process of proof. Any proved to be of required standard was returned into store for use. Of that which failed some was suitable for military exercise or royal salutes, some retained in separate store and the remainder sent to the mills to be repaired. The latter was either repaired under contract between Office and maker and returned for proof in the same way as new stock or, alternatively, sold outright to makers for repair for purposes of private trade. Such trade concerned sale to British mines or for export, either direct or via merchants. Unserviceable powder was that in which the grains had become either clogged due to slight damp or damaged and turned to dust. Gunpowder returned to Greenwich which had become wet while at sea or in store was unusable and therefore not sent again for proof. It was either sold to makers for their own use, in which case it could be dried and reworked or have the saltpetre extracted, or it was reworked for government stock as with any unserviceable powder.

In his military writings of 1672 Thomas Venn described certain methods for 'fortifying weak powder or that spoiled by wind, wet or air'. This could be achieved by mixing equal proportions of old and new powder, or by extracting and further refining the saltpetre before mixing it either with the original powder, or with new charcoal and sulphur.[3] As far as the makers were concerned, the reworking of unserviceable powder was preferable to the preparation of new, undoubtedly for reasons of convenience, speed, and finance. Usually the same price was paid by the Ordnance Office for this as for new powder but it had not required deposit for saltpetre, and possibly not replacement of both sulphur and charcoal. This preference is shown by the shorter interval between contract and delivery, and the fact that a contract for new gunpowder was frequently postponed in order to give priority to a subsequent contract for the reworking of old.

[2] See appendix 2, tables 1–4.
[3] Venn, *Military and Maritime Discipline*, p. 23.

A further contrast between the two wars was the quantity of powder supplied. In the nine-year period of the first war there was a combined total of 121,980 barrels of new and reworked powder, giving a mean annual supply of 13,553 barrels. In the eight-year period of conflict concerning the complete years 1755-62, the total was 115,948, giving a mean annual supply of 14,493 barrels. This difference was in favour of the Seven Years War, but considering the intensity of the latter conflict this figure would appear to have been surprisingly small. The possible reasons for this comparatively low supply in the face of so demanding a war will be discussed in later chapters.

Uncertain peace, 1749-54

The Treaty of Aix-la-Chapelle brought the usual sharp contrast between demand for gunpowder in war and in peace. Government requirements decreased, the price it paid was soon reduced and, finally, demand halted completely leaving little work for the mills other than in supplying powder for British mines and trade overseas. As the Ordnance Office had no further immediate need for new powder 1749 was characterised instead by the reworking at the mills of unserviceable stock returned from war, the majority of which was from naval ships. Reworked powder was sent back into store at Greenwich ready for future use. Contracts were agreed with eight of the wartime powder makers, with preference in terms of quantity given to the Faversham partnership of Pearse & Stevens.[4] Pearse had supplied the largest total of new and reworked powder during the war. During this first year of peace the partnership reworked 1,382 barrels compared with the annual totals of the other makers of between 605 and 760 barrels. The price of £1 a barrel which had been paid during the latter part of the war to all makers for new and reworked powder was continued until April 1749 when consignments entering store at Greenwich varied between 50 and 290 barrels each. Thereafter the price was reduced to £0 14s.[5] No further contract was made for new or reworked gunpowder after the end of 1749.

The period 1750-4 was characterised by problems not only for the mills but also for the Ordnance Board. The mills were underemployed

---

[4] WO 47/34, 27 January, 24 February 1749; Pearse & Stevens were to rework two parts in nine and the other seven men one part each. Although Ordnance minutes in 1749 sometimes refer to proof of new powder the bill books show that all powder delivered at this time was reworked, as referred to in the February agreement. Powder proved at the beginning of the year concerned contracts remaining from the war.

[5] WO 51/170-2, 174, January – April 1749.

while, peace being so uncertain, the Board had considerable difficulty in assessing demand. Most ordnance requirements could be stored indefinitely: gunpowder could not. The Board had to strive to reach the correct balance of stock at any one time. The peace treaty had left open the majority of the issues which had divided the nations involved in the war: Prussia and Austria competed for supremacy in Germany and Anglo-French rivalry overseas continued unabated, particularly in India and North America. Thus the Ordnance Board faced the continual possibility of a sudden large increase in demand for gunpowder and other supplies. Although it decided against further contracts at the end of 1749 its uncertainty about the international situation and therefore appropriate time to receive new powder was particularly evident during 1753 and 1754. Mistiming of immediate or future requirement resulting in premature contracts could be serious for the Board in terms of finance and space.

The eight powder makers submitted a proposal on 15 December 1749 'to make new powder and repair old'. At the Office's department at Old Palace Yard, Westminster the lieutenant and surveyor generals and other members of the Board considered the makers' request to prepare powder for the Office for £0 17s 6d or, alternatively, 30 lb of saltpetre for each barrel. In addition, they proposed that for every three barrels of wet powder of which they relieved the Office they would return two barrels of new.[6] This may have been the wet powder dried and reworked or new powder employing the saltpetre extracted from it; in the latter case the makers would, presumably, retain the saltpetre equal to the quantity contained in one barrel. Because of the uncertainty of the current international situation the Board was not yet ready to discuss further contracts. It did venture subsequently to agree with a proposal made by Robert Norman of Molesey that he could be one of the three intended for contracts after he had stated his personal acquaintance with the Speaker of the House of Commons.[7] However, in reality the Board did not consider such contracts again for the next three and a half years. There is no record whatsoever of any powder being supplied to the government between December 1749 and those contracts of December 1754. This was therefore a difficult period for both the Office in assessing munitions requirements at a time of steadily increasing international tension, and for the makers who were in great need of work. Several claimed later that the demand for powder from private trade had been so small that 'many of the mills were unused and would in the process of time become ruinous'.[8]

6 WO 47/34, 15 December 1749.
7 WO 47/35, p. 110, 13 February 1750.
8 WO 47/46, p. 8, 1 July 1755.

In June 1753 the Board decided to reprove powder returned from Dort and Flanders since the war. Of a total of 2,755 barrels proved at Greenwich only 1,195 were found to be serviceable for return to store.[9] In September it was decided that action should be taken on the large quantity of returned powder accumulating at Greenwich, including that 'decayed, damaged and wet'. The Privy Council authorised the Board to have this 'repaired, exchanged or otherwise disposed of'.[10] John Walton and the partnership of Chauncy & Vigne were the only makers to purchase such powder, although it is not clear if they were the only men to request it. In the absence of current government employment the sale of all powder produced at the mills at this time was private, the majority to merchants. In September Walton wrote to the Board to express his 'great want of 800 barrels of repairable powder to work up for a public service' (non-government trade) for which he was willing to pay £2 10s a barrel. This price was based on the market price of saltpetre while new powder delivered to the Office already contained the latter's saltpetre supplied to the mills at the signing of contracts. Considering this to be 'an advantageous price', and obviously pleased to clear some of the redundant stock, the Board asked its treasurer to receive the £2,000. By 12 October the powder had been weighed and transferred to Walton's own barrels to be shipped from Greenwich for the Waltham Abbey mills. A further 400 barrels were sold to Walton in November. Although a total of 600 such barrels was sold to Chauncy & Vigne between November 1753 and January 1754, their proposal to supply powder was not accepted.[11]

The Board's action in proving 2,750 barrels of returned powder and selling 1,400 of unserviceable stock between September and November 1753 only partly met the Privy Council request. As late as March 1755, it was reported by the Ordnance storekeeper at Gravesend that there were 5,080 barrels of powder which had not been moved and 'aired' for about six years. Careful movement of the barrels and therefore of the powder in them was intended to prevent clogging of the grains. However, by that date immediate action was necessary to assess government stock and the storekeeper was ordered to inspect such stock and report the quantity still serviceable.[12] Supporting the probability that much surveying of stock was left until some months after the first British forces had left with Braddock for North America in January 1755 were the many entries in the Ordnance bill books during that year concern-

9 WO 47/42, 23 June, 10 July, 3 August 1753.
10 WO 55/354, p. 220, 14 September 1753.
11 WO 47/42, pp. 147, 274, 7 September, 16 November 1753; WO 47/43, pp. 14, 140, 17 January, 7 March 1754.
12 WO 47/45 p. 197, 11 March 1755.

ing the work of the Office coopers. This work involved the surveying of stock by opening, reheading and moving barrels of powder, and the repair of barrels.[13] Furthermore, it was April 1755 before the master general requested the first inter-war assessment of the exact quantity of gunpowder in each of the outport magazines.[14]

Meanwhile, on 17 July 1753, a further proposal was made for contract; this was from Jonathan Eade, one of the suppliers in the previous war and partner of Alexander Bridges of Ewell. The proposal, to supply a minimum of 300 barrels of new powder annually, was considered at a Board meeting at the lieutenant general's house in North Audley Street. The Board reported that each barrel should be prepared from 80¼ lb double refined saltpetre, 15 lb charcoal, and 12¾ lb refined brimstone; the total composition was to be divided into three separate parcels of 26¾ lb saltpetre, 5 lb charcoal and 4¼ lb brimstone, each of which was to be worked for five hours to reduce the entire quantity of 108 lb to 100 lb. The makers were to abide by the Board's decision at the testing or proof of powder and to collect that which failed.[15] The saltpetre from the Office would be at the same refraction as agreed between the Office and East India Company and would be double refined at their own mills. For each barrel of new corned powder they would accept 40 lb of government repairable powder instead of money. They would also deliver two barrels of new powder for every three of wet with which the Board wished to part; these were to be 'filled and rammed as usual'. No part of this powder would be incorporated into the new.

It is of interest that the partnership proposed contracts only for new supply 'to secure a modest profit' and not for the reworking of old, for they felt 'their credit would suffer from the uncertainty of the composition of such powder'. They were willing to contract for seven years. In spite of the makers' comment on old stock there is no reason to consider that, once reworked, this was inferior to new: as already noted, twenty-two per cent of powder supplied in the previous war had been reworked at the mills.

The Board's uncertainty about the most appropriate time for boosting stock continued. Initially it was enthusiastic but later all negotiations were suddenly stopped. A contract was to be prepared and 36 lb of powder received on trial, with two men acting as securities against the sum of £2,000. These were Philip Cantillon, a London merchant and prominent holder of land near the Ewell mill, and Zephaniah Eade, sailmaker of Wapping and probably a relative of Alexander. The

13 WO 51/180 p. 168, 30 September 1755.
14 WO 47/45, p. 371, 6 April 1755.
15 WO 47/42, p. 41, 17 July 1753; this is discussed in more detail in ch. 10.

powder was delivered to the Tower for trial while grough saltpetre for the contract was to be provided by the Office on receipt of a deposit of Navy Bills.[16] By 7 September the plans had been changed dramatically. The lieutenant general cancelled delivery of the twenty tons of salt-petre and ordered that the deposit for its receipt be returned. The Office solicitor was to 'draw up a case to be laid before the attorney general for his opinion on the procedure between the Board, and Eade & Bridges'.[17] No reason was given for the sudden change in plan. Although the need for British armed forces and ordnance stores in North America became apparent by the end of 1754, it is obvious that after further consideration plans for the preparation of new powder were thought to be premature. It is also possible that when old powder was reproved in the summer of 1753 more may have passed than had been foreseen. It could be said that the Board's change of mind over this contract was correct in view of the comparatively small scale of the conflict in North America at that date and the fact that no British force had yet been sent. Clearly, the decision was not an easy one in the rapidly changing political circumstances of the day.

The view that one war was frequently the forerunner of the next is illustrated here by factors linking the War of the Austrian Succession and the Seven Years War.[18] Under the peace treaty of 1748 many territorial matters were left unsettled in Europe and North America and, at the time of consideration of the above contract there was already evidence of mounting hostility in the latter location. This was particularly evident in the Ohio Valley, a significant fur trading area previously controlled by Indians. 'The Ohio became the critical area of Anglo-French tension'.[19] After a long tradition of friendship with Britain the Iroquois now had an uneasy neutrality in the area, while allegiances of other tribes to British and French changed frequently.[20] Both nations aimed to consolidate their positions with regard to Indian allegiance and territorial gain. France was not only gaining strength here but was also infiltrating Nova Scotia, location of an important British naval base. Britain advised colonial governors in 1753 to resist further French encroachment in the area and to organise an inter-

16 SRO Northey Muniments 2238/10/8, Map of River Hogsmill, Ewell, November 1753; WO 47/42, p. 68, 3 August 1753.
17 WO 47/42 p. 144, 7 September 1753.
18 C. R. Middleton, 'The administration of Newcastle and Pitt: the departments of state and the conduct of the war, 1754–60, with particular reference to the campaigns of North America' (Unpublished Ph.D. thesis, University of Exeter 1969), p. 1.
19 R. C. Simmons, *The American Colonies: from settlement to independence* (1976), p. 276.
20 Ibid., pp. 275–6.

colonial conference to discuss the situation; this was to be the Albany Conference of the following year. Warnings to the French by the Virginian Assembly were rejected and in April 1754 a defensive fort built by the latter on the Ohio was captured by the French and re-placed by Fort Duquesne, resulting in the first official conflict of this period of 'peace'. The possibility of a 'Plan of Union' with an agreed intercolonial fund for defence in terms of men and ordnance require-ments was discussed at the Albany Conference in June, attended by seven colonies. Views were varied, no such agreement made, and Par-liament did nothing to enforce one. The colonies decided instead, albeit in theory, that men and supplies should be sent in proportion to population.

With the government's decision of October to prepare an armed force and ordnance supplies for North America the Board now had to agree contracts immediately for the supply of gunpowder. In spite of valid reason for the delayed decision concerning new supply, it is sur-prising that the Board did not do more to implement fully the Privy Council's request of September 1753 to clear the large amount of powder returned from the previous war by selling a larger quantity to the mills, or to have some of it reworked for return to stock. This would have been very much more practical than holding on to considerable amounts of useless stock at this time.

Escalating conflict, 1754–5

The continuous and ever increasing need for gunpowder from the time of mounting hostility in 1755 to the start of peace negotiations at the end of 1762 produced higher demands on Office and mills than ever before. Gunpowder was required for all military forces and naval ships leaving Britain and for defence at home. In order to examine supply against the background of war and sources of demand it is necessary to consider the main areas of conflict and the interaction between war strategy and politics.

American colonial defence was the responsibility of the respective governors who were expected by the British government to finance their own defence needs. This included the supply of gunpowder from their own stock, acquired from the powder duty levied on all merchant ships arriving in port.[21] The initial action in 1755 was considered not as offensive, but only as immediate necessary defensive aid for colonists against the French. It was only when defence requirements greatly exceeded supply that colonial governors had to request aid from the

21 See ch. 6.

Ordnance Office via the Board of Trade. After the declaration of war in the following year when the Newcastle ministry decided that further territorial gain by the French should be halted, land retrieved, and colonial defences further reinforced it was acknowledged that the colonists could not possibly provide the ordnance requirements previously expected of them and that even more substantial help was required.

Meantime, in March 1755, as a direct response to the intensification of international rivalry in North America, Parliament voted the extra finance necessary to augment British military and naval forces.[22] Large numbers of men were now required. Both forces had been reduced to their peacetime strength in 1748, largely as a result of Parliament's long established fear of both expense and possible interference in civil affairs of a large standing army. 'Between 1748 and 1754 problems of defence were always superseded in Parliament by political and financial considerations.'[23] Gordon says of the Army in this period that the efficiency which produced the long tale of successes was efficiency of command and courage: it was not the result of alert preparation. Between the wars its needs were openly and deliberately neglected. The country remained in dread of a standing army, and numbers were increased by vote from Parliament when trouble was imminent and promptly reduced when trouble was over as in 1748, 1763 and 1783.[24]

At the beginning of 1755 the Army consisted of 40,000 men distributed between Britain, Ireland, the colonies and other bases overseas. By 1758 Ligonier, commander in chief of land forces, had 90,000 men under his direction, 54,000 of whom were in Britain and Ireland and the remainder in North America, Gibraltar and the East and West Indies.[25] Considerable organisation was also required to increase the size of the Navy involving ship building, the fitting of ships with guns and gunpowder by the Ordnance Office, and the recruiting of crews. It could not be mobilised quickly in emergency because of a shortage of manpower and inefficient administration. The Cabinet decided on the commission of seventeen warships for immediate service in North American waters, and in anticipation of the order the Admiralty had already requested permission to begin recruiting men. Accordingly, the Privy Council authorised the Admiralty to begin the press, to make the payment of bounties to volunteers, and to recall British seamen serving in foreign vessels. The Admiralty was forced to rely on compulsion as

22 Cobbett, *The Parliamentary History of England 1753–1765* (1813), xv, 518.
23 Stephen F. Gradish, *The Manning of the British Navy during the Seven Years War* (1980), p. 29.
24 Hampden Gordon, *The War Office* (1935), p. 33.
25 H. C. B. Rogers, *The British Army of the Eighteenth Century* (1977), p. 25; Rogers states that the establishment for 1756 was 49,000.

the principal method of manning the fleet because Parliament and the nation at large had failed to devise an efficient method of recruitment. In January enlisted seamen were at the normal peacetime figure of 10,000. Between January and November 1755, ninety-five additional ships were commissioned and over 29,000 more men recruited, although this became inceasingly difficult during the year as large numbers deserted or became sick.[26] Such difficulties caused considerable trouble for the Ordnance Office for not only was the departure of warships delayed but also crews had to be moved suddenly from one ship to another to make up numbers; this caused confusion when ships were being fitted. Shortage of men could also delay ships carrying ordnance stores overseas either because the naval convoy accompanying them lacked a crew or because the ordnance crew had been taken by naval press gangs.

In January the Ordnance Office also had to prepare gunpowder and other stores for four new regiments of Artillery to accompany the East India Company to India. The trading interests of the French and English East India Companies were in a permanent state of friction, a situation heightened further by rising international hostility and declaration of war. Although the two powers were to remain rivals in the south, Calcutta and Bengal, the latter an important source of saltpetre, were retrieved from France in 1757. British forces overcame French power in India in 1761.

The sudden increase in the armed forces, commencing in 1755, was not the only reason for the increased demand for gunpowder: other factors were the number, nature, length, and intensity of campaigns, nature of the terrain, methods employed by the opposition, and the amount of powder lost as a result of damp during transportation. In the absence of extant records of powder contracts or proof for the War of the Austrian Succession it is impossible to compare the intensity of demand in the two wars or the ability to meet it. What the sudden increase in forces did cause was a sudden need for new powder in large enough quantities to be shipped with the military forces to North America, and to supply the many new warships in commission. Of particular value is the fact that detailed extant records of gunpowder supply and distribution are available for the Seven Years War, a war extensive not only in time but geography, in which new types of offensive took place, and which was for the first time supplied not only from independent, but also national gunpowder mills.

[26] Gradish, *British Navy*, pp. 30–2.

Contracts

The escalation of hostilities in 1754 and armed conflict in 1755 produced a need for more cannon, arms, ammunition, and gunpowder and
for such stores as gun carriages, entrenching tools, flags, horses, and
hay. Gunpowder was required at home for army training and defence,
for the military forces sent to North America, those accompanying the
East India Company, those eventually sent to the Continent in 1758,
and for the Navy both for Channel and foreign service. Supplies were
received at the main magazine at Greenwich from where they were
sent for the fitting of naval ships at the other seven outport magazines
at Portsmouth, Chatham, Plymouth, Sheerness, Upnor Castle, Woolwich, and Gravesend and Tilbury, to the ten garrisons of Berwick,
Edinburgh, Stirling, Fort William, Carlisle, Pendennis, Hull, Chester,
Jersey, and Guernsey, and to the five British naval bases at Minorca,
Gibraltar, Antigua, Jamaica, and Nova Scotia.[27] A lesser quantity was
also sent to the Tower for testing small arms and to Woolwich, not only
for ships but for filling shells, proving cannon, making fireworks for
official displays, and for training the Artillery. It was also used for firing
salutes at the Tower and St James's Park.

The Board's eventual decision in November 1754 to increase its
powder stock arose as a direct result of British plans to retake North
American territory lost to the French, and the consequent need for
ordnance supplies.[28] Military troops and an artillery train were sent
under Braddock in January to coordinate the regular British and provincial forces in North America in an attempt to regain the area of Fort
Duquesne but Braddock was defeated long before receiving additional
ordnance. In April a naval squadron was sent under Admiral Boscawen
to intercept French reinforcements off Louisbourg but with many of his
men suffering from fever he was unable to complete the task and
captured only two ships, the *Lys* and the *Alcide*. These were later
brought to Britain and stripped of their powder and guns.[29] It was these
incidents which eventually resulted in the cessation of diplomatic relations between the two powers and in French plans early in 1756 for the
invasion of England and the taking of Minorca, Britain's naval base, for
the defence of trade in the Mediterranean.

Contracts for powder involved the supply of an agreed quantity
prepared in a certain manner and proved to be of required standard.
Although initially the time allowed for delivery was specified, apart

[27] WO 54/113 March Quarter 1755.
[28] BL Add. MS 33046 fos. 297, 299, 29 September, 1754; fos. 313, 315, 360
undated.
[29] Adm. 1/4010, 4 December 1755.

from occasional financial incentives offered by the Board for speedy delivery of powder during the war, contracts did not specify dates for delivery and there is no evidence of forfeit for delay. The main variation between makers was the quantity submitted, that passing proof, and the nature of the deposit to the Board for the receipt of saltpetre. A separate contract was agreed for each delivery of a certain number of barrels of powder; this was either 242½ or 485 according to the choice of the maker, who then usually dealt in the same amount at each contract throughout the war. Varying numbers of barrels, each containing 100 lb of gunpowder, were conveyed to Greenwich at intermittent intervals until sufficient quantity had been received and passed proof to satisfy the contract. Details of the completed delivery and date of issue of the respective bill of payment were entered in any one of a number of current Ordnance bill books. The interval between the date of completion and payment during the war varied between six weeks and four months and immediately one contract was completed another was agreed. Powder passing proof was put into store and that which failed collected by the makers at their own expense. The deposit for the saltpetre supplied by the Office varied between Navy Bills, East India Company Bonds, South Sea Annuities, and Ordnance Debentures, and each new contract was made subject to a new deposit or to the current deposit being retained. For 485 barrels, 20 tons of double refined saltpetre were required, for which the deposit was £1,200. Among those attending proof sessions at Greenwich were the surveyor general, clerk of the deliveries, the storekeeper, their clerks, and the proof masters from the Tower. The quantity under proof at any one time varied between 350 and 2,080 barrels per session, the latter occurring on 29 January 1762.[30] Undergoing separate proof was gunpowder of the East India Company, purchased privately from various of the makers under government contract.[31]

Although the exact method of the initial communication between Ordnance Board and powder makers at this time is not stated, contracts were agreed with Pryce of Faversham on 16 November 1754, and on 6 December with Walton of Waltham Abbey and the partnerships of Eade & Bridges of Ewell, and Chauncy & Vigne of Oare, all of whom had received contracts in the previous war. Further contracts were agreed with four other makers in April 1755 and with two others, on the same terms, at Hounslow and Chilworth in 1757 and 1759 respectively. Apart from powder imported from Holland between 1756 and 1758 these mills were, for reasons already discussed, the sole source of supply. There was no public advertisement for submission of tenders for

30 WO 47/59, p. 86, 29 January 1762.
31 WO 47/56, p. 422, 5 December 1760.

any ordnance store at this time and although this was changed in 1783 there is no evidence that the new procedure included gunpowder.

Pryce's proposal, on which his and the December contracts were based and which was similar to that of Eade & Bridges earlier, was to supply 485 barrels of gunpowder a month or 4,850 a year 'if the Board shall have occasion for same'. The Board was soon to need as much powder of the correct standard as possible. This proposal was based on certain conditions. For the preparation of the powder, which would undergo the usual proof at Greenwich magazine, he would receive from the Office quantities of grough saltpetre partially refined by the East India Company according to the refraction settled between that Company and the Board; this provided an indication of the degree of impurity, which at this time was agreed at fifteen per cent. This allowed for double refining of the petre at the mills ready for the incorporation process. After the five hours of intense mixing and grinding of the three ingredients the saltpetre would be in the desired proportion of 75 lb for each barrel of 100 lb of gunpowder. Instead of saltpetre the Office could opt to supply one barrel of unserviceable gunpowder from which saltpetre could be extracted. On receipt of either, Pryce would make a deposit with the Office treasurer, returnable at completion of the respective contract. Good charcoal and the best refined brimstone or sulphur were to be used and the whole was to be worked under the mill stones for at least five hours, as in the proposition of 1753. If the Board was unable to deliver saltpetre he would receive instead unserviceable powder valued at £2 10s a barrel in a quantity equal to that of the new powder he was to supply. He undertook not to use any part of this powder in the preparation of new, and would also be willing to take wet powder from the Office 'rammed in the usual manner' at the rate of three at a time, for which he would return two barrels of new. (In this way he would be rewarded with the contents of one barrel). He would pay the Office cooper for heading up all barrels of his own failed powder or government powder which was repairable or wet, and provide his own barrels for removing it at his own expense. Finally, he proposed that payment for each barrel of new powder supplied was to be in the form of materials; this was to be either such quantity of grough petre as would amount to 25 lb of double refined petre, or 31¼ lb of repairable or unserviceable powder, at the option of the Board. An exception to the time agreed for delivery was to be made in case of unavoidable delay caused by explosion.[32] The possible reasons for these alternative suggestions to money payment were twofold. Firstly, Pryce may have considered that the Office would be more likely to agree readily to non-money payment which would rid

[32] WO 47/44, pp. 288, 291, 303, 333, 18, 26 November, 6 December 1754.

it of unserviceable stock; secondly, private trade at this time was more lucrative and possibly payment more speedy, and the saltpetre could be used profitably for this market.

Some idea of the need for government contracts is conveyed in the later comment by the powder makers to the Board in which they referred to the detrimental effect of peace, low demand, and mills unemployed and near ruinous. Although several of these men are known to have purchased old powder from the Board for reworking for private sale this would not have stimulated enough demand to keep mills and employees fully occupied, a situation confirmed by a communication between John Walton and the Board of January 1754: 'Mr Walton desires 400 barrels of repairable powder at £2 10s that he may be enabled to keep his mills at work until the Board shall contract with him.'[33]

With the Seven Years War and the eighteen months which preceded it came complete contrast: the highest demand for gunpowder that the Board had yet known and unprecedented pressure on the makers. However, the demand did not only come from the Ordnance Office. It also came privately from the much increased opportunity to market a material so necessary for expanding overseas settlement and trade and also as a result of Anglo-French conflict, trade competition, and the need to protect that trade; this was particularly so in the case of the African slave trade and the varied trade with North America. From the underemployment characteristic of the period prior to 1755 the makers were now to receive not only opportunity but also pressure from two very different sources. Having avidly awaited government contracts, they were now tempted to supply merchants for export at the same time as, or even at the expense of, the Ordnance Office. The shortage of gunpowder which the government was to experience during 1755 was to continue throughout the war. Although shortage may have occurred during previous wars, it is unlikely to have been of the same order, for so concerned was the Office about high demand and short supply that for the first time an Act was passed to prohibit the exportation and coastwise movement of gunpowder without licence.

Gunpowder supply, 1755

Requests for gunpowder for the armed forces increased considerably from January 1755, particularly with preparation for Newcastle's plans for North America. However, to the consternation of the Board the initial deliveries were slow. So concerned was it, that at a meeting at

[33] WO 47/43, p. 32, 24 January 1754.

Old Palace Yard, Westminster the surveyor general ordered that the four makers be requested to make immediate delivery to Greenwich. This was to little effect. The partnerships of Eade & Bridges and of Chauncy & Vigne continued to be unproductive, while of 610 barrels delivered from Walton on 22 March only 145 were of the required standard, and of Pryce's 100 barrels not one was passed. As a result further letters were sent to the two former partnerships on 27 March repeating the plea for speed in delivery.[34] By 29 March Greenwich magazine had at last received a delivery of 158 barrels from Chauncy & Vigne, although only about one-eighth of this quantity proved to be satisfactory. Of a total of 964 barrels which had now been delivered from Chauncy & Vigne, Pryce, and Walton, no less than 785 had failed to pass the Office proof, thus leaving a meagre 179 barrels to go into store.[35]

With a squadron of naval ships being fitted for Boscawen's expedition to the Atlantic and British military forces being equipped for Braddock's campaign, this was a most unsatisfactory situation. The low quantity of powder delivered so far, compared with unserviceable powder purchased from the Office, confirms the makers' involvement in private trade. Although lacking in official status such trade was, as the Board later realised, more remunerative.[36]

Eade & Bridges, with no delivery at all as yet, were obviously working almost entirely for such trade. They had agreed contract in December 1754 yet purchased 200 barrels of unserviceable powder at a time from government stock in each of the months of January, February, March and April for their private use. At £2 10s a barrel the total cost of purchase was £2,000.[37] The Board refused such requests in May and June in an unsuccessful attempt to speed the supply of new powder from the mills. Not until 26 April did this partnership make its first delivery when the negligible total of sixteen barrels arrived at Greenwich. Of these only two passed proof and the remaining fourteen were returned. An explosion at their Ewell mills in June added to the delay.[38] Pryce, and Walton were the first to submit enough powder of required standard to fulfil their respective contracts; this was in May. Not until November did Chauncy & Vigne, and Eade & Bridges complete their first contracts.[39]

34 WO 47/45, p. 269, 27 March 1755.
35 Ibid., p. 461, 16 May 1755; for method of government proof, see ch. 10.
36 WO 47/58, pp. 256, 274, 8, 15 October 1761.
37 WO 51/193, p. 157, 31 March 1755; WO 47/45, pp. 35, 135, 393, 14 January, 21 February, 25 April 1755.
38 WO 47/46, p. 566, 13 June 1755.
39 WO 51/198, p. 12, 15 November 1755; WO 51/179, p. 217, 22 November 1755.

It is extraordinary that the Office continued to sell unserviceable powder during 1755 at the expense of supplies of new stock. The contracts stated that old powder could be obtained in two ways; in lieu of saltpetre at the discretion of the Board or instead of money payment, the latter the most usual method. It was therefore not in direct connection with contracts that the majority of unserviceable powder now came from the Board but by direct purchase. Such sale by the Office not only helped it to clear its stores but was intended as an incentive to the makers to provide more new. This was totally misjudged as the more old powder sold to them the more time the makers spent on private trade. Pressure on the Office to sell a further 900 barrels of such powder in March came as a result of problems at Greenwich magazine. Because of cracks in the north-east wall all stock had to be removed from the upper floors to the outports and Gillingham Fort. Unserviceable stock had to be sold and a new site, Purfleet, chosen for a magazine.[40]

In view of the small quantity of gunpowder which had been delivered by April, the date set for Boscawen's departure, the Board decided to contract with additional makers but instead of 485 barrels a month, obviously an unrealistic goal, the quantity agreed was less. Those now contracted were the partnerships of Robert & James Norman of Molesey, Edward Pyke & Thomas Edsall Sr & Jr of Dartford, James Underhill & Thomas Ravens of Bedfont, and William Taylor of Worcester Park. These new contracts were on improved financial terms. It was agreed that payment could be in money, at a minimum rate of £0 17s 6d or, alternatively, as 36 lb of dry repairable powder or 28 lb of refined saltpetre per barrel.[41]

Not surprisingly, makers already under contract petitioned the Board on 1 July on the difference in remuneration, stating that they had submitted to the Board's terms at contract because of underemployment when many of their mills were unused. Since then the present armament had caused 'difficulties by the raised price of all materials required for manufacture and of workmen's wages'. They prayed the Board 'take the same into consideration and put them on a like footing with the other makers'. The Board agreed reluctantly, on condition that their powder improved in quality.[42] Until November 1756 payment of the makers' choice was saltpetre which could be used for private trade, and it was only after a long interval that the Board decided, for that reason, to stop this method of payment. Whatever form payment took, entries in the Ordnance bill books refer only to the

[40] WO 47/44, p. 366, 17 December 1754; WO 47/45, p. 191, 10 March 1755.
[41] WO 47/45, p. 353, 15 April 1755; see appendix 2, tables 3 and 5.
[42] WO 47/46, p. 8, 1 July 1755.

money value of £0 17s 6d a barrel. The type of payment was recorded in the Office minutes. After this time all petre for such trade was purchased on the open market.

Three of the four most recent makers made their first delivery within a month, with an initial success at proof in striking contrast to those before them. However, ordnance stores for the forces leaving to join Braddock in May, together with continual requests for fitting naval ships, maintained pressure on both Office and makers. This resulted in a desperate plea by the Board to hasten delivery on 6 May and again on 10 June, by which date only Taylor and Pryce had responded.[43] There is no evidence in extant Ordnance records of any penalty imposed by the Board for poor delivery or constructive comment for improving quality.

Meantime, the Board continued to sell old powder. This is puzzling, but the reason for it is perhaps indicated in a minute of 4 August 1755. This expressed the fear, even worse than that its makers might spend time working for private trade, that they might employ for that private supply the best quality Office saltpetre intended specifically for government contracts. On this date Pryce requested a further 200 barrels of old powder 'as he was at present in great want of powder for supplying the merchants'. The existence of such activity was therefore clearly recognised by the Board. The surveyor general, in the presence of the lieutenant general and clerk of the Ordnance suggested that: 'the other makers also be furnished with what they have requested to encourage them to be expeditious in sending new powder into store and also to prevent their working up the Office petre for the merchants to use'.[44] Pyke & Edsall, together with Underhill & Ravens, responded to the offer and paid the usual price of £2 10s a barrel. Probably because of their poor record to date, Chauncy & Vigne were told a week later that no old powder could be spared for them, yet the Board readily complied with Walton's request for 300 barrels when offered the higher price of £3 a barrel. This was in spite of the fact that Walton clearly stated that this was to prepare for the merchants while his saltpetre was drying in preparation for new powder for the Board.[45] The Board demonstrated its concern that saltpetre might be misused with the result that government powder might receive short measure, when it suddenly ordered an analysis of a barrel of new powder from Chauncy & Vigne at the Royal Laboratory at Woolwich; it was found to contain the required seventy-five per cent.[46]

The efforts of the Ordnance Office to meet demands for new powder

---

43 WO 47/45, pp. 490, 544, 26 May, 10 June 1755.
44 WO 47/46, p. 123, 4 August 1755.
45 See appendix 2, table 4.
46 WO 47/45, pp. 283, 570, 29 March, 13 June 1755.

resulted in a complicated system of balancing stock between one magazine and another in order to have a sufficient supply at the right place at the right time. There was no simple one-way flow of powder between makers, central stores and the armed forces but, instead, a continual movement of barrels from one store to another together with a complex reverse flow of both unserviceable powder from the Navy back to Greenwich for reproof and of contracted powder returned to the mills after failing proof. For this purpose the Board began to ask its outport officers, at regular intervals, to report the quantity in store, that for distribution and that required for completion of stock. This was later formalised by monthly returns sent on the last day of each month to enable the Board to assess its overall position.[47]

With increased Anglo-French hostility caused by Boscawen's attempts to intercept the French fleet and Braddock's to recapture lost territory, the demand for powder increased further. Yet, by the end of September 1755 only four of the eight makers had delivered sufficient to fulfil their first contracts. The most productive to date was Walton with 970 barrels.[48] Three others had supplied enough for some payment by the year's end although they were still well below their stated target. The remaining four had not yet submitted enough of good quality for any payment. The lowest quantity passing proof was that of Eade & Bridges.

The powder makers were not the only suppliers with whom the Ordnance Office experienced delays in delivery and poor results at proof. This applied also to such iron masters as Morgan in South Wales, the Crowleys in the Midlands and south-east England and, from 1764, the Carron Company of Scotland.[49] Between 1756 and 1763, twenty-two per cent of all guns submitted for proof at Woolwich were rejected.[50] One of the worst rejections for the Carron Company was in peacetime, in May 1767; of 100 guns submitted, 63 were rejected.[51] Iron masters and powder makers had different problems. The latter had little, if any, work in peacetime. This compelled them to take every opportunity of employment in war. However, they were near London and apart from the occasion when Benjamin Pryce's powder cargo from Faversham mills was delayed in the Thames Estuary by Customs officers because of the absence of licence required by the above legislation,

47 WO 47/48, p. 433, 6 November 1756.
48 WO 51/194, p. 276, 31 May 1755; WO 51/196, p. 65, 4 September 1755.
49 R. H. Campbell, Carron Company (Edinburgh 1961), pp. 83–4; M. W. Flinn, Men of Iron, The Crowleys in the Early Iron Industry (Edinburgh 1962), p. 154; L. J. Williams, 'A Carmarthenshire Ironmaster in the Seven Years War', Business History, 2 (1959), 32.
50 Williams, 'A Carmarthenshire Ironmaster', 33.
51 Campbell, Carron Company, p. 84.

and certain delays experienced by Edward Pryce from Chilworth, the makers had comparatively easy transportation. In contrast, iron masters suffered many delays resulting from hazards of coastal transportation to Woolwich and the constant need to apply for such licences. However, the iron masters, who were more fortunate with peacetime employment, often ceased some of their private trade when under the considerable demands of war in the attempt to fulfil government contracts. The powder makers had no intention of so doing.

So concerned was the Board at low supply and the indifference or inability of the makers to produce more that on 15 October Ligonier, lieutenant general of the Ordnance, informed the secretary of state, Holderness, that because the Board suspected that the makers were producing for export the latter should be prohibited. This resulted in the legislation, in force throughout the war, intended to prohibit private trade in guns and gunpowder. In practice, it was aimed specifically at gunpowder in order to force the powder makers to concentrate more on supply to the government.[52]

The period 1740 to 1755 clearly demonstrates the problems experienced by the Ordnance Office and gunpowder makers in the face of greatly fluctuating demands for gunpowder. The Office found it difficult to judge whether to sell its large stock of unserviceable powder remaining from the War of the Austrian Succession, and when to agree contracts for the supply of new stock. From mid-1754, and increasingly from the beginning of 1755, conflict in North America gathered pace. This resulted in the sudden demand for gunpowder. After a six-year interval of peace the powder makers welcomed the long awaited government contracts, but international conflict brought increased demand not only from the government but also from private trade. In attempting to maintain both markets the makers failed to provide the quantity agreed. It was this situation which eventually resulted in the prohibitive legislation on private trade and, a few years later, the purchase of Faversham mills.

[52] See ch. 7.

3

War and Politics, 1756–63: the Background

A study of gunpowder supply during the Seven Years War must be placed in the context of the main events and the close interactions between war, war strategy, and national and international politics. This war, with the preceding year of Anglo-French hostility, was the most intensive and geographically extensive to date. Whitworth describes it as the most complicated series of military operations so far conducted, while Kennedy considers that it can 'lay a far stronger claim to the title of the first world war than many others before or since'.[1] The fact that it placed great pressure on both Ordnance Office and gunpowder makers further supports Savory's view that it marked the greatest upheaval the world had yet seen:

> The Seven Years War . . . strode the world. Fighting took place in the Philippines, India, the Mediterranean, Spain, Portugal, and West Africa; in Germany, Austria, and on the coast of France; in North America, the Caribbean and Cuba; by sea and on land. All the Great Powers were involved; Austria and the Empire; Russia and France; . . . Sweden and, later, Spain, against Prussia and England with Hanover and their mercenary allies, and later Portugal.[2]

International conflict and declaration of war

The British military and naval action of 1755, aimed at recapturing land in North America from the French, resulted in the cessation of Anglo-French relations, and in French plans at the beginning of 1756 for the invasion of both Britain and Minorca. Affairs in Europe became more complex. The increased Anglo-French conflict in North America increased in turn the threat to George II's electorate of Hanover.

[1] Rex Whitworth, *Field Marshal Lord Ligonier* (Oxford 1958), p. 198; Paul M. Kennedy, *The Rise and Fall of British Naval Mastery* (1976, 2nd edn 1983), p. 98.
[2] Sir Reginald A. Savory, *His Britannic Majesty's Army in Germany during the Seven Years War* (Oxford 1966), p. vii.

Conflict on the Continent with Hanover at its centre, and the degree to which Hanover should be defended, were to be among the main sources of British political controversy throughout the war; yet if France took Hanover it would increase her chances of dominating Europe. In exchange for subsidies Hesse and Russia agreed to provide troops to help Britain protect the electorate against France and Prussia. To neutralise the effect of the Anglo-Russian alliance Prussia joined Britain, in the protection of Hanover, in January 1756. With the French plans for invasion of Britain there was a sudden increase in warships to protect the British coast, and Hessian and Hanoverian troops were brought to strengthen home defence. At the same time preparations were made to send further military forces to North America and a naval fleet to relieve Minorca. In response to the earlier Anglo-Prussian alliance, one was formed between France and Austria in May. In spite of Britain's efforts at defence the French had by this time taken Minorca, the act which resulted in war.

As far as Holland was concerned there was a refusal to agree to a British request for 6,000 men, in spite of the Anglo-Dutch defensive alliances of 1678. In May a position of neutrality was declared with regard to Britain and France.[3] As a result there were no new Anglo-Dutch trade agreements at this time, a point to be of significance regarding importation of Dutch gunpowder.

Although concentrated on the Continent and North America the war was very much more widespread:

> In effect two wars were running concurrently. In the first Frederick the Great of Prussia fought for the existence of his kingdom against the combined forces of Russia, Sweden and Austria. In the second Great Britain, together with Hanover and its little group of west German allies, faced the French at sea, in the New World, in the Indian sub-continent and in Westphalia. In Germany the British and Hanoverians, as allies and auxiliaries of Frederick, stood back to back with him, each defending the other's rear.[4]

In addition to the problem of recruitment was that of desertion and disease among seamen, particularly in the early years of the war. For the Ordnance Office this posed the additional problem of the premature return of naval ships to port and the constant need to check the amount and condition of the powder stock of each vessel before departure with fresh men. The shortage of men meant that Britain could not

---

[3] Alice C. Carter, *Getting, spending and investing in early modern times* (Assen, Netherlands 1975), p. 143.
[4] Ian R. Christie, *Wars and Revolutions: Britain 1760–1815* (1982), p. 45.

at this point take the offensive at sea. Gradish considers that Pitt's influence on the increase of the land forces and later the Militia is undisputed, but that he was never as successful in finding a workable solution to the naval manning problem.[5]

Britain declared war on France in May 1756. The crisis that was to develop in the ensuing six months brought to a head the instability of the British political situation.[6] Subsidies to the Continental allies, military and naval failures, the loss of Minorca, and ministerial mismanagement of the conflict brought outrage from the public against Newcastle, effectively encouraged by Pitt. Newcastle's unstable government, in existence until the summer of 1756, though supported by the King was weakened by mismanagement and lack of a suitable commoner to lead the House of Commons. Pitt's antagonism to Newcastle had been further increased and was to have a marked bearing on the political situation and conduct of war. Pitt publicly opposed the subsidy treaties and had been dismissed from office at the end of 1755, but he voiced the feeling of many including Leicester House, the City, and many independent members of Parliament.[7] Pitt's anti-Hanoverian views were to change within the year.

Problems multiplied. In August 1756 Frederick, concerned about the mobilisation of Russia and Austria, attacked Saxony against British advice thus precipitating the need for an Army of Observation in Hanover for the following year; this was partly sustained by British subsidies. Completing the year of catastrophe was the French capture in the autumn of Fort Oswego on Lake Ontario, an important trading post with the Indians. The deteriorating situation overseas, used to advantage by its opponents, brought down the administration in November. It was replaced by a Ministry led nominally by the Duke of Devonshire but in reality by Pitt. This was shortlived, confused, and ineffective, largely because of limited support for Pitt in the House of Commons and from the King.[8] Under this Ministry the troops brought from the Continent earlier in the year to strengthen British defences against possible invasion were returned, and British forces in North America were increased when stronger measures were proposed against France.

Pitt attempted to please both the King and his own supporters. He

[5] Gradish, *British Navy* (1980), p. 47.
[6] BL Newcastle Papers, Add. MS. 32996, fol. 423, 10 May 1756; Marie Peters, *Pitt and Popularity* (Oxford 1980), pp. 46–7.
[7] E. J. S. Fraser, 'The Pitt-Newcastle coalition and the conduct of the Seven Years War, 1757–60' (Unpublished D.Phil. thesis, Oxford University 1976), pp. 6–7.
[8] Lucy S. Sutherland, 'The City of London and the Devonshire-Pitt Administration 1756–1757', *Proceedings of the British Academy*, 46 (1961), 147.

was heavily dependent on support from the City and from Tories in the House of Commons who not only wanted the Hanoverian troops returned and a Militia Bill but also to avoid direct involvement on the Continent. Pitt's attitude changed once in office and needing royal support and he failed to keep certain pledges to his supporters. Fraser considers that Pitt's past pronouncements were now a serious handicap. He began to support previous government policy of protection for Hanover and requested financial support from Parliament for an Army of Observation in Hanover of Hanoverian, Hessian and Brunswick troops, and a subsidy for Prussia to secure Frederick's promise not to make a separate peace with France. He also supported the alliance with Prussia which he had earlier opposed. To what extent he had any choice is difficult to assess. In his conduct of war Pitt was prepared to take decisions fundamentally opposed to earlier commitments but was careful not to endanger his main sources of support. So that the Prussian subsidy might appear more acceptable he emphasised that no British troops were to be sent to Europe, but in his gradual move towards more extensive Continental involvement even this was to change.[9] Similarly, Pitt championed the Militia Act when out of Office but was less sure of its worth once in. This Act was unpopular with many, including Newcastle. There were others, including the independent members of Parliament, who considered a militia preferable to a standing army. With his need for support from the independents he did not oppose the Act which was passed in June 1757. Embodiment of the Militia, which took place in 1759 resulted in the need for more arms, ammunition, and gunpowder.[10]

Pitt's policies, particularly those concerning Hanover, convinced neither the King nor Cumberland, commander in chief of the allied army, but when the coalition was terminated in April 1757 there was public outrage and after three months without a government the King was compelled to accept Pitt again, but in coalition with Newcastle.

Main events of war, 1757–8

By mid-1757 the military situation on the Continent was alarming. The Prussians had been defeated at Kolin, were in retreat from Bohemia and were threatened by the Swedes and Russians now in alliance with Austria. A further pact had been made between France and Austria to recover Silesia from Prussia. In July the French seized Emden, an important Prussian port and main line of communication

9   Fraser, 'Pitt-Newcastle coalition', 8–11, 109.
10   WO 55/359, p. 158, 9 July 1759.

with England. Cumberland was defeated at Hastenbeck on the Weser leaving Hanover open to invasion from the west. When, as a result, Cumberland was forced to resign his post, Ferdinand of Brunswick was appointed in his place. Adding to the gloom was news from North America that with inadequate troops Loudoun had failed to take Louisbourg and that Fort William Henry had been captured. By summer the position had worsened and immediate action was essential in both Europe and America. In August Pitt suggested increased financial support for Prussia and further subsidies to Hanover and Hesse in the following year. There were hurried plans to reinforce Loudoun's army for the 1758 campaign and to send an expeditionary force to attack the French coast at Rochefort, employing marines and land forces protected by the fleet.[11] One of several such undertakings this was intended to divert French attention from its European campaigns, and in general proved more acceptable to the British public, to the future King and supporters at Leicester House, and to the City than the possibility of sending troops to Hanover. These expeditions, dependent on the Ordnance Office for arms and powder, were viewed by Newcastle as a risk to home defence in that too many troops were employed overseas, while the forces themselves disliked combined military and naval operations. Pitt emphasised that if necessary the troops could be returned home with speed. After Cumberland's resignation Ligonier was appointed commander in chief of British land forces and Sackville replaced him as lieutenant general of the Ordnance.[12]

In the plans for America for 1758 Amherst was to command an expedition with the aid of Howe and Wolfe to attack Louisbourg while Loudoun was to attempt the retrieval of frontier territory. An early attack on Louisbourg was vital in order to block the harbour.[13] The preparation of gunpowder, ordnance and ammunition for these activities was task enough for the Ordnance Office and its manufacturers but confusion over the shipping being loaded for America and the coastal raid against France added to their difficulties. Reinforcements for America were not completed until nine months after the original planning with the bulk of troops and ordnance stores leaving England in February. Middleton considers that this was mainly due to primitive communications between departments of state, unpredictable weather made more noticeable when combined with poor administration, indecision, inadequate planning, and lack of common sense. Departments, by their own standards, executed their tasks competently but it was not

11 WO 55/357, pp. 22, 37, 39, 43, 8 July, 3, 4, 8 August 1757.
12 WO 47/50, p. 425, 23 December 1757; orders for North America were sent by a secretary of state.
13 Whitworth, *Lord Ligonier*, p. 239.

a period of reform or dramatic change. Success was accomplished with the same administrative machinery as had sufficed in England in all wars since the end of the seventeenth century. He suggests further that the government lacked understanding of the difficulties of preparing for Atlantic crossings: 'Ministers in their ignorance remained incurable optimists.'[14] Therefore, in view of the fact that communication between Ordnance Office, Admiralty, and secretaries of state was cumbersome, it was a considerable achievement on the part of the Office that it managed as effectively as it did to link powder supply from the mills to the armed forces in many parts of the world.

The expedition to Rochefort was an amphibious operation involving tactics of quick landing, raid, and embarkation, a method unfamiliar to army officers of the day. Estimates of the necessary quantities of gunpowder and ammunition would have been difficult, for the Army, Navy and Ordnance Office were more familiar with the preparation and use of equipment for more conventional inland warfare. Whatever the expedition or campaign the master general, or other member in his stead, attended Cabinet meetings to advise on appropriate ordnance requirements. The relevant secretary of state would then make an official request to the Ordnance Office for preparation of a certain number and size of guns, small arms, ammunition, and gunpowder, together with any of a large variety of ordnance stores. For this expedition ships loaded with troops and stores gathered off the Isle of Wight in August, sailing from Spithead in early September with troops unaware of their destination until at sea. Only the small island of Aix was taken and the ships returned prematurely. 'The expedition was a disastrous failure and it seemed to be a fitting end to an undistinguished year for British arms both on land and at sea.'[15]

During the winter of 1757–8 the Admiralty was able to man squadrons to serve in the Baltic, West Africa, and Cape Breton and although that under Hawke was so short of men due to sickness that only six of the twenty-two ships assigned to him were available, he managed to intercept a number of French war and troop ships leaving France for Louisbourg. This was part of Pitt's scheme; while the French were prevented from dispatching reinforcements British forces moved freely to areas of conflict overseas.[16] The blockade of French ports continued throughout the war, with ships returning as necessary to replenish ammunition. The key position of Louisbourg on Cape Breton Island at the mouth of the St Lawrence was taken from the French by Wolfe in

[14] C. R. Middleton, 'A Reinforcement for North America, Summer 1757' *Bulletin of the Institute of Historical Research*, 41 (1968), 59–72.

[15] Gradish, *British Navy*, p. 43.

[16] Middleton, 'Administration of Newcastle and Pitt', pp. 5–6.

the summer of 1758, although it was then too late in the season to proceed to Quebec. Once again war strategy and politics were closely interlinked for the capture of Louisbourg strained relations between King and coalition, and France was now more likely to concentrate its efforts on Hanover. Although Ferdinand saw a possible peace as the only alternative to further reinforcement from Britain Pitt wanted the war to continue in order to derive full benefit from French disorder and therefore to acquire more territory. As a consequence the pressure continued on both Office and powder makers.

On the Continent Frederick had defeated the French and Austrians at Rossbach and Leuthen respectively by the end of 1757. Ferdinand forced the French to evacuate Bremen and in February 1758 a supporting naval squadron forced the French from Emden.[17] The subsequent British occupation of Emden was an unpopular move with the House of Commons, the City, and Leicester House. To help the allied army drive the French behind the Rhine in April a further diversionary coastal raid was planned, this time against St Malo. By late May troops had been assembled off the Isle of Wight under Marlborough, master general of the Ordnance, and Sackville, later lieutenant general. The Admiralty was concerned about the amount of shipping necessary both for the assault (150 ships) and for its protection. This assault was to include cavalry, marines, artillery, and guards with specially designed landing craft together with an artillery train prepared by the Ordnance department. Although French ships and stores were set alight the town was not successfully attacked due to a combination of factors such as difficulty in moving the artillery train, bad weather, illness, and shortage of drinking water.

By mid-1758 an increasingly offensive strategy against French colonial and naval power was in operation. Plans included stronger naval squadrons off the French coast to block French reinforcements going overseas and cripple trade, and further raids and expeditions against French possessions abroad. The war strategy was not Pitt's alone. The position of secretary of state did not confer unlimited authority. Any major decision conveyed by Pitt was usually the result of consultation between many people and departments, and his letters of communication were simply the official method of expressing decisions made at Cabinet meetings.[18] To exactly what extent war policy and therefore demand for military stores were influenced by Pitt is a matter for conjecture. Middleton considers that as the main lines of the war had already been determined before Pitt came to power he was, as much as anyone, a prisoner of events. Fraser believes that he had very definite

---

17 Whitworth, *Lord Ligonier*, p. 247.
18 Middleton, 'Administration of Newcastle and Pitt', pp. 352–3.

personal views and subtle but effective ways of putting most of these into effect, although Whitworth considers that it was Ligonier, as commander in chief of land forces and from July 1759 master general of the Ordnance, who had more influence on the military strategy decided within the Cabinet than has been generally realised.[19]

One of the most significant decisions of the war was that made in June 1758 to send a British military force to the Continent to support Ferdinand. On 30 June Pitt asked the Ordnance Board for guns, ammunition and powder for three battalions of Foot and detachments of the Royal Regiment of Artillery to embark for Emden.[20] The King, who had previously backed Newcastle, transferred his favour to Pitt as a result of the latter's support for Hanover. Leicester House, previously behind Pitt, was highly critical of the expedition particularly concerning the consequent diminution of defence troops at home.[21] At approximately the same time came news of Frederick's success at Custrin and, to add to the success of Louisbourg, a successful coastal raid against Cherbourg. However, these were followed by another disastrous attempt on St Malo in August, again with an amphibious force. Due to bad weather and poor planning the troops were stranded ashore and many of the Guards Brigade were lost in the eventual retreat. Such raids were then temporarily abandoned.

Military forces were sent to Africa in April to reinforce the trading base of Fort Louis on the Senegal and to capture the island of Goree.[22] In the autumn troops were sent to strengthen the number in North America. Although an attempt on Martinique, intended as a potential exchange for Minorca at the eventual peace, was unsuccessful Guadeloupe was captured from the French in May. Some of the forces remained there while the others went to Halifax to join those gathering for the attack on Quebec. In these undertakings the Ordnance Office continued to play a key part, fitting ships with guns and powder and sending all necessary equipment for the troops. Preference was now given to those ships bound for America with men and ordnance stores to join Wolfe. There was therefore difficulty in recruiting enough men for ships intended for service in the Mediterranean and the East Indies, and for the continued blockade of French ports. For the 277 ships in commission by April the Navy was 7,000 men short of the 82,000 required.[23]

---

[19] See Fraser, 'Pitt-Newcastle coalition'; Middleton, 'Administration of Newcastle and Pitt'; and Whitworth, Ligonier: for the political aspects of this war, the studies of Fraser and Middleton are among the most detailed accounts available.
[20] WO 47/52, p. 6, 4 July 1758.
[21] Fraser, 'Pitt-Newcastle coalition', p. 254.
[22] WO 55/358, pp. 11, 74, 6, 9 September, 4 October 1758.
[23] Gradish, British Navy, p. 48.

Gunpowder from Holland

After their declaration of neutrality in May 1756 the Dutch traded impartially with both sides. They continued to ship timber and permit the passage of artillery from Scandinavia to France and also supplied gunpowder to the British government to help boost stock. This continued until the sudden change in the international situation in 1759.

Although always called 'Dutch' by the Ordnance Office, it is unclear how much of the gunpowder imported from Holland was actually manufactured there. That imported officially from Middlebourg and Amsterdam played an important part in Britain's national stock between 1756 and 1758. Absence of such imports would have added further to the difficulties of the Ordnance department in the initial years of war, just as did its absence during the four years to follow. Royal warrants were issued by the Privy Council to the Ordnance Board for the importation of 10,000 barrels of Dutch powder in each of the months of January and December 1756, 7,000 in September 1757, and 1,000 in May 1758 at a cost of £4 8s a barrel.[24] Such warrants meant the Board could insert the cost of purchase in the next annual financial statement to Parliament. A copy of each warrant was then forwarded to the Treasury so that it could prepare its own warrant for the Customs officers to permit free importation and landing of the powder at Tilbury. Customs staff were paid one guinea each for each ship attended during unloading.[25] Although the first consignment was intended for storage in the Tower, in practice the main store throughout this period was the magazine at Tilbury, while the remainder was distributed immediately to the other outports. Samples of powder were tested at the Tower but when testing of English powder was so stringent it is surprising that no official trials appear to have been undertaken on behalf of the Office on the Dutch powder before it was shipped from Holland. No record of the Tower results survives but the Board regarded Dutch powder as inferior to British.

The monthly returns submitted to the Board by the Ordnance officers at the six outport magazines of Greenwich, Upnor, Gravesend and Tilbury, Portsmouth, Sheerness, and Plymouth between November 1756 and August 1759 detail the proportion of Dutch to English powder in store at any one time; from this can be seen the significance of Dutch stock.[26] There was a total of over 6,000 barrels of Dutch powder in store by the end of 1756, mainly at Tilbury and Gravesend. By

[24] WO 47/48, p. 599, 23 December 1756; WO 47/50, p. 189, 14 September 1757; WO 47/51, p. 525, 27 May 1758.
[25] WO 55/357, p. 42, August 1757; WO 47/51, p. 159, 15 February 1758.
[26] See appendix 2, table 8.

January 1758 this total had risen to 14,470, the highest stored quantity of such powder recorded during the war. This was in sharp contrast to the 2,840 barrels of English powder in stock, the lowest total of the war to date. Not until September of that year did the English total surpass Dutch after which the absence of the latter became noticeable as stock gradually diminished.

These returns form a valuable record of the monthly state of government powder stock during a three-year period of war. However, they were intended solely for purposes of assessment by the Board of the current state of powder stock available for use in its magazines on specific dates. The state of stock could be compared between different dates but the returns could not, and were not intended to be used for assessing either the pattern of movement of powder or the quantity sent into, or issued from the magazines in the intervening weeks. Although the returns give also the quantity 'under orders for issue' (the quantity of stock planned for imminent issue to the armed forces), it is impossible to judge what proportion, if any, had actually been issued by the date of the next monthly return. Also, although the quantity was known of all Dutch powder arriving at Tilbury together with all new and repaired powder successfully proved at Greenwich, there is no way of assessing exactly when such powder became included in stock ready for entry in the official monthly returns. Some returns, such as those of May 1757, included a separate entry on the quantity of powder either ordered to be sent or actually in transit between one magazine and another but not included in the official total or that 'under order for issue'. Such a figure, though an important part of the entire government gunpowder stock for the month in question, was just a fraction of the much larger daily movement.

In particular, there is no way of estimating the exact proportion of Dutch powder issued during any one month from any particular magazine, although it was established in 1758 that powder issued to ships of the Royal Navy should be one-third Dutch and two-thirds English.[27] One further factor which made impossible the assessment of the quantity of gunpowder entering and leaving magazines between the monthly returns was that the importation of Dutch powder was sometimes undertaken in secret and referred to only in private correspondence. It is obvious that when, on 5 January 1756, the Duke of Marlborough as master general received a royal warrant to order the importation of 10,000 barrels from Holland, this was not the first such order of the period; the Ordnance Office and Admiralty were corresponding currently concerning convoy for 1,000 barrels of powder from Middle-

27 WO 47/51, p. 232, 7 March 1758.

bourg. Purchase was to be kept secret from the Office staff.[28] An indication of secrecy in the previous war is given in correspondence of April 1757 between Holderness and surveyor general Frederick when the latter was asked to seek evidence of Dutch importation in 1740. He found reference only to the quantity and added 'I find it was kept a profound secret and none of the transactions entered in our minutes.'[29]

Early in 1759 there was a marked change in Anglo-Dutch political relations and consequently the importation of Dutch powder ceased completely. The Dutch government, until now neutral and trading impartially with both Britain and France suddenly, and to Britain's alarm, appeared to favour France. It was now transporting large cannon from Scandinavia to Dunkirk in its own ships under a neutral flag. The cannon were for the use of the French in their preparation for an invasion of Britain. Britain protested to Holland and threatened to prevent all Dutch ships trading between the Baltic and the Texel. Some were captured and as a result the Dutch opted to renounce all trade in arms with the two powers and prohibited the passage of all munitions from Dutch territory.[30] Although initially this prohibition delayed shipments of cannon to France, thus aiding the British successes of 1759 and hampering French plans for the invasion of Britain, the cessation was in practice temporary for shipments to France recommenced. Furthermore, Holland was at this time exporting saltpetre to France for use in the preparation of gunpowder. Although both powers managed to purchase munitions in Holland to be sent via inland waterways to the respective armies on the Continent during the remainder of the war, there is no evidence that Dutch gunpowder was ever supplied direct to the British troops in Germany.[31]

The termination of powder supply from Holland was undoubtedly due not only to the continuing uncertainty about Anglo-Dutch relations, but also to the increasing danger of conveying powder laden vessels across open sea. As early as December 1756 it was decided between Ordnance Board and Admiralty that a 20-gun ship would now be the most appropriate convoy vessel. This was due to the difficulty in shipping the powder secretly and thus the danger that French emissaries might know of it and 'send advice thereof to Dunkirk as they did last time'.[32]

[28] Adm. 1/4010, 14 January 1756.
[29] SP 41/38, 23 April 1757.
[30] Carter, *Getting, spending and investing*, pp. 151–4.
[31] Ibid., p. 156.
[32] Adm. 1/4010, 7 December 1756; in spite of this, private shipments in arms and powder continued; WO 47/48, p. 546, 7 December 1756.

War, 1759–63

The year 1759 was one of success for Britain in North America, Germany, West Africa, and the West Indies and not least in the defence of Britain itself. Coinciding with Wolfe's departure for America in February came news of further plans for a French invasion of Britain. The consequent need for more men led to the embodiment of the Militia. At the same time more troops were required in India, Germany and North America, those for the latter location to replace large numbers lost during the harsh winter.[33] As a further safeguard against invasion five new batteries were established along the south coast, and a mobile force of troops and ships was stationed off the Isle of Wight ready for rapid deployment to any part of Britain. Destinations included Scotland threatened by a coalition of Sweden and France. An artillery train was prepared by the Ordnance Office and dispatched to Fort George in Scotland, and arms and powder supplied to the citizens of Bristol, Liverpool, and Aberdeen.[34]

In August, Ferdinand defeated the French at Minden, Amherst took Crown Point, Ticonderoga, and Niagara in North America and even more important, Wolfe took Quebec; only Montreal was still in French hands. In the autumn French ships at Dunkirk, Brest, and Quiberon Bay still waited for an opportunity to invade Britain. British ships in the Channel and Mediterranean continued to intercept French reinforcements for America. This included Hawke's squadron which maintained a five month blockade in changeable weather with sick men who were continually having to be replaced from Portsmouth. In October, movement among French ships brought full alert in Britain although when a French squadron left Brest in November to collect its troop transports in Quiberon Bay it was overcome by Hawke; this, combined with the defeat of another French squadron in March 1760, brought to an end any immediate fear of invasion. With additional forces needed on the Continent, in the East Indies, and for taking both Montreal and Martinique, independent companies had to be raised and new regiments formed. With the Militia and the augmentations of 1760 (excluding the Irish establishment) there were now almost ten times as many troops as at the start of the war, over 200,000 men in total. This number was to rise even further in 1762 when Spain entered the war.[35] Added to this was the vast increase in the Navy. These brought increased pressure on the Office.[36]

[33] SP 41/38, 4 June 1759.
[34] WO 55/359, p. 165, 26 July 1759; WO 55/361, p. 64, 31 October 1760, including 150 barrels for the defence of Liverpool.
[35] Whitworth, *Lord Ligonier*, pp. 316–17.
[36] SP 41/38, 3 May 1760.

Although Amherst succeeded in taking Montreal in September 1760, Ferdinand was only partly successful against the French due to sickness among his men and eventual shortage of arms. He defeated the French in Hesse but not in Cassel. No other British troops were sent although one further coastal raid was planned to divert French attention from Hanover. The King was enthusiastic but concern was expressed by Ligonier, now master general, about the short notice for ordnance preparation and the lateness of the season, and by Newcastle about a decrease in troops for home defence. This raid involved preparations of the Army, Navy, and stores on a scale never before seen in Britain. Furthermore, it was undertaken in the utmost secrecy and entitled variously 'special' and 'secret' expedition in Ordnance records. Even the Board had no idea of the destination, so there were obvious difficulties in estimating the quantity of gunpowder needed. The goal was Belle Isle, a fortified island off Brittany. Marching orders were given to 9,000 troops to assemble at Portsmouth in October 1760 and one of the largest artillery trains ever prepared by the Office accompanied them by road from London; this included twenty-one tons of gunpowder.[37] Eventually a naval survey was undertaken of the terrain; it was found unsuitable for landing and in December the expedition was postponed. The detailed preparations of the Office came to nothing and all troops and ordnance stores assembled off Portsmouth came ashore. Sudden changes of location, cancellation, or postponement of a plan like the 'secret expedition' to Belle Isle made continual demands on Ordnance staff. Stores had to be prepared for all intended campaigns, whether or not they took place, and reassembled, inspected, and put into safe storage in the event of changes in plan.[38] Belle Isle was eventually captured in June of the following year.

With continuing indecisive action in Germany in 1761 and Ferdinand's ideas for a separate peace with France, the Cabinet decided that prior to peace, the cost of war in Germany should be offset by further territorial gains, including St Lucia, Dominica, Martinique, Mauritius, and more land in America. In August Spain announced its intention to enter the war with France against Britain unless peace was made by the following May. Spain resented among other things the British presence in Gibraltar and its claim to the restitution of Minorca by the French. The British naval squadron off the Spanish coast and the

[37] WO 47/56, pp. 254, 265, 270, 295, 441, 5, 8, 10, 17 October, 12 December 1760.
[38] This procedure will be illustrated in subsequent chapters; the term 'Cabinet' employed here is as defined by Gradish; 'that small group of Privy Councillors who were confidential ministers of the Crown . . . frequently known as the "Inner" Cabinet'. (Gradish, *British Navy*, p. 11)

forces on Guadeloupe and Belle Isle were strengthened, an expedition sent to Martinique, and further military forces raised. As the shortage of seamen continued the Admiralty requested reinstatement of bounty payments to volunteers and local aid in finding recruits.[39] By October 1761 the threat of Spanish intervention in the war prompted Pitt to seek his colleagues' consent to a pre-emptive strike. On their refusal he resigned, although the government did eventually find it necessary to declare war on Spain in January. The year 1762 marked a turning point:

> During the campaign season of 1762 British military and naval might, now at its peak, smashed through Bourbon resistance to an almost unprecedented series of triumphs. In the Caribbean the British seized French Martinique, Grenada, and the neutral islands and also Spain's leading island base at Havana in Cuba. From India an expedition was launched against the Philippines, and Spain had also lost Manila before the end of the summer.[40]

In Germany the British and allied force maintained its position until early in the year when Russia and Sweden made peace with Prussia, and Austria was deterred because of fear that Russia might support Prussia. In May, controversy within the ministry over war in Germany reached a climax and when aid was granted to Portugal against Spain, at the expense of the subsidy to Prussia, Newcastle resigned. He was replaced by Bute. The involvement of Portugal occurred as the result of French and Spanish awareness of the commercial value to Britain of Lisbon; Britain went to Portugal's aid when Spain entered the country in April. Gunpowder for this involved not only that provided by the Office for British troops but that sold privately by certain powder makers to the Portuguese.[41] The combined army's success against Spain was one factor in the termination of this war. The partial collapse of France's eastern alliance system and British successes in the Caribbean and western Pacific left the Bourbon powers no alternative but to submit.[42] Peace negotiations were commenced in the autumn and the Peace of Paris was signed on 10 February 1763.[43]

The events of the Seven Years War, in which Britain and France and their various allies fought in many parts of the world, were complex from many points of view. The initial political instability in Britain, exacerbated by the loss of Minorca, controversy about

[39] Ibid., p. 50.
[40] Christie, *Wars and Revolutions*, p. 46.
[41] WO 47/59, p. 551, 25 June 1762.
[42] Christie, *Wars and Revolutions*, p. 46.
[43] WO 47/61, p. 160, 21 March 1763.

Hanover, and political difficulties with North America, was calmed by the more stable administration of Newcastle and Pitt. The political situation changed again later as the indirect result of involvement with Spain. This all produced, in turn, unprecedented pressure on the Ordnance Office in its effort to supply the enormous demand for gunpowder for the armed forces. Although importation of Dutch stock played an important part initially this ceased in 1758, at the same time as demands on the Office were increased by the decision to send forces to Germany.

4

Gunpowder Supply
in the Seven Years War

The severe problems with gunpowder supply continued into 1756 and increased further with the declaration of war in May. It is unlikely that the Ordnance Office could have foreseen either the scale of demand or the degree of difficulty in meeting it. It might seem that experience should have been gained from previous wars but there was no reason why the Office should suppose that a routine quite satisfactory in the past would not suffice again. It did not take delivery of the quantity agreed and much of what it did receive did not pass the official testing or proof. Conversely, the suppliers, faced in peacetime with slump and dependency on the comparatively low requirements of merchants took every opportunity in war to satisfy two markets simultaneously – government and private trade. Both now sought more powder than ever before. Within the hours and limited technical knowledge available it was impossible to satisfy both fully at the same time and inevitably it was the government, which paid less but which demanded powder of a higher quality, which was at the greatest disadvantage. Government contracts were long awaited, highly sought, and prestigious. However, continuity in production of powder of high quality demanded not only valuable time at the mills, which the makers were often loath to provide when merchants were more easily satisfied, but also good organisation and accuracy in technology. Neither of these had yet been considered in detail, let alone attained. In spite of legislation to prohibit private exportation without licence this trade continued; powder merchants and even the makers themselves obtained licences with little difficulty.[1] It soon became evident that the Act was virtually useless and throughout the war the Office struggled to balance increasing demand with unsatisfactory supply. The end of gunpowder imports from Holland after 1758 added to its difficulties.

With regard to the responsibility of the Ordnance Office towards the armed forces at this time, it was never in possession of sufficient gunpowder to run the service with the ease and efficiency it would have desired. There is no evidence for any part of this war that it could

---

[1] See ch. 7

not meet the demands made by the respective secretaries of state on behalf of the Army. Stock for campaigns in North America and Germany, and for the defensive artillery trains at home was usually supplied direct from the main magazine at Greenwich; although heavy demands were made on this magazine in its role as source of supply for all other British magazines at home and abroad, it was nevertheless the reception point for new stock from the mills and as such was never entirely deplete. It was ships of the Royal Navy which posed most problem. All such ships returning to port, for whatever reason, had to have their powder stock surveyed and replenished if the grain appeared damaged or damp from its time at sea. Although difficult to quantify such requirements did eat heavily into the Office's stock. Most difficulty was experienced at the height of the war in the winter of 1761–2, when demand was at its greatest to date and stock at its lowest; then ships at Portsmouth and Plymouth were forced to set sail without their full complement.

It was the continuing shortage of powder throughout the war rather than the dramatic dearth at its height that put the greatest pressure on the Office. At no time did it appear to have experienced a complete absence of stock at several outports simultaneously but there were frequent delays while supplies were moved from one magazine to another in an effort to balance stock and meet immediate requirements. As far as overseas naval bases were concerned the Office always attempted to meet the immediate demands of their storekeepers, but when stock at Greenwich was particularly low there was often delay in dispatching the full amount at any one time while the priorities between one base and another were evaluated. The overwhelming problem for the Ordnance Board was that it received far less powder than the quantity originally agreed at contract and less than expected from subsequent agreements or financial incentives.

Gunpowder supply, 1756

Although more gunpowder of the required standard was delivered during 1756 than in the previous year, no individual mill produced that agreed at contract. The Underhill & Ravens, and Walton partnerships produced most. Only Chauncy & Vigne of Oare produced less than in 1755. This partnership's cessation in supply between May 1756 and August 1759 and low overall supply was probably due to reasons of age for both men died in 1760; Chauncy was 70. The degree of success at proof of each maker varied considerably. There was no necessary correlation between improved quantity submitted to Greenwich for proof and improved percentage actually passing; sometimes quite the reverse.

Although some makers reacted to the financial incentives offered by the Board in 1757 and 1761 by increasing their output in general, none achieved the original annual quantity agreed. The Board was less interested in annual totals than in reliable weekly deliveries, and less in intermittent excellent results at proof than in regular reasonable ones. It was the marked fluctuations in quantity and standard of powder received which caused as much concern to the Board as the general shortage.[2]

With the outbreak of war and general political uncertainty the Board required information on current stock. From its request of 2 April for a report on stock at the outport magazines resulted the automatic monthly returns issued by the outport officers until August 1759. On 29 June 1756 it ordered staff to prepare a statement of all outstanding contracts together with dates of agreement and degree of completion. Pryce, and those whose contracts were on the same terms as that of December 1754, had supplied a total to date well below the 485 barrels a month, or 4,850 a year for which allowance was originally made. Even with the lowered expectations agreed with the other powder makers in the spring of 1755 only the partnership of Pyke & Edsall had submitted quantity to date anywhere near that stated.[3]

Problems and incentives, 1757–8

In spite of the official importation of Dutch powder during the previous year the state of stock continued to be a matter of concern in 1757. The Office purchased some separate consignments of Dutch powder in April when the master general was informed by the secretary of state that 6,000 barrels of powder were being offered for sale in Holland by the envoy to the King of Prussia. The British minister at the Hague was asked to negotiate purchase based on the fact that 'powder for His Majesty's service costs £3 14s a barrel, including the hazle hooped barrels'. As with the regular official imports of Dutch powder, the contractors for the sale were Pye and Cruikshank.[4] In May of the following year a further 500 barrels of Dutch powder were purchased from the merchant Richard Oswald at £4 16s a barrel; this included free delivery plus removal of all which failed proof, in this case 200 barrels.[5] Alarmed by the competition from Oswald, Pye and

[2] See appendix 2, table 6 and, for example of variability in proof, see ch. 9.
[3] WO 47/47, p. 689, 29 June 1756; see appendix 2, tables 5–7.
[4] WO 47/49, p. 415, 26 April 1757; for official importation of Dutch powder see ch. 3.
[5] WO 47/51, pp. 509, 633, 16 May, 16 June 1758.

Cruikshank proposed delivery of a further 1,000 barrels 'of the best and strongest proof at £4 12s a barrel'. The Board agreed, providing all that failed proof was returned to Holland. Although a sample of English powder was sent to the contractors for comparison there is no record of agreement to the transaction.[6] The only other references to such powder offered during the war were to 1,000, and 4,000 barrels in March and August 1759 respectively, the first of which was offered by a Peter Fearon, stored on his ship at Shields 'of the same proof as that made use of by the government of Russia'. There is no record of acceptance of either.[7]

The Devonshire-Pitt coalition ended in April 1757 and was replaced by the more stable administration of Pitt and Newcastle. International conflict continued unabated and by the summer the Ordnance Office and powder makers were experiencing the highest demand on supplies yet. Increasing numbers of British military and naval forces were being prepared for departure on the 1758 Louisbourg campaign and a combined force was being fitted out for an amphibious assault against the French coast at Rochefort for August to divert French attention from the allied army in Hanover. An example of the size of request to the Office was that made by Pitt on behalf of the Crown on 28 January 1757. He requested a battering train for the British forces in North America which was to include ordnance of various sizes, mortars, and shot, for which the Board calculated a requirement of 2,000 barrels of powder. It was to be ready to sail on 12 February. Total stock at the outport magazines on 31 January was 8,426 barrels of English powder and 5,768 Dutch, of which 4,274 and 2,352 barrels respectively, were already under order for issue; therefore, this one consignment for North America, not yet accounted for in the report of stock, represented a high proportion of the total available.[8]

Correspondence between Pitt and the Board on 26 July concerning a request from the East India Company for purchase of ordnance stores illustrates the shortage. The Board reported that it could supply the brass ordnance, shells and shot, but in view of the present emergency it could not provide gunpowder without the greatest inconvenience to its own service.[9] Adding to the continuous pressure on supply was the large amount of gunpowder expended. This was partly due to the inaccurate flintlock weapons which necessitated firing volleys of shots by word of command to an entire group of men rather than single shots

6 WO 47/52, pp. 78, 141, 21 July, 9 August 1758.
7 WO 47/53, pp. 369, 408, 27 March, 6 April 1759; WO 47/54, p. 141, 10 August 1759.
8 WO 55/356, p. 190, 28 January 1757, Pitt to Marlborough; WO 47/49 p. 44, 7 February 1757; see appendix 2, table 8.
9 SP 41/38, July 1757.

at individual targets.[10] Large amounts of powder were used in this way by the North American colonial forces fighting alongside the British, whereby the former made a 'most intolerable and inconceivable consumption' of powder.[11] A large quantity was also used in naval salutes. The Board reminded the Admiralty at the beginning of the following year of a regulation of 1688–1731 according to which, due to the quantity of powder consumed, salutes were forbidden in time of war unless to ships or castles of foreign princes.[12] It was once again concerned about the effect this would have on stock and from April 1758 no salutes were to be allowed by the Navy in wartime unless specified.[13] Nevertheless, gunpowder continued to be used in celebratory fireworks. These were prepared by the comptroller of the Royal Laboratory at Woolwich for the King's birthdays, for the firing of guns on forts, castles, Tower wharf and St James's Park for the King's coronation in September 1761, and for the various individual victories of the war.

Until the beginning of 1757 the main efforts by the Board to improve supply were confined to three main methods. These were firstly, to restrict by legislation the export activity and associated commercial interests of its gunpowder makers; secondly, to cease temporarily the sale of returned gunpowder to the makers and, thirdly, to introduce certain financial incentives for good results. The Board had hoped that the quantity which passed proof would rise once the competition of the merchants had been decreased by the above legislation, but it failed to eliminate this alternative market and was forced to offer certain financial incentives. In January 1757 the Board decided that 'in order to encourage them (the powder makers) to make powder better and to stand the Office proof they will be allowed from this day £0 2s 6d a barrel over and above their contract price for every 80 barrels that shall pass on proof out of each 100 barrels proved'.[14] This meant a minimum of eighty per cent success at proof of a minimum of 100 barrels actually delivered to Greenwich. The powder makers were requested a few days later to send in powder with the 'utmost expedition' and to ensure that it was of good quality as the Board had granted them 'an indulgence in price for that purpose'.[15]

As it supplied the saltpetre to the mills, the Board had some control over the cost to the makers of the powder they prepared for the government. Although the price of sulphur is known at import (£0 9s – £0 11s

10 Rogers, *The British Army*, p. 68.
11 Stanley Pargellis, (ed.), *Military Affairs in North America 1748–1765* (New York 1936), p. 278.
12 WO 47/51, p. 177, 21 February 1758.
13 WO 55/357, p. 180, 14 April 1758.
14 WO 47/49, p. 19, 7 January 1757.
15 Ibid., p. 47, 11 January 1757.

per cwt), insufficient detail of market or local prices of sulphur and charcoal, or wood for charcoal, make it difficult to ascertain the exact profit made by the makers on powder supplied to the Office. Therefore, payment at this time had to cover costs which included charcoal, sulphur, labour, the transportation of powder to Greenwich and of failed powder back again, and the transportation to and from Rotherhithe to collect saltpetre. The makers retained their own barrels. In March, the arrangement for the above incentive had to be modified for by no means did every delivery or quantity undergoing proof from individual makers consist of a minimum of 100 barrels. The Board decided that if four-fifths of each man's total delivery passed proof it should be monied at £1 a barrel but otherwise at £0 17s 6d.[16] This incentive lasted until November 1762. The Board was more strict with this more clearly defined reward than with those previously. The results varied between obvious improvement at some mills, improvement with either output or proof results at others and, for some, no appreciable difference at all.

Assessment of the effect of this incentive requires study not only of the number of barrels passing proof but any link between the number passing and the percentage passing of the total delivered. Among those who responded most positively were Eade & Bridges. This was not immediate, but by a gradual increase of the annual quantity submitted from 332 barrels of which fifty-one per cent passed proof in 1757, to 1,606 of which ninety-five per cent passed in 1760. The Waltons' total rose from 3,676 barrels submitted (of which eighty-two per cent were successful) in 1757, to 3,826 (ninety-six per cent successful) in 1760; although their total quantity passing proof was not as high in 1761, the additional financial incentive did result in a higher percentage passing proof of the total submitted that year. This was a total of 3,536, which was ninety-nine per cent of the total submitted (3,572). During 1758, their first whole year under contract, Smith & Hill gradually increased their total output but retained a low annual percentage passing proof. Instead of any obvious concentration on improving quality they appear to have submitted larger quantities for proof to compensate for those which failed. Between June and December their percentage pass rates for individual deliveries dropped as low as thirty-eight, forty-one, and thirty-two per cent respectively. This partnership managed only a low percentage pass rate compared to output throughout the war. On the other hand both Taylor and Benjamin Pryce increased their percentage passing proof rather than their total quantity; Taylor was the only maker who actually achieved the reward of £1 a barrel for every one passing proof during the period of this incentive. The changes which

16 Ibid., p. 260, 11 March 1757.

occurred show that for certain makers this incentive did have some effect but viewed overall there was not the general marked improvement at which the Board had aimed. Although the weekly, rather than annual results demonstrate a large number of successful rewards of £1 a barrel there were still also many at the old price of £0 17s 6d. To achieve a marked rise in stock, more was required than the minimum result necessary to achieve the reward.

The disappointing totals of both powder submitted and that passing proof at this time demonstrate that there must have been problems at the mills in not only achieving, but maintaining good results. There is no evidence during any part of the war that the Board checked whether the manufacturing process at individual mills conformed with certain stipulations agreed at contract. Even for those powder makers with a particularly low percentage pass rate at proof there is no sign of direct investigation or constructive communication by the Board regarding individual methods. Although with high demand this might be considered as surprising it is rather unlikely that the Board had much positive advice to offer, given its experiences at its own mills at Faversham from 1759 and the general lack of contemporary knowledge on the subject.[17]

It is most unlikely that this was a situation where, because a greater amount could be earned more readily from private trade, the powder makers lacked the impetus to attempt a high standard for the government and made the positive decision to sell direct to the merchants all powder failed by the Office. There was no advantage to be gained from this. Not only did they have to finance all transportation to and from Greenwich, but powder intended for the Office contained the Office saltpetre; they had to make a deposit of £1,200 for twenty tons of grough saltpetre for 485 barrels. If powder which failed proof was sold to merchants the saltpetre content would have to be replaced. The cost of the grough petre for each 100 lb. of powder was £2 10s. The price of replacing petre at the India House sales was higher.[18] As it would not have been worth selling failed powder to the merchants, and merchants were satisfied with stock of lower standard anyway, it would have been reworked at the mills and resubmitted for proof. Nevertheless, the use of Office saltpetre in merchants' powder was something the Ordnance Board always feared because it believed merchants paid a higher price for each barrel purchased. In practice it is unlikely to have happened on any great scale, and certainly not regularly. It was time that makers gave to private trade rather than failed Office powder or an insignificant amount of Office saltpetre.

17 See chs. 9 and 10.
18 For saltpetre, see also ch. 10 and appendix 2, table 9.

Gunpowder makers found it difficult to maintain a high standard of workmanship for a number of reasons in addition to the time it spent on private trade. These included high demand, the limitations of organisation, and the limited scientific and technological knowledge within the industry at the time. The only extant eighteenth century results at proof prior to this war were those of a year of peace in 1749. When comparing the two periods it is interesting to note that for much of this war results at proof were lower than in 1749. With gunpowder reworked for the Office in that year the average success at proof was ninety-nine per cent for Eade, and for Chauncy & Vigne, and between ninety-four and ninety-eight per cent for the other six makers. This may have been because private trade was not offering such strong competition and because the powder was not new but reworked. Comparison between results at proof during this war in general, and the years 1760 and 1761 in particular is equally interesting. From the latter it appears that, although only for a limited period, certain makers actually managed to sustain an improved standard at proof when under severe pressure. They were probably giving more attention to detail; certainly considerable effort went into achieving the required standard at this time.[19]

The main change during 1757 was the agreement for contract in July with the group of Edmund & John Smyth, and Edmund Hill of Hounslow mills in Middlesex. They managed to complete their first warrant by May 1758 in spite of an explosion at their mills two months previously.

Gunpowder from British and French ships

With the temporary cessation in 1755 of the sale of unserviceable powder by the Office for reworking at the mills, that from ships returning to port began to accumulate at Greenwich. By March 1757 there were over 2,000 barrels of repairable powder in store at Greenwich magazine. There was also a similar quantity fit only for salutes or military exercise, or too dusty or wet to be any use at all. Of a total of 14,280 barrels of all grades of gunpowder in all outport magazines, fourteen per cent was unserviceable but considered repairable, and sixteen per cent not even fit for repair.[20] In February 1757 the Board decided that some of its mounting stock of unserviceable powder employing valuable space at Greenwich should be reprocessed at the mills

---

[19] See ch. 10.
[20] WO 47/49, p. 377, April 1757.

and made available for immediate use.[21] Not until March 1758 did it decide to move more of this unserviceable powder but instead of having it reworked at the mills it made it available for direct sale. This decision, which appears to have been the result of a combination of further increase in quantity from ships returning to port, and a request by the Walton brothers for such powder for private use, reversed the policy of the previous three years.[22] Why there was no question of having it reprocessed to boost serviceable stock is unclear.

The Waltons offered £3 5s a barrel but rather than agreeing immediately the surveyor general announced that the price would be based on the quantity of saltpetre in each, determined by the current value of saltpetre on the open market. At the most recent India House sale the price was £5 3s a cwt. It was estimated that each 100 lb barrel of powder was worth approximately £3 10s. This was based on the current market price and on the fact that in June 1753 the comptroller of the Royal Laboratory reported that an average of 66¾ lb of saltpetre per barrel was extracted from 100 barrels of unserviceable gunpowder. Nevertheless, the Board decided to agree with the price suggested provided makers purchase the quantities requested of them, and not only English but Dutch. With regard to Eade & Bridges specifically, unserviceable powder would only be sold in proportion to the quantity of new which passed proof, a stipulation obviously based on the partnership's exceptionally low overall pass rate of fifty-one per cent for the previous year.[23]

It was not until 1761 that for the first time since the start of war unserviceable powder was again made available as an alternative to money payment for new. The attraction for the powder makers of repairing or reworking unserviceable powder under government contract as an alternative to the preparation of new was discussed earlier when comparing this war and that of the Austrian Succession. The attraction concerning the acquisition of such powder for private trade, either by direct purchase or as payment, was for similar reasons. Powder considered 'not fit for immediate service' was divided into 'triumph, repairable, dust, wet, damaged, and not yet proved'. Triumph was only suitable for salutes, military exercise, and celebratory fireworks while repairable was where grains might be slightly damp, clogged, or damaged but considered suitable for reworking at the mills for return to government store alongside new stock. Dust and damaged had most or all of the grain broken, and that which was wet had probably been

---

[21] Ibid., p. 142, 7 February 1757
[22] WO 47/51, p. 230, 4 March 1758.
[23] WO 55/2, p. 121, 6, 7 March 1758; WO 47/51, pp. 234, 252, 7, 10 March 1758.

affected by sea water. Powder sold by the Office could belong to any of these categories. There were several ways of preparing such powder at the mills for sale to merchants, depending on its condition. It may only have needed further incorporation or mixing, followed by corning or formation into grains. Alternatively, it may have been enough to mix a proportion of the unserviceable powder with an equal quantity of new. If the powder was unsuitable for reworking, the saltpetre, as the main and most expensive ingredient, was extracted for further refining before being mixed with new charcoal and sulphur. To do this the mixture was soaked for several hours in fresh water, the water then strained off, and the process repeated several times. All extracted liquid was then boiled and cooled to retrieve the saltpetre contained in it.

The magazines also held powder from those French ships captured by the Navy or by privateers. This was offered for sale to the Office which then subjected it to proof. That which passed was added to stock but it is impossible to state the total quantity involved as this was not listed separately in the Officers' returns from the magazines or recorded in negotiation between the Board and the agents for the captors. The unloading and inspection of 282 barrels from the *Lys*, captured by Boscawen before the declaration of war, took five coopers and nine labourers a whole day in October 1756, but there is no indication of the quantity actually taken into store. All unsuitable French powder had to be removed from Greenwich at the captors' expense and when, in February, only one of 200 such barrels passed proof the agent requested that the remainder be delivered to a Mr Vaughan, who wished to show a sample to Walton at Waltham Abbey mills.[24] From this it is evident that much of the French powder unfit for the Office eventually found its way to the mills and was prepared for export. The price paid by the Office for such powder at the beginning of the war was £3 10s a barrel but as the need became greater this was raised in October 1758 to £4 16s for serviceable, and £3 11s for triumph.

Problems of supply, 1758–9

Louisbourg was taken by Wolfe in the summer of 1758 but a further raid against the French coast, intended to divert French attention from the allied army in Germany, proved unsuccessful. For this attack Army, Marines, and the naval fleet protecting them all required ordnance, ammunition and gunpowder. It was also needed by warships waiting in the Channel to intercept French supplies en route for North America, for the continued demands of the Army in that colony, for defence of

[24] WO 47/49, pp. 451, 480, 7, 13 May 1757.

other colonies, and for training an expanding military force in Britain. At this point the commander in chief of Land Forces had 90,000 men under his general direction in Great Britain, Ireland, North America, Gibraltar, and the East and West Indies. Powder or its constituents were also lost in accidents. For example, in June 1757 the Waltons lost about one third of their twenty tons of saltpetre when a barge sank between the Rotherhithe granaries and their Essex mills, and the following month ships under Admiral Holburne returning from North America were forced to throw guns and powder overboard in a storm.[25] Storms were also responsible for a number of accidents in which powder was lost off the south coast on its way to the outports.

So considerable was the demand on Office and mills by 1758 that when the Waltons stated that they were willing to work on Sundays in order to provide more powder the Board requested that others do likewise. It also summoned the powder makers to attend a meeting on 21 February to state the exact quantities to be supplied within the year.[26] Attempts to meet these clearly defined promises were far from satisfactory. Of the seven men involved only two managed the specified quantities. These were the Edsalls and, surprisingly considering their past record, the Eade & Bridges partnership. Both the Waltons and Taylor almost reached their targets but Norman, Underhill & Ravens, and Smith & Hill were well below. Pryce, who had made no such promise, had less passing proof than anyone although this was probably because his business was decreasing as he planned to sell his mills to the government. It was at this meeting in February that the Board's concern about low supply and competition from merchants produced one of the most interesting proposals of the entire war: that the powder makers should be informed that 'for every mill that is erected new and works only for the Government and produces in twelve months 300 barrels at least that pass proof the Board will allow a premium of £50 for each mill, allowing six months from this day for erecting the same and that the mill shall work only for the Government as long as the Office shall require it'.[27]

The only immediate response, and that a negative one, was from William Taylor of Worcester Park mills who was ill and 'wished to be excused from erecting any more mills as this may be injurious to his family'. The term 'mill' would have referred to an individual unit, powered by water or horse, employed for any one of the various stages in the process.[28] There were varying numbers of such units in each mill

---

[25] Ibid., p. 557, 3 June 1757; WO 47/50, p. 31, 14 July 1757.
[26] WO 47/51, p. 55, 17 January 1758; see appendix 2, table 5.
[27] WO 47/51, p. 181, 21 February 1758.
[28] Ibid., p. 208, 28 February 1758.

complex. This can be seen in the later responses from Smyth and Hill in March 1758 and September 1759. The first was a result of an explosion at their Hounslow mills near Twickenham which prompted an immediate letter to the Board. This reported that on 11 March the partnership had 'the misfortune to have their powder mills blown up and could not determine to venture any further in so hazardous a business but as the Board had offered an encouragement for the erecting of Horse Mills they prayed their case may be taken into consideration'.[29]

This request was subsequently defined as £500 towards the necessary rebuilding. When the Board declined, the request was lowered to 'some encouragement' to which the former promised some attention once rebuilding of the mills was complete and the quantity of powder ascertained. By 2 June they had built 'three pestle mills and one horse mill'. They also hoped to build two further pestle mills and to make between 2,000 and 2,500 barrels of powder annually.[30] There is no record of the Board's response or of any encouragement which may or may not have been given. That its original offer referred to one mill unit rather than a complex of several such units is confirmed by that partnership's correspondence of September 1759. It stated that if the same 'encouragement' could be given as was offered in March 1758 it would erect two pestle mills capable of making 400 barrels a year.[31] The request was refused, for by that time the government had acquired its own mills. The Ordnance Board must have realised that incentives were of dubious benefit. When, in spite of failing to reach their target for 1758, the Waltons stated that they would provide as much as possible if paid £1 for all passing proof, the offer was rejected.[32]

On 27 June 1758 Pitt asked the Office to prepare to fire the guns at the Tower and St James's Park for the victory of Prince Ferdinand of Brunswick on the Lower Rhine on the 23rd of the month.[33] In July came one of the most significant tactical decisions of the war when the government decided to send military forces to Germany; this involved the Office in provision of even greater quantities of gunpowder.

The year 1759 was one of success, with the capture of Quebec from the French and of territory in Germany, West Africa, and the West Indies. It was also a year of change in that, for the first time ever, powder mills were purchased by the Crown. These were Faversham mills, purchased in May, with the intention of boosting stock and

29 Ibid., p. 267, 14 March 1758; see also ch. 1.
30 Ibid., pp. 282, 348, 556, 17 March, 7 April, 2 June 1758.
31 WO 47/54, p. 224, 3 September 1759.
32 WO 47/53, p. 473, 28 April 1759.
33 WO 55/357, p. 180, 14 April 1758; WO 47/51, p. 662, 27 June 1758.

lessening dependence on the private mills. After the sale Benjamin Pryce recommended Edward Pryce of Chilworth in his place.[34] At the same time Chauncy & Vigne returned to agree a further contract but made a disastrous start when all 150 barrels submitted in August failed proof. Not until July 1760 did they complete their contract for 242½ barrels, a surprisingly low quantity over so long a period. While this partnership was obviously the least satisfactory, that most favoured to date was Edward Pyke & Thomas Edsall Sr & Jr. of Dartford which appears to have worked only for the government. Overall, it had the most success at proof. Pyke left the partnership in 1757 but the Board continued to retain confidence in the Edsall family. When, in December 1758, the latter informed the Board that delay in delivery was due to necessary repair to their mills they were requested 'to exert themselves in delivering powder as expeditiously as possible, their powder having proved much to the satisfaction of the Board'.[35]

Supply as a whole continued to be variable during 1759 and ranged from 1,265 barrels passing proof from Norman of Molesey, to 3,199 from the Waltons at Waltham Abbey. This represented seventy and eighty-one per cent respectively. Edward Pryce, who had commenced supply in May had 519 of his 570 barrels passing proof, while Faversham mills, starting as a national concern in September, totalled only 47 out of 637 barrels passing proof. No official targets were set and although the total supplied for the year was an increase on 1758 it was far from satisfactory. Of those mills which supplied during the entire year the total submitted was still far from satisfactory and only four achieved over eighty per cent success at proof. The gravity of this situation can be seen from the official returns of the state of powder at the outport magazines for August 1759, the last to be recorded during the war. This shows that the total in store was only 4,447 barrels (eighty-six per cent English and fourteen per cent Dutch), the lowest since such records commenced in November 1756. This was due to the combination of poor supply and the gradual decrease in Dutch stock since import ceased more than a year before.

The Office had other problems. For example, there were now almost 3,000 barrels of unserviceable powder at Greenwich. These took up valuable space yet in spite of being suitable for reworking and returning to store the Board still feared they would be prepared for trade if sent back to the mills. Furthermore, the performance of the Faversham mills, initially intended for the reworking of unserviceable stock, was so far disappointing. It was not only repairable powder which was

---

[34] WO 47/53, p. 473, 28 April 1759; it is unclear if the familes were related. For business relationship see ch. 9.
[35] WO 47/52, p. 444, 2 December 1758.

taking up time and space at Greenwich but also over 6,000 barrels of powder returned from ships which, though unsuitable for leaving on board, had not yet been resubjected to proof. At the time of severe shortage in 1760 the Board retained even failed powder at Greenwich; there is no evidence to show that such powder was ever distributed.

Although gunpowder had to undergo strict testing at proof there were certain occasions when even that strong enough to pass was subsequently criticised. This was usually for its consistency and weight, mainly due to inadequately corned grains resulting in too high a dust content. In May 1759 the Board ordered that although powder from Smith & Hill had passed proof, it was so dusty that it should be sifted before weighing and the siftings returned. Later that month and again in September the clerks at Greenwich reported that gunpowder not only from Smyth & Hill, but from Benjamin Pryce, the Waltons, and Taylor, was of such consistency that the coopers had to 'force it down by violence into the King's barrels, which would soon cause it to clog'. So light and dusty was the powder that it had to be sent in extra large barrels. The offending men were ordered that 'if they do not remedy this evil their powder will be refused'. The problem persisted for in March 1760 the Portsmouth officers reported that ninety-nine barrels recently received from Smith & Hill were so dusty and the grain so tender that they had sent one back to Greenwich for inspection. The Board requested that the entire batch be returned to London and the makers be told that if they could not find a better method of corning their powder they would receive no further contracts.[36] In May gunpowder from Edward Pryce, and from Smith & Hill was compared with some from Underhill & Ravens. On filling a pound measure with powder from each of the three makers, it was found that that from Underhill & Ravens weighed 17½ oz. while that from Pryce, and from Smith & Hill weighed 13¼, and 13 oz. respectively.[37] While the Office acted thus on gunpowder of poor consistency, it was quick to defend its powder against complaint regarding performance in the field. Quantity and standard of gunpowder, guns, and ammunition alike attracted the wrath of men in action in various wars.[38] Ordnance stock could be damaged by bad weather, by handling or storage and, although in theory still the responsibility of the Board, once beyond British shores these were in practice beyond its direct control. Recorded official complaints to the Board in the minutes of the surveyor general concerning

[36] WO 47/54, p. 271, 413, 573, 15 September, 11 December 1759; WO 47/55, p. 261, 22 March 1760.
[37] Ibid., p. 431, 23 May 1760.
[38] For instance, J. A. Houlding, *Fit for Service: The training of the British Army 1715–1795* (Oxford 1981), p. 145.

quality of powder in this war were comparatively few. These included difficulties in the use of powder by a gunner on south coast defence duties at Newhaven in 1761, which were put down to his ignorance at pointing the gun and, in December 1762, the Portuguese Minister's disatisfaction with powder recently purchased from the Office for use against the Spanish in Portugal; although to be fully investigated this was, nevertheless, considered to be due either to damage or change of stock after embarkation.[39]

Demand for gunpowder increased even more with further threat of French invasion during 1759. It was needed by the Militia embodied in June, by new batteries along the south coast, by the mobile force of troops and ships ready for immediate movement to any part of Britain, and by Hawke's Channel squadron which continued to intercept French supply ships. It was also required for the artillery train for Fort George, and for the defence of Bristol, Liverpool, and Aberdeen. During the late summer and autumn concern over defence at home was balanced by success overseas. On 29 November Holderness conveyed the King's request to Ligonier for the firing of the guns at the Tower and St James's Park on 29 November to mark successes at sea and on land in North America, and particularly the taking of Quebec. The guns were fired the following day on Pitt's report that the fleet under Hawke had overcome the French at Quiberon Bay. The defeat of yet another French naval squadron in March 1760 considerably lessened the threat of French invasion.[40]

Severe shortage and extreme measures, 1760–1

So concerned was the Board during 1760 about stock for the supply of further campaigns on the Continent, for additional British forces for the East Indies, for the taking of Montreal and Martinique, and for further increase of the armed forces, that it took certain action, unprecedented at least in this war. On 19 July it requested that all powder intended for the government be sent from the mills to Greenwich whether or not contracts had been arranged. In addition, Greenwich officers were ordered to retain all powder failing proof until further orders. Finally, and with some degree of panic, it ordered the proof masters to go to each of the makers' magazines and purchase all powder they could find in any way fit for service, with leave to the makers to

---

[39] WO 47/58, p. 38, 14 July 1761. For storage in North America, see ch. 6; WO 47/60, p. 416, 13 December 1762.
[40] WO 55/360, p. 7, 28 November 1759, Holderness to Ligonier; ibid., p. 18, 30 November 1759, Pitt to Ligonier.

draw on the Board for its value.[41] Such orders made little, if any difference to the Board's plight. The preparation of twenty-one tons of powder in October for the secret expedition to Belle Isle increased the difficulty. The fact that this was eventually cancelled and all powder brought ashore again in November from the ships lying off the Isle of Wight, and that in the same month Britain celebrated Frederick's victory over Austria in Germany was of no immediate consolation to the Board. Although the powder would eventually be available for use, each barrel first needed thorough checking on the dockside to ensure serviceability, which simply added to the general pressure on the Office at this time. The following year brought no relief. Both the annual total of powder delivered to Greenwich and that actually passing proof were well below the totals for the previous year.[42] In one order alone, for Portsmouth in December, 1,000 barrels were required immediately for naval ships in port. Output from Faversham mills was disappointing and on 20 May the Faversham officers were included with the other makers in a plea from the Board to 'deliver all powder they had by them and to use all possible expedition in the making of more'.[43] Once again, dual celebrations in July at the capture of Pondicherry and Prince Ferdinand's victory over the French in Germany brought the Ordnance Office little direct relief.

Concern in Britain mounted in August when Spain threatened to enter the war, and Pitt resigned as a result of the Cabinet's refusal to make a pre-emptive strike against Spanish ships. International tension increased. A meeting between Ordnance Board and powder makers on 8 October at Old Palace Yard to discuss the serious need for powder was to no avail for a few days later the Board wrote to the master general in its greatest desperation yet. It stated that due to various expeditions and the vast increase in the Army and the Navy, demand greatly exceeded supply from the mills. So low was stock as a result that the Board was experiencing considerable difficulty in refitting naval ships. As all efforts to improve the situation were in vain, because of the demands of the merchants who paid more than the government, the master general was 'ernestly desired to think of such expedients as may effectively prevent the ill consequence that may arise'.[44] This was put before the president of the Privy Council and the King. The Board was requested to cease all permission for the export of gunpowder, and to send to Portsmouth 500 barrels of powder from the transport ships lying off Belle Isle. In addition, the Tilbury storekeeper was to send 700

[41] WO 47/56, p. 57, 19 July 1760.
[42] See appendix 2, table 7.
[43] WO 47/57, p. 338, 20 May 1761.
[44] WO 47/58, pp. 256, 274, 8, 15 October 1761.

barrels of returned powder to be proved at Greenwich and the store-keeper at Greenwich to report immediately on the result.[45] The powder makers were then offered an advance for one month from 26 October of £0 5s a barrel for every 100 passing proof, provided that 80 passed out of each 100 and that they delivered the full quantity agreed. Agreements were as follows: Waltons 400; Edsalls 300; Underhill & Ravens 250; Smith & Hill 240; Normans 220; Edward Pryce 200; Eade & Bridges 180; Taylor 160; and Chauncy 100. Of the nine only four fulfilled their contracts: Underhill & Ravens, Norman, Eade & Bridges, and the Waltons. Edward Pryce was refused the new price when his 200 barrels were delayed at Guildford due to lack of craft to carry them down the Thames.[46] Payment during both that and the subsequent months was based on either £1 5s for the above agreement, £1 for the agreement of January 1757 still in progress or, if satisfying neither, the original £0 17s 6d. The pricing of a completed contract could be complicated. One example was that of Smith & Hill of 3 April 1762 when, of the 485 barrels, 10 were monied at £1, 242 at £1 5s, and 233 at £0 17s 6d.[47]

The Waltons asked for the increase in price not only for the 400 barrels but for 213 delivered on the day of the agreement, at the same time stating that they were erecting an additional mill. The Board's agreement prompted another proposal from the pair but this time, not surprisingly, without success. In spite of the ban on all powder export for an indefinite period, they sought approval for the sale of the 250 barrels of trade powder they had at their mills to certain London merchants for export to Africa. The master general was informed that although these makers had, to date, supplied one quarter of all gunpowder passing proof, they could have supplied much more if they had not worked for the merchants, a serious matter in view of the state of powder stock. The request was refused.[48] Certain powder makers continued openly to prepare powder for export. As with the Waltons, it was no surprise when Taylor was refused his request of May 1762; he 'desired leave to employ his mills for the next month to make some merchants powder'.[49] Of more interest to the Board was the Waltons' next proposal on 19 February:

to employ their mills entirely in making gunpowder for this office for one year from 1 March next and not to make any powder for any

45 Ibid., p. 276, 20 October 1761.
46 Ibid., p. 371, 24 November 1761.
47 WO 51/219, p. 157, 3 April 1762.
48 WO 47/58, p. 330, 6 November 1761.
49 WO 47/59, p. 439, 25 May 1762.

person whatever without the Board's leave and consent except the liberty of working up their dust, in consideration of the Board's allowing them £1 5s for the workmanship of every barrel that shall pass proof.[50]

The Board approved immediately.

On 24 November it was decided that the incentive of October should be continued for a further month; it was then renewed each month until 26 November of the following year. Although there is no record of the outcome the Board took the unusual action at the December 1761 renewal of asking the makers the quantity of powder they had at the mills fit only for merchants.[51] Although this may have been in order to assess the precise extent to which each maker was currently involved in private trade it is unlikely, for it was not until April 1762 that the Office first showed any direct sign of interest in linking its information on quantities of trade powder at the mills with that on the identities of merchants purchasing it for export. It is more likely to have been yet another sign of the Office's immediate desperation at powder shortage in that it was now prepared to consider the use not only of powder which had failed poof but even that intended for trade. However, there is no record of it actually resorting to such a measure.

It was between November 1761 and March 1762 that proposals were received from Baugh, Ames, and Strachey of Bristol who ran Woolley mills near Bath, and from the Liverpool merchants for their mills at Thelwall, Cheshire. A proposal was made by the former to provide 500 barrels by 1 January at £4 7s a barrel, followed by 500 more within the next two months. The powder would be stored in a magazine after proof at their own expense until required for distribution. Initially, the Board agreed and it prepared to send samples of powder of the desired standard as a guide, together with barrels which could be used as a pattern for local coopers. However, on 30 March the company eventually gave up their attempts to gain contract after all samples sent to the Tower had failed proof. Samples sent from Thelwall failed proof likewise.[52] Reasons have already been discussed for the Board's decision not to risk contract at this time, even though in dire need of powder, and knowing that a certain proportion at least would

50 Ibid., p. 153, 19 February 1762.
51 WO 47/58, p. 449, 26 December 1761.
52 Ibid., pp. 329, 342, 6, 10 November 1761; WO 47/59, pp. 27, 205, 222, 345, 12 January, 8, 11 March, 22 April 1762; WO 55/3, p. 31, 9 March 1762; Brenda J. Buchanan, 'A Comment on the Manufacture of Black Powder', *Industrial Archeology*, 2 (1976), 76–8.

probably have passed proof if submitted to Greenwich in larger quantities.

Climax and depression, 1762–3

1762 was a year of sharp contrasts, with British successes overseas and complaints from the Admiralty to the Ordnance Board about shortage of gunpowder at home. Shortages reached a climax in the first half of the year and peace negotiations began towards the end of the second half.

In spite of Britain's earlier decision to delay action against Spain, war was eventually declared in January, and when Portugal was invaded by Spain in April Britain went to her aid. As a result, the Ordnance Office sent men, equipment and stores to Portugal between April and June. These included two companies of Artillery, together with brass howitzers, iron ordnance, 4,000 barrels of gunpowder, ammunition and other stores which, arranged through de Mello, the Portuguese ambassador in London, cost the King of Portugal over £149,893. Included in the consignment was a total of 280 barrels of powder from seven of the makers, but mainly from the Waltons. This sale via the Board was mostly powder which had recently failed the Office proof for which payment was £5 a barrel, and also eighty barrels of powder from the Waltons originally intended for the merchants; for this they agreed £4 10s. Payment by de Mello to the makers was to be made once he had received the subsidy for aid for Portugal from the British Treasury.[53]

In January the Ordnance officers at Plymouth were 'so distressed through want of powder' to refit the ships returning to port that they were compelled to let the *Hero* proceed to Spithead 160 barrels short of her proportion in the hope that she could be supplied at Portsmouth. Although too late for that vessel an immediate order was given for 500 barrels to be found from other magazines. Portsmouth was no better endowed and on 29 July the Board received a complaint from the Admiralty about 'the great want of powder for the fitting out of His Majesty's ships there'. Having already recognised such shortage the Office had that morning dispatched 350 barrels by water and 400 by land, a meagre quantity in view of the current requirements of this port but obviously as much as could be spared.[54]

During this year there was a certain irony about the nature of supply to the Ordnance Office. The early part of the year saw one of its worst

---

53 WO 47/59, pp. 530–1, 544, 18, 23 June 1762; see also ch. 3.
54 Ibid., pp. 65, 544, 22 January, 23 June 1762; WO 47/60, p. 88, 29 July 1762.

shortages to date because of high demand and inadequate supply from the mills, yet when the supply of gunpowder from those mills eventually reached the highest recorded level of the war so far the Office no longer wanted it. During the first half of the year the weekly supply from certain mills was particularly poor. The Edsalls submitted nothing between March and May, Edward Pryce delivered nothing between April and June, while Chauncy & Vigne, after sending nothing in April, sent only 125 barrels between May and July, of which 112 failed proof. The latter partnership ceased production entirely in October. However, over the year as a whole six of the makers produced higher individual annual outputs than ever before in this war, the highest quantities coming from the Waltons of Waltham Abbey, Underhill & Ravens of Bedfont, and Norman of Molesey. This resulted in both a greater total supply submitted to Greenwich and, though not the highest percentage to pass proof, a higher total passing proof than in any preceding year of the war.

The autumn of 1762 brought the sharp contrast which heralded peace. In October the Board told the powder makers that it would not allow the current year's contracts to be completed the following year. A request from the Waltons to have 300 barrels of their powder proved for a purchaser, the East India Company, which might once have met with some antagonism was now accepted. In November Smith & Hill offered to supply all the powder they could produce on the same basis as the Waltons' arrangement of the previous February but, not surprisingly, the surveyor general advised the Board that it would be unwise to so engage with any of the makers when 'its needs were now not so pressing'.[55] On 23 November the financial incentive of October 1761 was terminated, leaving only outstanding contracts to be honoured. By December the Board's difficulty lay not with shortage of powder but with lack of space to store the large quantities arriving from ships returning to port. The stark contrast is shown in correspondence between the Ordnance Office and the Admiralty. The former, obviously experiencing difficulty in finding storage space, asked the Admiralty's permission to store on board ships lying at Plymouth, Portsmouth, Chatham, and Sheerness as much powder as their magazines could take until official arrangements could be made at the outports.[56] In order to alleviate the situation further the Treasury approved purchase of a storehouse near Upnor Castle to take 1,000 barrels of powder from ships returning from Portugal and the Continent, the unloading of which was supervised by Customs officials. There were 1,500 barrels

---

[55] Ibid., pp. 343, 363, 16, 23 November 1762.
[56] Ibid., pp. 365, 417, 23 November, 13 December 1762; Adm. 1/4012 13 December 1762.

awaiting storage at Plymouth alone, which had to be shifted to prevent keeping ships in commission longer than necessary, together with 300 from the Royal Laboratory containing powder from case shot and shells.[57]

With the peace treaty of March 1763 came the termination of the prohibitive legislation. The year saw only the completion of outstanding contracts for there were no others until 1765. The only immediate commercial link with the Office at the onset of peace was the purchase of unserviceable powder for private use. When Smith & Hill failed to complete a contract of October 1762 until August 1765 the Office did not react at all. On March 22 the guns on Tower Wharf and in St James's Park were fired to mark the end of the war. For the majority there was joy but for the gunpowder makers there was, once again, the dreaded calm of peace after the demanding, yet rewarding storm of war. The two most significant actions taken by the Ordnance Office in response to gunpowder shortage were the Act to prohibit exportation or coastwise movemement of gunpowder without licence, and crown purchase of Faversham mills. In addition, there were the various incentives for improved supply, the eventual cessation of sale to the makers of unserviceable powder for their own use, and a continual balancing and movement of stock between one magazine and another in an effort to meet daily demand. With little doubt, the Seven Years War was the most testing period to date for both Ordnance Office and mills. The Office had the dual responsibilities of assembling sufficient gunpowder from the mills for the demands of the Army and Navy, and of distribution to a wider geographical area than ever before. Making these responsibilities more onerous was the fact that at few times during the war did the powder makers deliver more than the bare minimum agreed at contract and usually far less. There is no indication that shortage of powder in Britain directly changed the course of military action overseas, although certain campaigns in North America were undoubtedly affected by delays in dispatch. Certainly, the Ordnance Board experienced difficulties in attempting to meet demand. However, there is no indication that the frequent delays in the dispatch of gunpowder from British shores in the storeships bound for North America were ever directly linked with inadequate stock, for most of the stock for these consignments came directly from the main magazine at Greenwich. Delay in embarkation caused by shortage of gunpowder was usually confined to naval ships supplied at the outports, and even that happened mainly at the height of war.

The Ordnance Office, faced with an unprecedented demand for gunpowder, did not receive the quantity expected. Throughout the war

57 WO 47/61, pp. 36, 141, 153, 19 January, 11, 16 March 1763.

it made various unsuccessful attempts to obtain more cooperation from the powder makers, who themselves had considerable problems in achieving a product of a satisfactory standard and in the necessary quantities, especially when trying to balance the demands of government and private trade. Peace offered little demand but war, particularly this war with its parallel opportunities of demanding government contracts and increased private trade, offered too much. Yet to make any real investment in the expansion of industrial plant, when peace would inevitably bring slump, would have been high risk indeed. The legislation intended to limit the private trade in gunpowder proved to be virtually ineffective. Although not immediately obvious, there were definite reasons for this. The result of the crown purchase of Faversham mills in 1759, intended to boost government stock, was disappointing. It is important to ascertain the degree to which blame for inadequate supply can attributed to either the Office or mills. Certainly, time spent in producing gunpowder for export meant less powder submitted to Greenwich for proof. However, there must have been additional factors involved in the greatly varying results of that proof which involved powder from the crown mills at Faversham too. The possible reasons for both the lack of effect of the legislation, for the very varied standard of gunpowder at proof, and for disappointment with Faversham mills will be the subject of later chapters.

PART TWO

THE ORDNANCE OFFICE
AND GUNPOWDER DISTRIBUTION

5

The Army and Navy

Obtaining gunpowder from the mills for Greenwich magazine was just
one stage in the Ordnance Office's chain of supply for the armed forces.
Equally important was the second stage, that of distribution, which
could be either direct or indirect. Direct distribution was from Greenwich to the main garrisons and other large defence establishments, to
the Army in the field, and to colonial governors. Indirect distribution
involved an intermediate stage, for lesser defensive forts and castles
received their powder via the larger establishments, and naval ships
received theirs via the outports.[1]

Procedure

All Ordnance establishments in Britain and overseas submitted annual
requests for stores for the following year. These were included in the
Office's annual estimate to the Treasury to be presented to Parliament
for the expenses of land and sea service.[2] The Board was given appropriate monthly sums for the year concerned from the total agreed for
current service. All exceedings for which no allowance had been made
were submitted with the estimate for the following year.[3] Quarterly
proportions were drawn by the Board for discharging storekeepers of all
ordnance stores issued after their accounts had been cleared by the
treasurer.

---

[1] See appendix 2, table 10.
[2] WO 47/58, pp. 250, 336, 6 October, 10 November 1761.
[3] WO 46/8, 22 September 1758, Frederick to Treasury; WO 47/49, pp. 79, 126,
21 January, 4 February 1757; WO 55/356, p. 87, 19 January 1757, warrants.

The efficient distribution of gunpowder and other ordnance stores was vital to the conduct of war. The quantity of powder issued was based on discussion within Cabinet meetings attended by the master general of the Ordnance and the first lord of the Admiralty who advised on military and naval strategy and ordnance requirements. Once a plan of action had been agreed the relevant orders were given to the master general and his Board for the preparation and dispatch of men, equipment and stores in the quantities listed.

The preparation of stores for the Army was the result of an order of the lords justices of the Privy Council conveyed by a secretary of state. Among the responsibilities of the secretary of state for the Southern Department (Pitt from June 1757) were the British colonies, including North America, and Spain, France, and Turkey. Holderness, for the Northern Department, was responsible for North Britain and the North European states, including Holland and Germany. This method applied to the annual allowance of powder for the regiments in Britain and for the Militia, to artillery trains for the defence of south east England, and to powder for those military troops and artillery trains sent overseas. The Ordnance Board required a royal warrant for the cost of these stores to be included in the next report to Parliament. This too was sent by the secretary of state on behalf of the King and in theory either accompanied the order in Council or followed it. In practice the routine was not always as clear and proved to be a source of constant concern to the Board. Thus although the Cabinet was the focus for discussion the Privy Council was responsible for the formal orders and warrants on which the Board depended. The role of the Privy Council in this context is by no means straightforward.

Orders for guns and gunpowder for ships of the Royal Navy and the Marines came from the Admiralty. As with land service supply that for sea service had to be fully accounted for; only in this way could the cost be approved by Parliament and funded by the Treasury.

Requests from the secretaries of state and Admiralty, together with the steps taken by the Office to arrange issue, transportation, and reception of gunpowder at its destination, involved numerous scattered entries in the Ordnance records. Gunpowder might be shipped on its own or as part of a general consignment of ordnance stores, the most common of which would be large iron or brass guns of various sizes, small arms, and ammunition. Where distribution was regular and routine and not the result of royal command, as in the case of garrisons and naval bases, the quantity was not always specified. For artillery trains and other consignments for the British Army in the field the precise size and weight of guns and quantities of powder and other stores were usually recorded.

The Royal Navy

Among the most important duties of the Office was the supply of gunpowder, in large quantities during this war, to ships of the Royal Navy. Once the number of ships was approved by Parliament the Admiralty informed the Office of the guns and gunpowder it needed and provided information on the identity, size, and location of every ship to be supplied. No ship was ever provided with powder without instructions from the Admiralty commissioners to the Board and, in turn, the Board's written authority to the outport officers. This was for Channel service, such as the squadrons protecting the British coast and blockading French ports, and for foreign service which included the ships along the North American coast, and those in the West Indies and the Mediterranean. An assessment of the quantity of powder needed was based on the number and size of guns on each ship, which in turn depended on the ship's size and function as established by the Royal Navy. Supply at this time was at the rate of 540 barrels for a ship of first-rate of 100 guns for foreign service, and 490 for Channel service.[4]

There were two main elements in the supply of naval ships. The first involved the fitting of existing ships or those newly constructed in royal or private ship yards with guns, gunpowder and ammunition. The second was resupplying those ships with the necessary gunpowder every time they returned to port. Gunners had to provide an account to the Ordnance officers of all powder expended, were charged for any unaccounted for, but were paid one shilling for each serviceable barrel returned. Whenever a ship returned to port for refitting or with sick men all remaining barrels of powder were opened by the Office coopers. The powder underwent a meticulous inspection by the officers, was sent back on board if satisfactory or returned to the main store at Greenwich for retesting if damp or damaged. The vessels were then cleansed and smoked to inhibit the spread of fever. The Navy therefore ate deeply into the nation's powder stock at this time. Yet this was an aspect of supply which could not be calculated with accuracy. The problem was exacerbated by a considerable increase in the size of the Navy during 1755. It would be impossible to compare the quantity of gunpowder issued to the Navy in this, with any other war. It would be feasible to compare lists of naval ships of each class in service in different wars and therefore their quota of gunpowder when fitted for service where the dates of fitting and identification of ships could be   ·

[4] WO 55/1739, Ship Establishment Book, 1716; WO 55/1743, Ship Establishment Book, 28 April 1743; Adm. 1/4010 5 April 1755; Adm. 2/531 p. 349, 17 July 1761.

traced in the Ordnance minutes. However, it would be more difficult to trace the course and function of each ship: it was not unusual for the Admiralty to order certain ships to be changed from one duty to another in wartime and this might considerably affect the number and size of guns used and therefore the quantity of powder required. In the absence of outport accounts of issue to ships and of complete ships' logs or gunners' accounts it would be even more difficult, if not impossible to establish how frequently each ship returned to port and how much powder was issued to it. On gunpowder, the records of the Office for this war are more detailed than for any other in the eighteenth century and provide considerable information and insight into the pattern of distribution. However, as with other wars of the period, it is impossible, in the absence of complete records, to calculate the total quantity of powder allocated to a particular outport, entering it, or being issued from it. The most detailed figures to survive are the monthly statements of gunpowder remaining at the eight outports but these do not include the total quantity actually issued. Except for imported Dutch powder stored initially at Tilbury, which usually formed one-third of the issue to each ship, all powder for both Army and Navy came initially from Greenwich.[5] None was issued without the Board's written order and none was purchased locally.

Two principles governed distribution. Firstly, there was a specific allowance for each outport, garrison, fort or castle, and each December all Ordnance storekeepers (or master gunners at the smaller forts) submitted their demands to complete the allowance for the forthcoming year. These came before the surveyor general for approval and the necessary arrangements were made to value and procure the quantity demanded. All storekeepers of Ordnance stores at home and abroad were discharged of stores issued in the previous quarter only after examination of their accounts by the clerk of deliveries.[6] Secondly, there was an additional allowance of powder in wartime, specifically to the outports. Its size was based on advance details to the Office supplied by the Navy Board via the Admiralty which detailed the location, number, and class of each naval ship, those already in commission and those under construction or repair. Such information was requested by the Office in February and July 1755, June 1756, and annually thereafter. There were similar requests concerning ships stationed overseas to allow estimation of powder required at the overseas Ordnance bases.[7] The Office did not benefit in full from such

5   WO 47/51, p. 232, 7 March 1758.
6   WO 47/46, p. 533, 16 December 1755; WO 47/55, p. 102, 5 February 1760.
7   Adm. 1/4010, 29 June 1756; Isaac Schomberg, *Naval Chronology* (1802), iv, 32–7.

advance knowledge because of the pressure on supplies caused by the unavoidable frequency with which ships returned to port, and because of the overall shortage of supply. The climax of such shortage, as stated earlier, was in 1761 and 1762 when some ships had to leave Plymouth and Portsmouth without their full complement.

For the distribution of gunpowder from Greenwich to the outports or garrisons in Britain and abroad shipping was arranged by Richard Bennet, Ordnance purveyor for sea. Contracts with ships' masters who at an agreed price were usually willing to travel within Britain or overseas resulted from public advertisements in the press or at the Royal Exchange. The comparatively short route to Portsmouth and Plymouth was undertaken when possible by the Office's own sloop *Montague* or by those masters such as John Smith of the sloop *Faversham* who tendered their vessels regularly to the Office. Most consignments of powder were of between 300 and 500 barrels.[8] As Bennet had to find the most suitable ship at the most reasonable price he inspected all proposed vessels and reported to the Board on their condition, size, and tonnage and on the tonnage of stores each was capable of receiving. He was responsible for ensuring that craft were suitably fitted for maintaining powder in as dry and safe a state as possible during transportation; once contract was agreed he checked loading. The price paid for transportation was usually the same as that paid by the merchants, but when competition between masters was keen it was often less in order to obtain government contract. Although the price was not always recorded that agreed with Smith for the *Faversham* in June 1755 was £0 14s a ton to carry 300 barrels to Plymouth, while for Guernsey and Jersey he charged £1 12s a ton. In September the price agreed with Hayward Chambers, master of the *Charming Betsey* laden with stores for Portsmouth was £0 10s a ton, while by 1758 the price agreed for Plymouth was £0 15s.[9] All vessels carrying ordnance stores were supposed to be convoyed. To avoid repeated requests from vessels bound for Portsmouth and Plymouth it was arranged between the Board and the Admiralty at the beginning of the war that masters of ships apply to Admiral Smith in the Downs for convoy to Spithead, and to the commanding officer at Spithead for convoy to Plymouth. Sometimes, as in September 1759, delivery also involved Milford Haven for which convoy was provided at Plymouth.[10] In spite of convoy, the Board often asked its officers at Gravesend, Sheerness, and Dover to report viewing of such ships as they passed to ensure masters did not delay. In November 1759 Bryant, storekeeper at Dover Castle,

8 WO 47/54, p. 430, 24 November 1759.
9 WO 47/45, p. 523, 3 June 1755; WO 47/51, p. 81, 26 January 1758.
10 WO 47/59, p. 234, 16 March 1762; Adm. 1/4010, 20 August 1755.

reported that the sloop *Sincerity* laden with guns and gunpowder for ships at Portsmouth had sunk in a storm at the Pier Head. He was ordered to salvage what he could and procure another vessel to complete the mission.[11]

Payment for transportation to the outports was only for the outward journey unless there were stores to be returned to London, such as unserviceable guns or gunpowder from ships returning to port. As both sides were keen to make all possible use of vessels, in order to save time and money and to avoid the nuisance of having to take in ballast to manage rough seas, close contact was maintained with the outport officers for news of further contracts. A master preferred to wait a few days in port for unserviceable stores to accumulate and for the relevant permission from London to carry them than to return empty handed. Characteristic of the distribution pattern throughout the war was the intermittent transfer of powder from one outport to another to overcome the general shortage at Greenwich. When, in May 1755, Upnor Castle needed 800 barrels of powder for ships and Greenwich could send only 250, a total of 900 barrels were sent from Tilbury. It is probable that a large proportion of this powder was Dutch. In March 1761 it was Upnor's turn when 600 were sent from there to Plymouth.[12] Gunpowder was also sent from Greenwich for ships fitting at such ports as Hull, Leith, Aberdeen and Milford Haven. In October 1756 the *Resolution* carried guns and powder to Aberdeen for the *St Ann*, while the *St Andrew* sailed with same to Leith for the *Princess of Wales*, at £1 4s, and £1 respectively, both £0 4s less than the current price for merchants. In July 1756 powder was sent to Kinsale to supply naval sloops patrolling the Irish coast.[13] The outports also served the Marines from sea service stores. Like the Army, they could be provided with their half-yearly issue from the allotted annual proportion, provided written confirmation was given to the storekeeper that the previous half year's allowance was nearly expended. In June 1755 it was agreed that each company be allowed one barrel yearly for exercise and training while on land.[14]

The Office appears to have done everything possible to ensure that gunpowder and other stores reached the right place at the right time. With hindsight it is possible to see how administrative arrangements regarding convoys could have been improved but, given current conditions, the serious delays which did occur were undoubtedly beyond the

11 WO 47/54, p. 428, 23 November 1759.
12 WO 47/45, p. 495, 27 May 1755.
13 WO 47/48, p. 281, 1 October 1756.
14 WO 47/45, pp. 346, 609, 15 April, 26 June 1755.

direct control of that particular department alone. An example was when the Admiralty agreed on 25 March 1757 to provide the *Enterprise* as convoy for the *London Packet* laden with ordnance and powder for fitting ships of the Royal Navy at Hull; when the ordnance vessel arrived at the Nore on 2 April as arranged, the *Enterprise* had departed. Another convoy was arranged for this and other vessels en route to the Shetlands but that too had sailed before the Board even received the Admiralty instructions. Yet another convoy had to be organised. No one side wanted to be kept waiting for loss of time meant loss of money. A combination of factors was involved including delay by the Ordnance vessel, unrealistic Admiralty timing, an impatient convoy captain and, above all, lack of liaison between the two departments.[15]

The other main cause of delay in distribution was the impress of crew on Ordnance storeships, particularly in the early years of the war. This could cause failure to reach convoy and delay in the delivery of gunpowder to Ordnance bases in Britain and overseas. In May 1756 Richard Beales, crewman of the *Isaac & Elizabeth* laden with powder for Portsmouth, was impressed and put on board a naval tender at Tower Wharf. As with others impressed at the same time from the *St Ann* with powder for British ships in Jamaica, each impress delayed stores for the Navy itself.[16] When hiring ships the Office agreed protection from the press but this received little recognition from the Navy Board. There were faults on both sides. The Navy was desperate to find men, while the Ordnance Board did not always ensure at contract the correct number of signatures on the protection form, or check hired crews fully enough to eliminate the pre-existing naval links to which the Navy Board usually made claim.

Water carriage was always the cheapest form of transport and therefore that chosen for gunpowder, guns, and arms which were heavy and bulky. Storekeepers were ordered to send in their annual demands early so that 'the expense of land carriage be avoided'. The only time powder was sent by land was in an emergency. Due to imminent declaration of war and threat of invasion in March 1756, 500 barrels of powder had to be sent quickly by road to Portsmouth and Plymouth for their garrisons. This required 40 waggons, 80 men and 240 horses.[17]

15 WO 47/47, p. 479, 7 May 1756; Adm. 1/4011, 25 March 1757.
16 Adm. 1/4010, 12 January, 6 March, 13 May 1756.
17 WO 47/47, pp. 264, 348–9, 12 March, 1 April 1756.

Garrisons and other defence establishments in Britain

Mounting conflict, threat of invasion, and the eventual declaration of war caused the Ordnance Office to survey and strengthen its defence establishments and stores throughout Britain during 1755 and early 1756. In many cases gunpowder stocks were found to be inadequate or unserviceable because of lack of attention since the previous war. In January 1755 all Ordnance storekeepers of garrisons, forts and castles (or, as in smaller establishments, master gunners) were ordered by the Board to report their state of stock, and the Ordnance officers at the outports to survey master gunners' stocks at the smaller establishments within their respective divisions. The Plymouth officers reported in February that thirty-two barrels of powder at St Nicholas Island were clodded and the hazel hoops worm eaten. The Portsmouth officers found that twenty-one barrels of powder at Calshot Castle were all unserviceable, and the officers at Upnor Castle that powder in store at Gillingham Fort was 'decaying'. All were replaced from the respective outport land service stock.[18]

In September each Office department had to list all ordnance stores issued during the years 1754 and 1755, including powder for land and sea service in Britain and overseas and whether for outport, garrison, or field service. In January 1756 the Office examined the state of ordnance and powder stores at the establishments in the Cinque Ports division, and in March assessed the quantity necessary to complete the field trains and garrison stocks in the Portsmouth and Plymouth divisions. As a result Portsmouth received 1,000 barrels of Dutch powder immediately to be stored in the town magazine for any necessary supply of troops. This was separate to sea service stock at the outport. At the same time the surveyor general studied the demands for stores at all other garrisons, forts and castles. The supply which resulted included 330 barrels of powder for the additional new defence works at Dover Castle and 264 for the new batteries at Plymouth Citadel.[19] In May assessment was made of stores required at the coastal defence batteries of England and Wales and in July of those for the defence of the coasts of Dorset, Devon, and Cornwall in particular. From any of these stores gunpowder could be issued for various regiments in those areas for training and exercise. The ten garrisons, the Cinque Port defences and some of the other larger defence establishments were supplied with powder direct from Greenwich, while the smaller defences were sup-

18 WO 47/45, p. 108, 14 February 1755; WO 47/47, p. 295, 19 March 1756.
19 WO 55/356, pp. 156, 162, 19 November 1756.

plied by the outport officers in their particular divisions.[20] From their land service stock the Portsmouth officers supplied such master gunners as those at the Portsmouth garrison and those, among others, of Calshot, Hurst, Yarmouth, and Carisbrooke Castles. Plymouth officers supplied, among others, Plymouth Citadel, Dartmouth Castle, St Nicholas Island, and Scilly Island.[21] As with the outports, distribution was based on the annual demands of each storekeeper or master gunner within his established allotted proportion and on the demands of the outport officers for land service supplies.[22] Increased defence included that for Scotland. In the summer of 1755 gunpowder and other ordnance stores were sent to Perth on the *Duke of Atholl* at £1, and to Inverness on the *Isaac and Elizabeth* at £1 12s a ton. Supplying the garrison at Fort William was obviously geographically more difficult. In January 1756 the master of the vessel *Happy Return* had only just returned from delivering the previous July's consignment of guns and gunpowder. He complained of the expense of the seventeen days needed for unloading and for the pilots bill for leading him from the Sound of Mull. The supply usually varied between English and Dutch powder; of the 500 barrels sent to Edinburgh Castle in May 1756, 100 were Dutch.[23]

The Army in the field and the Militia[24]

The quantity of gunpowder allowed for the Army in the field and for the Militia was clearly specified. All supply for regiments in Britain for training and exercise, for the Militia, and for British forces going overseas was discussed as part of a war plan by the Cabinet with advice from the master general.[25] Consideration of subsequent requests for supplies from the theatres of war overseas was based on reports and demands sent to London from the relevant commander in chief of forces. The Ordnance Office itself made an official estimate of the quantity of

[20] The Cinque Port defences as defined by the Ordnance Office; see appendix 2, table 10.
[21] WO 47/46, pp. 297, 549, 8 October, 20 December 1755.
[22] There is no available record of the proportions but these would have been based on consultation between master general & secretaries of state, and then ordered by the latter on behalf of the Crown.
[23] WO 47/46, pp. 106, 208, 31 July, 1 September 1755; WO 47/47, pp. 107, 464, 28 January, 1 May 1756.
[24] For distribution to the Army in North America and Germany see ch. 6.
[25] After the death of Marlborough in October 1758, there was no master general until Ligonier in July 1759. In the latter's absence his responsibilities passed to the lieutenant general.

gunpowder required for the specified number and size of guns and small arms. There was then intensive preparation to have the whole consignment ready by a certain date. Although there were often long delays in storeships setting sail for destinations overseas, there is no evidence that the Office was unable to supply the quantity of powder officially demanded of it either for the British military forces overseas or for those at home; that required for home defence was comparatively small. In theory, the Office was responsible both for storage of powder until required in the field and via its artillery staff for that in an artillery train at the site of battle. However, in practice it was impossible for the Board to oversee stock directly once it had been dispatched. As far as quantity in the field was concerned it was responsible only for supplying a sufficient number of barrels for the number and size of guns ordered of it by the respective secretary of state.

Methods by which official orders were conveyed to the Ordnance Office to issue stores were complicated, and could originate from any of several sources. Firstly, they could come from the Privy Council, as an order in Council resulting from a meeting of the Council at the Courts of either St James or Kensington and sent by the secretary of the lords justices on behalf of the latter and the Crown. Secondly, they could come as formal requests from a secretary of state on behalf of the Crown from the Council chambers at Whitehall. Thirdly, the order might come as a warrant from a secretary of state at either of the above courts, expressing the crown command for certain action and giving permission for the expense to be inserted in the next estimate to Parliament. Lastly, it might be as a combination of the latter two.

For full assessment of methods and their comparative importance it is necessary to study their individual roles. In comparison with the later Stuart period when 'policy was ceasing to be framed in the Privy Council and beginning to be initiated by the Cabinet' it is clear that by the mid-eighteenth century the planning process had developed further.[26] The role of the Cabinet had increased during the century with respect to the focus of discussion on war strategy and ordnance requirements, although the Privy Council continued to be the instrument of official communication. From Council registers and all extant orders in Council relating to the Ordnance Office and gunpowder during this nine-year period, it is obvious that the majority of such orders fell into three categories: requests by the special committee of the Council for Trade and Plantations for gunpowder for colonial governors, applications by merchants to export powder, and the supply of powder to regiments accompanying the East India Company. For these the Coun-

26 Tomlinson, *Guns and Government*, p. 18.

cil acted as an important central organ of administration, not in a decision making capacity but in sending the request to the master general for his advice followed by the formal order for him to act once that advice had been approved. Apart from the special committee for such matters as colonial defence, the Council could create temporary committees to consider particular requests. An example was that created to study a request from Jersey in 1755 for additional powder for the island's defence. The matter was referred to the master general, his advice approved and the order in Council issued for that advice to be put into operation. Therefore, orders in Council concerned the need for formal orders to the master general on certain less common aspects of gunpowder issue.

The method of request for issue of gunpowder to regiments in Britain or in theatres of war overseas, the heaviest aspect of military consumption, was in contrast. For this was employed either a written order from one of the secretaries of state at Whitehall, a formal warrant from one or other royal court, or a combination of the two. In theory it was one followed by the other in a two-stage request; in practice it was rarely as clear cut. The procedure was as follows: a decision or plan formulated in Cabinet resulted in the need for ordnance and stores for the Army, either for individual regiments, as part of an artillery train, or as subsequent additional supplies for that train. In many cases there was an initial letter to the master general from one of the secretaries of state at Whitehall conveying the royal request that he prepare an estimate of the ordnance and stores required for a given purpose. Once this request had been obeyed the secretary sent a warrant from one or other royal court. This was a formal command from the Crown to prepare and issue the stores according to the approved estimate, and containing a warrant to enter the cost of such supply in the Board's next estimate to Parliament. An example of a request from Whitehall followed by warrant was that concerning the artillery train to accompany Braddock to North America at the end of 1754. Robinson sent an order on behalf of the Crown from Whitehall to Ligonier, lieutenant general of the Ordnance, for a list to be prepared of stores and staff necessary to accompany twelve pieces of light ordnance. Once approved, Robinson sent a warrant containing the royal command from the Court of St James for the preparation and issue of the train, and warrant for the expense to be submitted to Parliament.[27] Some warrants were, as above, by 'His Majesty's command' while others were by 'the Lords Justices'. It is not clear whether or not every such Ordnance matter resulting in a warrant had been discussed at a Privy Council meeting. There is no indication of any such matters in

[27] WO 55/355, pp. 1, 12, 10 October, 25 November 1754.

the Council registers for this period. It is possible and far more likely that such warrants were prepared and issued from either St James's or Kensington by one of the secretaries either after the mere formality of agreement within a meeting of councillors or even solely in their name.

Not every order to the Office was as clear as this, with an initial request from Whitehall followed by warrant. Many requests from the Council chamber at Whitehall were in the form of direct orders to the master general to issue ordnance and powder from a list already prepared by the respective secretary of state. This had to be undertaken immediately with no time to be lost awaiting a warrant. At the height of war the Board had no option but to obey but was, nevertheless, at the obvious disadvantage of not possessing the warrant by which to submit the expense entailed. In such cases a warrant had to be requested by the Board after embarkation of stores, but there could be a delay of months before it was received. Often the matter was further complicated by additional requests for stores for the same consignment. Such problems were not peculiar to the period but were nevertheless accentuated by the scale of this war. For example, for a battering train of artillery for Loudoun in North America in January 1757 Pitt sent order from Whitehall on behalf of the Crown for immediate issue of a list of heavy brass ordnance and stores, including 2,000 barrels of gunpowder. Although preparation started immediately Pitt added several additional orders, including gunpowder, during the next few weeks but with warrant for none.[28] Orders from Whitehall also included instructions from secretaries of state for directing Ordnance storeships to Spithead to link with the troop transports for North America or Germany and for firing guns at St James's Park and the Tower to celebrate the various victories of the war.

The most common method of conveying orders to the Ordnance Office was the warrant alone. Filed with the very large number of warrants issued at this time are many separate detailed estimates of stores submitted by the Board; however, there is no evidence of accompanying preliminary requests from Whitehall to prepare such estimates in the first place. It is less likely that all such preliminary requests have been lost than that they never existed. It therefore seems that with this, the most usual method, the warrant was the order for immediate preparation and issue of ordnance, gunpowder and other stores. Detailed estimates of gunpowder, ammunition, equipment and artillery staff must therefore have been made and submitted immediately after receipt of the warrant, and at the same time as the Ordnance staff actually started to issue the stores involved. In such cases there

[28] WO 55/356, p. 190, 28 January 1757.

was no opportunity for loss of time. Any query from the secretary of state to whom the estimate had been submitted could be dealt with while ships were loaded; hence the reason for frequent subsequent additions of extra stores.

Whatever the method, no gunpowder was ever issued to the Army without an order on behalf of the Crown. Warrants issued for the supply of powder by the Ordnance Office to various regiments in Britain illustrate the increasing need for this material to prepare men for battle overseas. The first warrant of the period in May 1755 stipulated an annual supply of thirty barrels to each of twenty-six named Battalions of Foot in Britain, including the First Regiment of Foot Guards, and those of Wolfe and of Loudoun. Both were later involved in North America, the latter as commander in chief. This allowance applied to all such regiments raised subsequently and included the Hanoverian and Hessian troops in Britain to aid defence in 1756. The Board decided that ten of the thirty barrels should be of best quality for service and twenty 'triumph' for exercise, and that two-thirds of the latter should be either Dutch (fifty barrels of which were sent to the Tower for the purpose) or unserviceable, provided it was 'sifted, not wet, nor the corn broke.' The proper officers of the regiment were to inform the Board when requiring powder from their proportion so that the relevant storekeeper could have written permission for its issue, and were to certify to the latter that their last supply was almost expended.[29] In August 1756 an additional gunpowder allowance was ordered; four barrels of best and fifteen triumph for each Regiment of Foot, and two of best and eight triumph for each Regiment of Dragoons. The same allowance was ordered in June of the following year. However, in July all Battalions of Foot were to be allowed thirty barrels of triumph annually.[30] In December the allowance again increased not only for the Regiments of Foot but also those of Dragoons and of Horse. This was in various proportions, the largest of which was ninety barrels annually for the First Regiment of Foot Guards, sixty each for two other Regiments of Foot Guards and fourteen Regiments of Foot; some other Regiments of Foot received thirty each, the First Regiment of Dragoon Guards eleven, and various Regiments of Dragoons and the Royal Regiment of Horse Guards nine each.[31]

By May 1758 each of the marching regiments had been augmented from 700 to 900 men. As the former annual allowance was insufficient this was raised to fifty-six barrels, eighteen of which were best. This same extra allowance was given in 1759 also. Men of the Cavalry

[29] WO 47/45, p. 456, 16 May 1755; WO 47/47, p. 422, 23 April 1756.
[30] WO 47/50, p. 20, 9 July 1757; WO 55/356, p. 95, 13 August 1756.
[31] WO 55/356, p. 88, 9 December 1757.

regiments were each supplied with one pound of powder for service and two for exercise.[32] In the absence of further warrants concerning supply to the regiments at home it would appear that no further change was made and that the overall allowance of fifty-six barrels for the Regiments of Foot stood for the rest of the war. Regiments received their allowance as and when required from either Greenwich or the nearest defence establishment. For example, in July 1756 Colonel Hodgson's Regiment of Foot was provided with twenty-seven barrels from Dover Castle. In August 1757 powder was issued from Portsmouth land service stock for Lord Cornwallis's, Lord Loudoun's, and Kingsley's Regiments and Battalions of Buffs. Issue to the Militia from 1759 was by the same method as for the Army and in the same proportion.[33]

Powder for artillery trains was issued subject to warrant and to the ordnance specified. In March 1756 a train was prepared to attend the Hessian forces in Britain of 35 ordnance pieces of various sizes for which 470 barrels of powder were required. This train, which had 57 further pieces of brass ordnance added in July, was attended by the master and lieutenant generals and moved with 5 regiments of Artillery and 100 miners to encamp at Byfleet in order to be in constant readiness for possible invasion.'[34] Other trains were sent to such camps as those at Barham, Chatham and Dorchester.

Until Union, Ireland had its own regular army and a master general and Board of Ordnance centred in Dublin. Regiments sent overseas, as with Braddock, were usually first moved to the British establishment. Most of Ireland's gunpowder at this time was purchased by order of the lieutenant general and governor of Ireland from Lieutenant Colonel Philip Chenevix who prepared it there. This powder was for crown service, financed by the Treasury from the 'general revenue' but completely separate to that in British stock. The only recorded purchases were in 1751 (500 barrels at £4 12s each), in 1754 (1,000 at £4 17s 6d), and in 1756 (2,000 at £5 10s) These prices included Ordnance and Treasury expenses. When Irish stock was insufficient purchase was made from England. In 1755 an order was agreed by the Privy Council concerning 295 barrels together with a further unspecified quantity in 1756. However, in 1761 so short of supply was Britain that 1,000 barrels had to be purchased from Ireland.[35]

32 WO 55/357, p. 201, 3 May 1758; WO 47/54, p. 95, 26 July 1759.
33 WO 47/54, p. 78, 19 July 1759.
34 WO 55/355, pp. 234, 308, 12 November 1755, 1 March 1756; WO 55/356, 27 March 1756.
35 T 1 367/35, 26 June 1756; WO 47/58, pp. 322, 3 November 1761.

Ordnance bases overseas, 1755–7

During the Seven Years War gunpowder was distributed by the Ordnance Office to ordnance bases and colonial governors in many parts of the world. Although as war progressed ordnance stores were established at places such as New York, Boston, and Quebec, the main British Ordnance bases were initially in Gibraltar, Minorca, Jamaica, Antigua, Halifax and Annapolis in Nova Scotia, and St Johns and Placentia in Newfoundland. Each supplied land and sea stores for garrisons and the Royal Navy. Assessment of additional demand for naval supplies in wartime was based on lists from the Admiralty of shipping on service in the area. For any supply additional to the established allowance for each garrison, order was given by a secretary of state on behalf of the Crown. The duty of each storekeeper was to inform the Office in London regularly on the state of stock and to keep separate account of land and sea service issue.

The capacities of the magazines at Gibraltar and Minorca were not specified but for the former this was at least 10,850 barrels, the quantity in store in April 1757. By 1760 there were 4,239 members of the British Army at Gibraltar and 27 naval ships on service in the Mediterranean.[36] A report on the state of stores was received from each of the above storekeepers in February 1755 on which was based the Office's calculation of gunpowder required to complete stocks. The necessary arrangements were put in order and public advertisement made for the necessary shipping. Contract was arranged on 22 July with William Anderson, master of the ship *Smirncot* for Minorca, and with Zephaniah Eade for the *Sharpe* for Gibraltar. The latter was agreed at £2 2s a ton.[37]

As a result of the Ordnance Board's request to the Admiralty for convoy for 15 August, the intended date for completion of loading, the ships were to rendezvous at Spithead until a convoy vessel was available. Due to the need for speed with this consignment, the Board enquired of the Privy Council if the vessels should proceed alone. Although such intervention was unusual, the latter gave an immediate order to the Admiralty to provide convoy for the date specified. As the result of delay by a last minute Privy Council order for twelve men of the Royal Artillery to join the ship for Gibraltar, and therefore the need to move some of the ordnance stores to the ship *Essex*, the first two vessels were delayed in loading and did not leave until 24 August,

---

[36] Whitworth, *Lord Ligonier*, p. 317; Schomberg, *Naval Chronology*, pp. 37–42.
[37] Eade acted as security for, and was probably a relative of powder maker Jonathan Eade of Ewell mills, Surrey.

under convoy of HMS *Bedford*. The *Essex* had to await the protection of HMS *Chesterfield* on 15 November. The remainder of the annual proportion of stores for the Mediterranean bases was carried in February by the *Peggy* and the *Betsey*.[38] The difficulties of both government departments are obvious. Although request for convoy three weeks in advance gave the Admiralty adequate warning, that department knew from long experience the expense of such vessel awaiting storeships delayed in loading.

At the request of the Ordnance Office in May 1756 the Admiralty provided current detail of naval shipping in the Mediterranean so that those bases could be resupplied with powder and stores. This detail, together with information on ships sailing to the area under Byng, was received by the Office on 2 April. As a result it was decided to send 1,000 more barrels of powder to Gibraltar immediately. In addition, the Office received news in mid-April that stores were also required urgently for the Minorca base, for the naval squadron was due and the garrison was to be put in a state of defence. The supplies never reached Minorca, Byng failed to relieve the base, the French landed on 18 April, and St Philip's Castle was taken on 29 June.[39] Although heavy demand continued from Gibraltar the Board announced that supplies now required urgently in New York for Loudoun, commander in chief of forces in North America, should take precedence.

For the transportation of the 1,000 barrels due for Gibraltar contracts were, nevertheless, arranged on 11 May for three ships. These were the sloop *Susannah* of 70 tons, the *Endeavour* of 140 tons, and *St George* of 200 tons; William Jones, the master of the latter, made the proposal of £1 13s a ton and twenty days each for loading and unloading gunpowder, bedding, and timber, plus twenty days to await convoy. They arrived at Plymouth on 24 June.[40] Other ships taking the last of the gunpowder and other ordnance stores were the *Nancy* of 160 tons proposed at £1 15s in June, and the *Warren* proposed by Kemp, who had provided the *Peggy* earlier in the year. Accepted at the beginning of August, these were loaded by early September and arrived in Gibraltar on 26 November. Meantime, on 2 September, a further 1,500 barrels were to be sent as the result of the Office's estimate of what would be needed to complete the garrison 'in case of siege by sea and land, for six months'. With an order during loading for an increase in this quantity to 2,000 barrels more shipping had to be ordered. Among

38 SP 41/38, 4 August 1755, Ordnance Board to Amyand; WO 47/46, pp. 550, 567, 20, 23 December 1755.
39 WO 47/47, pp. 445, 461, 27 April, 1 May 1756; Adm. 1/4010, 30 March 1756.
40 WO 47/47, pp. 282, 470, 16 March, 4 May 1756; Adm. 1/4010 8 May 1756.

vessels proposed was the *Levant* by Kemp, but this was refused as 'too old, not proper and built in New England'.[41]

It was now, under considerable pressure, that the Office made an error of judgement. Secret negotiations, not minuted until December, were commenced in late August 1756 for the shipping of the Gibraltar consignment. Details of the transaction should have made the Board immediately suspicious. Richard Molineux, gunmaker, proposed five ships averaging 200 tons each, at £0 12s per ton per month for one month certain, after which one full months' notice was required before discharge, excluding notice within the first month; discharge was to be in the Thames. The ships were surveyed, contract agreed, and loading commenced. By early October and in spite of Molineux's assurance, the crew was still incomplete. On 2 November Molineux confessed that he was neither the owner of the vessels nor acting on their behalf. Although the ships were already loaded the contracts had to be cancelled. The Office was able subsequently to arrange a new contract with Sir Alexander Grant for the true owners.[42]

When 2,000 more barrels were ordered for Gibraltar on 28 October the whole transaction was faster. Contract was agreed for three ships at £1 15s a ton, and agreement made to sail forty-eight hours after loading with the bills of lading to be signed under penalty of £500. By 23 November they had all left Gravesend for Spithead.[43] In April 1757 1,000 barrels more were sent in part of 3,537 needed to complete the Gibraltar stock to 10,850 and taken in the *St George* and the *Endeavour* at the same price as those earlier.[44]

Gunpowder was also distributed to the Ordnance stores at Halifax and Annapolis in Nova Scotia, and to those at St Johns and Placentia in Newfoundland for garrisons and resupply of naval ships. In March 1755 the *Rachel* carried powder to St Johns at £2 a ton, an increase of £0 5s since the naval press, 'which entailed more liability with the crew'. In May a further quantity was sent together with some for the garrison at Placentia, the official allotted proportion for which was 220 barrels. The *Dorchester* was proposed for the consignment by John Adams at £3 a ton direct to Newfoundland. This was a rise in price stated by Adams to be due to 'the alteration in affairs which had risen the premium for insurance from four to ten per cent'.[45] Most consignments at this time appear to have been separate for Nova Scotia and Newfoundland although this depended on the quantity of stores in-

---

[41] WO 47/48, pp. 132, 180, 190, 13, 25 August, 2 September 1756.
[42] Ibid., pp. 305, 406–7, 532–3, 5 October, 3 November, 3 December 1756.
[43] Ibid., p. 396, 30 October 1756; WO 55/356, p. 178, 19 November 1756.
[44] WO 55/356, p. 255, 2 March 1757.
[45] WO 47/46, p. 92, 24 July 1755.

volved. If both bases required stores these would usually be shipped together but if the Ordnance staff at the first base could find a vessel locally to ship the stores to the second at less cost, such as occurred between St Johns and Placentia, they were ordered to do so. As shown by the agreement for the *Reward* the cost of freight to Nova Scotia had risen to £2 10s a ton by April 1756, although this was still £0 10s less than the current cost for merchants. In June the cost rose to £3, the same as for merchants, as seen by the agreement with John Reeks, master of the *Betsey* of 180 tons carrying powder and stores for both destinations. This vessel was loaded by mid-July but as all convoys for North America had already left it was delayed in the Thames until September. By April 1757 the cost of transporting 200 barrels of powder for St Johns and 150 for Placentia together with coal and 10,000 bricks was £3 15s.[46] At the same time more stock was shipped to the Halifax garrison and for Annapolis.

In the initial years of conflict gunpowder for the West Indies was mainly used to supply the Royal Navy in its task of protecting British commerce. It was in 1759 that Pitt abandoned the diversionary attacks on the French coast and began to operate a direct offensive in the West Indies to gain territory from the French.[47] At the outbreak of war Britain held New Providence in the Bahamas, Jamaica, some of the Virgin Islands and the Leeward Islands of Antigua, St Kitts, Nevis, and Montserrat, together with Barbados. Naval command was divided between the stations of Port Royal in Jamaica and of Antigua, and the quantity of powder delivered to each was largely based on Admiralty detail of ships on service there. Precise quantities within the established allotted proportions for each were rarely specified.

In March 1756, the *St James* was offered for Jamaica at £2 10s a ton if the quantity was 100 tons or less, and at £2 5s if more. The quantity of stores involved was eighty tons and even at this price was £0 10s less than paid by the merchants.[48] Soon after, contract was agreed for the *St Ann* with principal owners Drake and Long to take more powder to Jamaica, but once loaded there were difficulties with a press gang. Four of the crew were taken at Gravesend en route to Spithead and put on a naval tender; as a result the ship lost its convoy. The Admiralty refused to discharge the men as there had been too many similar incidents of what it considered to be naval men on ordnance ships, and to make allowance in this case would 'open the door to numerous applications, the granting of which would greatly distress the fleet at this time'. The

[46] WO 47/47, pp. 362, 367, 4, 6 April 1756; WO 47/49, p. 363, 5 April 1757; Adm. 1/4010, 15 July 1756.
[47] Julian S. Corbett, *England in the Seven Years War* (1907), i, 370.
[48] WO 47/47, pp. 146, 311, 323, 10 February, 23, 26 March 1756.

fact that such delay caused distress to the fleet in the West Indies and that Admiral Townsend had already written urgently from Jamaica for more powder appeared irrelevant to the Admiralty. To make matters worse, in spite of the crew's replacement in May, no convoy was provided until 13 September when the vessel finally left under the same protection as that for the *Mary Galley* with powder for the fleet at Antigua.[49]

Colonial governors

Until the Newcastle-Pitt administration there was some uncertainty on the extent to which the colonies should be assisted with defence supplies. Request for such aid from colonial governors was to the Privy Council via the Commissioners of Trade and Plantations. The decision on whether the request should be granted was the responsibility of the committee of the Council for Plantation Affairs, in conjunction with the master general of the Ordnance and his Board who advised on the request and the quantity and cost involved. A positive decision resulted in an order in Council to the Ordnance Office to arrange preparation and shipment and to insert the cost in the next financial statement to Parliament. All but one such request at this time was granted although in general the procedure was uncertain, slow and obviously of comparatively low priority as far as ordnance supplies were concerned.

The first such request for ordnance stores was from Governor Tinkler of the Bahama Islands on 18 July 1754. This was not passed by the committee of the Council for Plantation Affairs to the master general until January 1755. The Ordnance Board decided to send an engineer to examine the cannon already there, and although due to long disuse these were buried in sand and filled with stones they were retrieved and returned to use. Agreement was made in May for ammunition and 146 barrels of powder, the latter at an estimated cost of £627 16s, provided the Board require the governor to appoint an official storekeeper to guard the stores and make a six-monthly report on stock to London. This latter stipulation, based on an order in Council of 1745, was demanded of all governors thereafter.[50] Meantime, Governor Lawrence of Nova Scotia submitted a similar request via the Board of Trade. This was for completing the battery recently erected at

[49] WO 47/48, p. 211, September 1756; Adm. 1/4010, 23, 27 April, 20 May, 4 September 1756.
[50] PC 2/105, p. 182, 17 May 1756; WO 55/355, pp. 54, 128, 159, 24 January, 13 May, 14 June 1755.

Halifax harbour and included 7 pieces of iron ordnance and 400 barrels of powder. In its estimate of requirements the Ordnance Board advised a further 115 barrels of powder and an appropriate quantity of ammunition at a total cost to the government of £7,249.[51] Dispatch was delayed when the Privy Council ordered the Board to include with the shipment fourteen men to complete the Company of Artillery at Halifax. The stores were split between two vessels. Stillingfleet Durnford and John Croome of the Ordnance department of deliveries checked loading of the *Halifax* at Rotherhithe, and the *Cornwallis* at Horsley Down and Galleons respectively, and took the masters' receipts for powder and stores.[52] Lawrence's request for stores for the town of Halifax resulted in a consignment of 723 barrels of powder, ordnance, and ammunition on the *Charming Helena*. Loading was completed on 21 July and departure on 11 August. Although voyage should have been under convoy of HMS *Seaford* together with the *Keppel* laden with powder for Braddock in Virginia, the *Charming Helena* put to sea alone rather than be delayed further.[53]

A two-part request by Governor Dobbs of North Carolina in November 1754 was subject to an exceptionally long delay, caused initially by inadequate information from the governor himself. The advice of the master general and Board was sought in May 1755, with strong recommendation from the Board of Trade that the request be met. In his first request Dobbs asked only for thirty barrels of powder but the Ordnance Board stated that musket shot, flints and fine paper would have to be added. In the second, stores were required for Fort Johnson on Cape River, including iron ordnance of various sizes and 210 barrels of powder. The powder was priced at £129 and £903 respectively. As the result of time lost by Dobbs' inadequate information on the fort and its requirements there was a delay in preparing the estimate and this was not agreed by the Privy Council until 7 July 1756. Furthermore, various misunderstandings between Ordnance Board and Admiralty regarding convoy meant that it was not until the following spring that the consignment finally left Britain.[54]

The government's lack of interest in a request for ordnance stores from Governor Grenville of Barbados in 1755 clearly shows that its priorities lay elsewhere. No final decision was made on the subject until May 1756. Not until November did the respective consignment

[51] PC 2/104, p. 392, 7 May 1755; WO 55/355, pp. 40, 127, 17 December 1754, 13 May 1755.

[52] WO 51/194, pp. 264–5, 30 June 1755.

[53] SP 41/38, 9 October 1755; WO 47/45, p. 545, 10 June 1755; Adm. 1/4010, 10, 27 August 1755.

[54] WO 55/355, pp. 121, 136, 7, 31 May 1756; WO 55/356, pp. 84, 103, 7, 8 July 1756.

leave British shores for the West Indies. A further request for defence in the West Indies was made in August 1756 by John Sharpe, agent to the Board of Trade for the Island of Nevis, which in his view was, 'important to the revenue, navigation and commerce of the Kingdom'. Provision of twenty pieces of ordnance, ammunition, and sixteen barrels of gunpowder was agreed. The other two governors to request ordnance stores at this time were those of New York and of Georgia. The first, in October 1756, was refused. The Ordnance Board advised that the city had never been within the department of the Office, there were no plans on which to assess needs, and it would now be difficult to spare guns and gunpowder as a result of the needs of the garrisons in Britain. The second, on the same date, was successful in its request for thirty-one barrels of powder, muskets, and ammunition, largely because the Board of Trade considered that the colony, then without defence, to be of great importance 'as a barrier against the Spaniards, French and Indians'.[55]

Although methods of assessment and distribution of gunpowder within Britain and most military bases overseas were well established, those for the Army in North America were more complicated. Procedure for naval supply, which involved orders to the Ordnance Board direct from the Admiralty, were much simpler, even though there was severe shortage for ships at the height of war due to heavy demand. With hindsight it is possible to identify certain ways in which that department might have operated more efficiently, particularly with regard to transportation of stores. However, in most cases this would have necessitated simultaneous change in other government departments. To suggest that this would have been possible at this time would be to underestimate both the sheer volume of responsibility demanded by each department in time of war, and the many and varied restrictions of the day. Moreover, few could ever have foreseen the eventual intensity and extent of this war or the poor supply which would come from the mills.

[55] WO 47/48, p. 177, 24 August 1756; WO 47/49, p. 13, 4 January 1757; WO 55/356, p. 98, 151, 18 August, 13 October 1756.

6

North America and Germany

The main theatres of Anglo-French warfare during the period 1755–63 were North America and Germany. In North America British and colonial troops and Royal Naval ships were active throughout the period, while in Germany the British Army was involved from July 1758. All issue of ordnance stores to military forces in the field was the subject of order to the master general and principal officers of the Ordnance by the relevant secretaries of state on behalf of the Crown; orders were usually recorded in detail in Ordnance records and followed the method already discussed.

The very large number of stores involved in artillery trains included ordnance, small arms, ammunition, powder, laboratory stores for preparing ammunition, entrenching tools, waggons, horses, and spare wheels. The whole was in the charge of staff of the Royal Artillery, miners, and attendants. Reference will be made to all recorded shipments for these locations. Supply to Germany by the mid-eighteenth century was well established and routine. That to North America was certainly not. Emphasis will therefore be on the latter and especially on two main aspects: the complex political situation in the initial years of 1755–7 between the British government and her North American colonies regarding colonial defence; and the supply of the heavy demand for guns and gunpowder for that location throughout the war.

Britain and North America, 1755–7

In this initial period of conflict prior to the Newcastle-Pitt ministry, gunpowder supplied by the Ordnance Office was intended specifically for the main campaigns. These involved chiefly British forces, financed by Britain, under the successive commanders in chief Braddock, Shirley, and Loudoun. It was not intended for the subsidiary expeditions led by colonial commanders with colonial troops enlisted specifically for the purpose. At no time does there appear to have been any officially recorded decision on which men or expeditions, should or should not have ordnance stores supplied and financed by the British government. The entire question revolved round the degree to which the colonies were supposed to support themselves. Only under Pitt was it decided that colonial troops must receive adequate ordnance stores from Britain if they were to be expected to fight effectively alongside their British counterparts. Until then the issue was confused and many of the decisions on ordnance supplies piecemeal. While small arms and powder were supplied for one subsidiary expedition, they were not supplied for another and although an expedition might be supplied with powder for small arms it often had to find its own powder for cannon.

In his discussion of availability of gunpowder in North America in 1776 Stephenson refers to 'powder mills in ruins', to gunpowder in the colonial magazines which had 'lain there since the Seven Years War', and to the manufacture of the explosive as 'almost a lost art'.[1] This suggests local manufacture in the mid-eighteenth century, but there is no reference among Ordnance records of any contribution from such supply during the Seven Years War. Most of the local stock originated from the comparatively small official supply from Britain to certain governors for the basic defence requirements of individual colonies, from direct private trade between colonists and the British mills, or from port duty. The latter was arranged by individual Acts of Parliament for certain colonies between 1740 and 1773 whereby powder was provided by masters of all trading vessels entering North American ports. This was intended by the British government to furnish magazines for defence purposes and applied to Georgia, New Jersey, New York, North Carolina, and Virginia. This was at the rate of 'one pound of good gunpowder for every ton according to the tonnage of the vessel'.[2] When asked to estimate the powder requirements of Virginia after its governor requested ordnance stores in August, the Ordnance Board reminded the Privy Council that although cannon and shot could be supplied at British expense, the colony should already have powder from powder duty.[3]

Colonial defence supplies

The lack of unity between Britain and the North American colonies and between the colonies themselves, together with the unsettled British ministries of 1755 and 1756, did much to complicate gunpowder distribution at this time. The chief deterrent to order and responsibility

[1] O. W. Stephenson, 'The Supply of Gunpowder in 1776', *American Historical Review*, 30 (1925), 271.
[2] Leonard Woods Labaree (ed.), *Royal Instructions to British Colonial Governors 1670–1776* (New York 1967), i, 418–20.
[3] James Munro (ed.), *Acts of Privy Council of England, Colonial Series 1745–66* (1911), iv, 203.

in war finance was the failure of the British government to have a definite policy; from year to year everything was makeshift. The government missed the opportunity of creating some form of colonial taxation when those colonies were most in need of help.[4] This was particularly so in 1755 and 1756, before Pitt arranged regular reimbursement to the colonies for war expenses.

After the construction of Fort Duquesne by the French in 1754 the government decided that its American colonies required practical help in moving the French from the Ohio valley. In October it was arranged that two Regiments of Foot should be sent from Britain under Major General Braddock and two other regular Regiments of Foot be raised in North America itself, all to be financed directly by Britain. The latter were to be commanded by colonists Pepperel and Shirley and augmented by American Independent Regiments from New York, also under British pay. Braddock was appointed commander in chief and Shirley, the governor of Massachusetts, his deputy.[5]

Braddock arrived at Hampton, Virginia in February 1755, and it was at a conference at Alexandria on the Potomac River with Shirley and the governors of Virginia, New York, Maryland, and Pennsylvania that plans were finalised not only for the four expeditions against the French at Fort Duquesne, Niagara, Crown Point, and Beausejour but on the way in which gunpowder and other stores would be supplied. The most important expedition was to be commanded by Braddock against Fort Duquesne employing the regular British troops augmented as necessary by American provincials. The provincials would be provided by the colonies concerned to assist in a common defence. The 560 barrels of powder for Braddock's artillery train were obviously intended only for this expedition for there is no evidence of its use for any other purpose. The train was to be commanded by Captain Thomas Ord of the Royal Regiment of Artillery, previously stationed in Newfoundland, who was responsible to the Ordnance Office not only for the powder, ordnance, and hiring of horses and waggons to transport them but also for finding an iron founder to make additional shells for mortars.[6]

Of the two main subsidiary expeditions, one was to be commanded by Shirley to reinforce the British fur trading base of Oswego and to proceed against Fort Niagara, and the other by fellow colonial William Johnson against the French fort at Crown Point on Lake Champlain.

---

[4] Harry M. Ward, *Unite or Die* (Washington 1971), p. 98.
[5] R. C. Simmons and P. D. G. Thomas (eds.), *Proceedings and Debates of the British Parliaments respecting North America 1754–1764* (New York 1982), i, 24.
[6] WO 47/45, p. 120, 18 February 1755; WO 47/46, p. 65, 21 July 1755; WO 47/47, p. 18, 8 January 1756.

The plans for financing and supplying the latter were confused and unsatisfactory and those for Niagara not much better. This caused considerable related confusion in the distribution of gunpowder and other ordnance stores. The main reasons for this were uncertainty and mistrust between the British government and the colonial governors and assemblies, initial underestimation of difficulties in both communication and supply of men and stores over so great a distance, and over-ambitious military aims in unfamiliar and difficult terrain. Further difficulty resulted from both an initial lack of suitable men and ordnance supplies in North America and lack of intercolonial unity in defence policies.

Shirley's force of regular colonials was to be financed by the Crown and augmented by provincials supplied and financed largely by his own colony of Massachusetts. Johnson was to receive no crown finance at all. His ordnance supplies and force composed entirely of provincials and Indians were to be funded by Massachusetts, Virginia, New York, Maryland, and Pennsylvania. To these five colonies at the Alexandria Conference Braddock conveyed Britain's request for a common colonial defence fund but, as at the Albany Conference of 1754, the governors reported their assemblies' lack of agreement. Instead, they promised to help with men and supplies for Johnson according to the quota system in proportion to population, but requested British help in defraying the expense.[7] No decision was made on this point until the following year. Although the government attempted to rely less on the colonial quota system by supplying more British troops, the system remained throughout the war. This first year was far from satisfactory in terms of powder supply for either Shirley or Johnson, for instead of a reliable supply from the Ordnance Office they had to rely on the haphazard arrangement with individual colonies. This lacked any coordination whatsoever. Some sent powder to be used only by the troops they had supplied while others sent powder only to be used within their own provincial boundary.

Although Shirley did not draw on ordnance supplies consigned to Braddock the Office was requested in February 1755 to supply him with a small amount of gunpowder. Consisting of '12 barrels of gunpowder for the American Regiments', this was insufficient for total needs but with the pay, clothing, and victualling of his regular troops, together with 2,000 small arms and ammunition, it was obviously considered to be the agreed British contribution. The consignment arrived in Boston in May.[8] It is not surprising that the government did not supply the

[7] CO 326/28, 22 January 1756; E. B. O'Callaghan (ed.), *The Documentary History of the State of New York* (Albany 1849), ii, 648–52.
[8] WO 55/355, p. 50, 4 February 1755.

entire funding for Shirley's Niagara campaign for even the expense of raising the American regiments for this commander had been strongly opposed by Newcastle as first lord of the Treasury, and was only undertaken due to the persistence of Cumberland as captain general and Fox as secretary of war, with the support of Pitt and Anson.[9] Although Shirley was provided with 500 small arms from Virginia, as part of the consignment sent from Britain in 1753 to help with that colony's defence, and with brass and iron ordnance from the New York Assembly for the defence of Oswego, the source of most of his gunpowder is unclear.[10] He was assisted by members of the Royal Regiment of Artillery who were paid in America on behalf of the Ordnance Office by agents Thomlinson and Hanbury.[11] As most of the provincial troops for Shirley were recruited from his own Massachusetts this would have been the obvious place from which to procure his main powder. In addition, he requested powder from New York as shown in his letter to the Massachusetts General Court on 23 May. He also considered himself responsible for helping with Johnson's powder requirements, promising the latter that he would press the colonies concerned to supply the 800 barrels needed; 400 barrels were thus supplied for Johnson from Massachusetts alone. Shirley told the Court that as he also needed 600 barrels for his own Niagara expedition he thought it advisable that he and Johnson request some from New York and Philadelphia in case none was forthcoming from Boston.[12]

As commander in chief, following Braddock's death in July, Shirley was in a more advantageous position for acquiring the powder he needed and as a result sought a further 1,000 barrels. Although there is no record of the dispatch of this quantity the Office did send 625 barrels together with 10,000 muskets to Shirley at Boston in November.[13] It is unclear if, during his period in overall command in North America between July 1755 and his downfall in March 1756, Shirley intended to incorporate any of the official stock originally intended for Braddock into that for his own Niagara campaign. Certainly he ordered its removal from Hampton to the new military base at New York after agreement for the change between the governor of New York, the Board of Trade, and the Crown. However, a letter to the Ordnance Office in March 1756 from Ord, commanding officer of Artillery, suggests that there were difficulties; in this Ord stressed the need for

[9] Thad W. Riker, 'The Politics behind Braddock's Expedition', *American Historical Review*, 13 (1908), 747.
[10] *Pennsylvania Archives*, 1st series 2 (Philadelphia 1853), 354.
[11] WO 47/46, p. 66, 21 July 1755; T 1 377/85, 1757.
[12] C. H. Lincoln, *The Correspondence of William Shirley* (New York 1912), ii, p. 174.
[13] WO 55/355, p. 235, 12 November 1755.

Shirley to be supplied by the Office for his renewed offensive against Niagara, as the intermediate base of Oswego was British and the force to be employed from there against Niagara incorporated British men. It included those from his own Artillery Regiment.[14]

Supplies of ammunition additional to those prepared in Britain could be made in North America either in the field from materials supplied from the artillery train or ordered from a local foundry. Some of Shirley's ammunition was supplied by the Ancram furnace believed by its proprietor to be the only American furnace in blast at that time.[15] There is the suggestion in Ord's further correspondence with the Office that other foundries were in existence, at least by 1756, for he states that he would obtain 'such ammunition as could be found at Albany or the foundries thereabouts'. He had also received Shirley's orders to give directions for casting three iron howitzers.[16] In the artillery train provided for Braddock there were shot moulds and lead and iron bars for casting additional shot.

Although the five colonies at the Alexandria Conference had promised help with men and ordnance supplies for Johnson's expedition the response was, in practice, unsatisfactory and provision slow and uncertain, with some colonies waiting to see what others would give. Ordnance supplies and money to support the Indians was intended to be in porportion to the number of men promised by each area and the expense of artillery to be shared between all. However, in reality, Massachusetts supplied the most.[17] A member of Braddock's own artillery who was supplied to command Johnson's artillery train was shocked at the inadequacy of Johnson's ordnance and gunpowder.[18] Whether powder was supplied by Virginia is unclear, for in May 1755 Governor Dinwiddie was in doubt about what could be spared. As Virginia itself required powder Dinwiddie acquired 500 barrels at Braddock's death from Admiral Boscawen's naval squadron in North American waters 'to refill the empty magazine at Williamsburg and supply the new levies'. The supply of this naval powder plus 400 arms for Virginian defence stock was later agreed by the Ordance Board in the gunners' accounts of the respective ships.[19]

The efforts of 1755 were renewed in 1756 under Shirley, Webb, and Abercromby respectively, until the arrival of Loudoun as commander in chief in July, but the three main expeditions of 1755 and 1756 all

14 CO 5/1129, p. 26, 8 October 1755; WO 47/47, p. 493, 11 May 1756.
15 Theodore Thayer, 'The Army Contractors for the Niagara Campaign 1755–1756', *William and Mary Quarterly*, 3rd series 14 (1957), 36–7.
16 WO 47/47, p. 428, 23 April 1756.
17 O'Callaghan, *New York*, pp. 648–52.
18 WO 47/47, p. 493, 11 May 1756.
19 PC 2/105, p. 13, 27 January 1756.

failed in their ultimate aims. Both Shirley and the British government pleaded unsuccessfully for increased colonial exertion and unity in defence and were forced to accept continuation of the unsatisfactory colonial quota system in combination with British men and supplies.[20] With the inevitability of official war and government concern over the colonies maintaining even the quota system, a decision was made to reimburse them for the expense of action during 1755 in order that they might prepare for the following year. On 2 January Fox, for the Crown, asked the Board of Trade the sum it thought proper to ask of Parliament for the assistance of the British subjects in North America, whereby the Board sought the respective information from its own records, colonial agents, and the governor of New York. The latter had to admit that the provinces had never agreed on the establishment of any fund or quota of men for such services and asked the Board to apply its own judgement on the matter. This further illustrated the confused context in which gunpowder from both Office and colonies was supplied at this time.[21] The Board of Trade recommendations resulted in the decision to reimburse the colonies in proportion to their financial outlay to date, on what had so far been termed 'defence'. This established a pattern whereby the colonies provided provincials to augment the regular British and American troops, and sought annually the necessary reimbursement from Parliament. There were difficulties: payments were delayed and there was great variation in the enthusiasm or ability of the colonies to provide supplies for their provincial troops.

As is shown by the many Parliamentary debates on the subject, it became obvious during 1756 that many more regular troops were required in America not only for the increased offensives but in preference to the use of so many provincials. Under Loudoun, not only were more troops sent from Britain but the Royal American Regiment raised, all with British pay and supplies. The quantity of powder and other stores had to be increased accordingly and it was from this time that more reliance came to be made on British gunpowder and supplies rather than on the unsatisfactory colonial stocks, not only for provincials but, at the request of both Sir William Johnson and Abercromby, for the Indians.[22] Thus, during the period of disastrous failed expeditions against the French in 1755 and 1756, the loss of Oswego, the abandoned move against Louisbourg, and the loss of Fort William

[20] CO 5/1067, p. 93, 27 January 1756; for reference to the protection of North America, see J. Debrett, *The History, Debates, and Proceedings of both Houses of Parliament* (1792), iii, 235–7.
[21] CO 391/63, p. 6, 14 January 1756.
[22] Milton W. Hamilton, *Sir William Johnson: Colonial American, 1715–1763* (New York 1976), p. 231.

Henry in 1757, the pattern of distribution of gunpowder began to undergo significant change. After initial political confusion on the subject together with considerable colonial inefficiency and lack of concern, it was no longer to be a combination of British and colonial stock but almost entirely that shipped from, and financed by, Britain. As the war intensified so the supply to North America had to increase.

Gunpowder storage in North America

In theory, storage of gunpowder dispatched from Britain for the combined forces in North America remained the responsibility of the Ordnance Office until actually used in the field. A storekeeper appointed by the Office made local arrangements for safe storage and, still on its behalf, followed the directions of the commander in chief of forces in North America concerning the issue of stock from store and its transport between military bases. Responsible to, and paid by, the Office for maintenance of the artillery train accompanying the main expedition of the day, which included a large quantity of that stock, was the commanding officer of Artillery. In practice, it was impossible for the Office in London to be in full control of any of these aspects of stock once it had left Britain.

Francis Stephens, the first storekeeper to go to America, had risen to this post from that of Ordnance clerk at Woolwich. He was appointed in July 1755 to accompany the second dispatch of stores intended for Braddock. His salary and aid in searching for storehouses were provided on behalf of the Office by the agents Thomlinson and Hanbury. With the next dispatch for Shirley at Boston were included a paymaster, clerk of stores, and two armourers, the latter to deliver stores to persons authorised by the commander in chief, and to supervise subsequent deliveries from Britain.[23] This task was by no means simple. Commanders in chief, battle sites, campaign bases, and therefore location of stores, changed frequently at this time, while lack of purpose-built storage facilities and delays in correspondence between America and London added to the problems.[24] In his letter to the Ordnance Board from New York, dated 20 September 1756 and received in December, Stephens stated that he had unloaded the most recent ordnance storeships to arrive for Loudoun. He had then hired storehouses to receive some of the powder at a cost of £43 15s a year, together with three

---

23 WO 55/355, p. 237, 12 November 1755.
24 WO 47/46, p. 66, 21 July 1756; WO 47/47, pp. 20, 358, 642, 8 January, 2 April, 11 June 1756; Adm. 1/4010, 22 November 1755.

sloops to house the remainder in order not to detain the storeships.[25] Though responsible both to the commander in chief and the Ordnance Board it is obvious that his correspondence was merely a formality, for action had to be taken long before a reply was received from London. What must be considered in any assessment of the degree of efficiency or otherwise of the administration and management of gunpowder and stores over such large distances, is the enormity of the task.

Distribution to North America, 1755–7

Commercial storeships employed for the regular replenishment of British ordnance bases at home and overseas were usually arranged by the Ordnance Office; in contrast, the majority of those used for troops and ordnance stores for the combined British and colonial forces in North America, and the British forces in Germany, were arranged by the Admiralty. This was because of the much larger tonnage of stores and number of troops involved. The system was not formalised. On some occasions the Ordnance Office arranged the shipping alone and only approached the Admiralty for convoy; at other times it requested Admiralty assistance in arrangements, but had to ask the secretary of state to intervene when it received no cooperation. In the majority of cases the Ordnance Board informed the Admiralty of the precise shipping required, and only took responsibility itself once the vessels were ready for loading. All transportation was financed by the Ordnance Office.

With regard to the quantity of gunpowder for the Army in the field, whether in North America, Germany, or Britain, the Office did what it could to ascertain that barrels would be kept as dry and as stable as possible in transit, and therefore arrive in the quantity requested. However, the Board itself could not be directly responsible for inadequate stock in the field. Such inadequacy could be due either to misuse in action or to an inadequate quantity having been ordered in the first place. The Office issued the number, nature, and size of guns, and quantity of small arms, ammunition, and gunpowder demanded of it by the respective secretary of state. Insufficient powder at the scene of battle could be due, therefore, to misjudgement by the commander in the field, or the master general in London in discussion with other members of the Cabinet, of the size of artillery train or quantity of guns and gunpowder required; even more likely, it could be due to misjudgement of the nature, length, and intensity of the campaign involved.

The preparation of Braddock's artillery train in October 1754

[25] WO 47/48, p. 525, 3 December 1756; CO 5/1067, p. 176, 9 November 1756.

heralded what was to be a greater involvement by the British Army in North America than ever before. The train included 10 pieces of light brass ordnance, 4 brass howitzers, 1,400 muskets, and for all of these 560 barrels of gunpowder. Also included were 2 barrels of powder for filling shells together with 12 barrels and 2,000 muskets for the American Regiments under Shirley. Inclusive of salary for the artillery officers, engineers, artificers, and attendants accompanying the train, the entire cost as specified by the Ordnance Board to Parliament was £17,353. The three ships hired by the Office to take these stores linked with the two troopships at Cork and arrived in Virginia on 8 and 10 April respectively. Part of the stores were unloaded at Hampton and the remainder taken 360 miles up the Potomac River ready for Braddock's expedition against Fort Duquesne.[26] This order presented little problem, but this was not so for the additional stores ordered for Braddock a few months later. Considerable delay was caused for several reasons, one of which was an argument between the Privy Council, Admiralty, and Navy Board about who was responsible for arranging the necessary shipping. On 5 May 1755 Amyand, secretary to the Privy Council, presented the request for four pieces of light brass ordnance, ammunition, and fifty-five barrels of powder, totalling thirty tons in weight. The consignment, accompanied by storekeeper Stephens, did not leave Britain until the end of September.[27]

Worse was to come. These stores were to be transported at £2 a ton on the *Keppell*, of 180 tons, under Captain Arbuthnot. The usual twenty days demurrage each for loading and unloading was allowed by the master plus four pence a ton for each day in excess. Initially there was indecision about whether convoy was essential and on 21 July the Board considered sending her without, which resulted in the ship's master asking to be allowed 'the difference of the premium being advanced on chartering, from two and a half to fifteen per cent, on the ship's value being upwards of £1,400'. This was refused by the Office and convoy insisted upon by the Privy Council. Not until 10 August, with the vessel at the Nore awaiting further orders, was agreement made between Admiralty and Board on the subject.[28] This ship loaded for Virginia and the Bahamas and the *Charming Helena* for Nova Scotia were to go from Spithead under convoy of HMS *Seaford* but the master of the latter decided to put to sea alone to avoid possible delay. Delay

26 WO 47/44, pp. 187, 287, 297, 11 October, 18, 20 November 1754; WO 47/45, pp. 31, 383, 14 January, 22 April 1755; WO 55/355, pp. 7, 12, 10 October, 25 November 1754; Simmons and Thomas, *Proceedings and Debates*, p. 26.
27 WO 55/355, pp. 112, 202, 5 May, 13 October 1755; SP 41/38, 10 July, 9 October 1755.
28 WO 47/46, pp. 30, 105, 10, 31 July 1755; Adm. 1/4010, 10 August 1755.

there certainly was for on the arrival of the *Keppell* at Spithead the captain of the *Seaford* denied all knowledge of such plans. The Admiralty was informed; it was now 26 August. Braddock had long since ceased to need the extra powder and stores for he had been killed in action on 13 July. Even when the *Keppell* finally left Portsmouth during the last week of September she had to follow the convoy vessel into Plymouth to link with naval storeships before starting on a voyage now intended not direct to Hampton, but first to Boston and New York. After many weeks of awaiting a convoy she eventually crossed the Atlantic entirely alone, to arrive in Virginia on 5 January 1756, for only three days out from Plymouth she had parted from the Seaford in thick fog.[29]

On 8 and 23 October, 6,000 and 4,000 muskets respectively, plus ammunition and 625 barrels of gunpowder, were ordered for troops in Boston. These were prepared and loading already commenced when a further 4,000 muskets were ordered. Shipping had been arranged by the Admiralty for transportation from Spithead in HMS *Lynn* and merchant ship *Britannia*. The second order caused chaos. The Board expressed its displeasure at a meeting at Sheerness on 25 October as the first order would now be delayed for three weeks due to the need to view, engrave, number and pack the extra muskets. It also doubted if the two ships could manage the combined tonnage. The first consignment was ready to leave for Spithead by 12 November but the 4,000 arms and major proportion of powder and ammunition on the ships *Kent* and *Charming Betsey*, shipped from the Thames on 30 October, had still not arrived by 15 November because of bad weather. Not until 9 December did the loaded *Lynn* and *Britannia* sail for America. After they had sailed and the additional 4,000 muskets had been loaded onto HMS *Woolwich* at Sheerness it was discovered that 190 barrels of gunpowder and some ammunition from the order had been left behind at Portsmouth. Not until the end of January did the second group of ships depart, carrying the remainder of the powder and the other stores.[30]

Early in 1756 Loudoun was posted to North America with further British troops to take charge of what was by now a much increased force of regular and colonial troops. There were three main consignments of ordnance stores for him between March 1756 and July 1757, after which the position of commander in chief was taken by Amherst.

[29] WO 47/46, pp. 149, 198, 239, 12, 26 August, 18 September 1755; WO 47/47, p. 231, 2 March 1756.
[30] WO 55/355, pp. 195, 219, 221, 235, 284, 8, 23, 25 October 1755, 24 January 1756; Adm. 1/4010, 20, 29 October, 12, 22 November, 9 December 1755, 20 January 1756.

Loudoun's main aim in 1756 was an expedition against Louisbourg to be followed by one against Quebec. His first request to the government, conveyed to the Office on 26 March, concerned the needs of 12,000 men of the combined forces; this was for a total of 2,000 barrels of powder including 200 for service and 20 for exercise for each regiment together with 36 pieces of brass ordnance of varied sizes. This was issued from the stores at Tilbury Fort in April. Six vessels totalling 678 tons were to be ready for loading within a week before being linked to the troopships for convoy; four were at Gravesend and two at Deptford. However, on 7 April the additional orders began to be received which were to take up so much extra time. Initially just waggons and harness were requested but nine days later a further four ordnance pieces were ordered with gunpowder and ammunition in proportion, plus an additional thirty barrels each of English and Dutch powder. Powder was also to be sent for naval ships under construction in North America.[31]

This large consignment was further delayed by the decision that the King might send via Loudoun 'a large present to the Indians in the British interest in seeking Indian allegiance'. It included 90 barrels of gunpowder and 700 guns, together with bullets and lead bars. Although there is no record of its source, the powder appears to have been purchased privately from one or more of the mills. For this additional load the Office had to arrange twenty-eight more tons of shipping.[32] Additional orders and the management of extra shipping were delay enough but three weeks after the original order further disruption was caused when the master general requested that the 500 barrels of Dutch powder within it be exchanged for English.[33] Another, final order was made to the Office on 13 May, the last before the ships set sail 'a sufficient quantity of powder and ball to make up 36 rounds for 300 men on board the transports now in the Thames for New York'. The entire load then sailed. Storekeeper Stephens reported on the unloading in New York on 20 September and on Loudoun's order for the ordnance stores to be moved to join the main store there from Boston.[34]

With Pitt in office from Autumn 1756 reinforcements of men for North America were increased and, in view of the failed efforts of that year, a naval squadron was sent under Holburne for the combined military and naval operation against Louisbourg for 1757 to block French supplies and to act as a base from which to proceed to Quebec.

[31] WO 47/47, pp. 313, 355, 375, 407, 23 March, 2, 7, 16 April 1756; WO 55/355, p. 329, 26 March 1756; Adm. 1/4010, 2 April 1756.
[32] WO 55/356, pp. 20, 48, 7 April, 6 May 1756; CO 5/1129, p. 93, 29 July 1756.
[33] WO 47/47, p. 436, 25 April 1756.
[34] WO 47/48, p. 525, 3 December 1756.

Loudoun's next consignment of stores was increased correspondingly. The Navy Board was requested by the Admiralty to allow the Office to employ 1,600 tons of shipping for the purpose from that arranged recently for naval shipments, but with contracts and payment to be made by the Ordnance department. The loading was supervised by Bennet, the Ordnance purveyor for sea, together with the comptroller of the Royal Laboratory and the issuing clerks who reported on daily progress to the surveyor general.[35]

At the end of January 1757 a battering train of artillery was prepared for Loudoun which included 24 pieces of heavy brass ordnance, 26 brass mortars of various sizes, 2,000 barrels of gunpowder for the guns, mortars, and shells, and the necessary staff to accompany them together with a long list of such stores as ammunition, gun carriages, entrenching tools and means for making extra ammunition. The store-ships were to be ready to sail to Cork by 12 February to join the troopships.[36] However, once again there was a delay, for the two battalions of Scottish Highlanders who were to join Loudoun could not be fitted with the main dispatch and had to go in a separate ship convoyed by HMS Falkland to join the other six ships at Cork.[37]

At the same time the Office had to prepare powder for Holburne's naval squadron which was to accompany the above ships to New York for the combined offensive. This was no simple undertaking given the difficulties the Board was experiencing in obtaining sufficient stock from its powder makers at this time. It is therefore no surprise that having prepared the storeships well in time the Office was unable to have the naval ships at Portsmouth ready to sail for Cork until 16 April. It was 8 May before the troop and storeships, with the seventeen warships, five frigates, and twelve additional vessels were ready to sail for Cork. As stated by Corbett, this was 'all too late for any great success' as far as the attack on Louisbourg was concerned.[38] The accounts of John Knox, one of the men with the seven Regiments of Foot in Ireland sent on board the troopships, illustrate further the difficulties of this long crossing. All the ships were separated in high winds the day after leaving harbour and after reassembling and managing to keep together until 20 May many were again separated in thick fog. That carrying Knox proceeded alone in rough seas to reach the American coast almost eight weeks later but far too late to be of immediate

---

35 WO 47/49, pp. 79, 84, 96, 21, 24, 26 January 1757.
36 Ibid., pp. 107, 109, 147, 29 January, 9 February 1757; WO 55/356, p. 190, 28 January 1757.
37 Ibid., p. 345, 1 April 1757; Adm. 1/4011, 1 April 1757.
38 Corbett, England in the Seven Years War, i, 159.

assistance to Loudoun.[39] By this time France had broken the British blockade of French ports and reinforced her position at Louisbourg. Although Loudoun had moved troops and stores from New York to Halifax in early July for the attack on Louisbourg with Holburne, the entire endeavour was eventually abandoned on 6 August. This news would have taken many weeks to reach Britain and it was this time lapse, caused by large distances and wild terrain, which resulted in so much difficulty for the Cabinet in assessment of stores. Delays were increased further by the frequent need to give extra orders to the Ordnance Board for stores additional to the main consignment; this was usually due to subsequent requests to London from Loudoun. After his initial request for stores for troops and the artillery train, he asked for ten further pieces of heavy ordnance, six field pieces, four mortars and a company of Artillery. Even then the Cabinet had the problem of deciding whether the total requested would be sufficient for requirements by the time it was received. In all, five further additions were made to Loudoun's original request between 14 July and 8 August but the latter date, to say nothing of the date on which the storeships finally embarked, was already well after the Louisbourg expedition had been abandoned in North America. Among those additional requests were 680 barrels of gunpowder, 9 pieces of light brass ordnance, 20 mortars with powder and shells for 400 rounds, together with a further 132 barrels of powder and ammunition for two battalions. Also included were carpenters, wheelwrights, miners, and smiths.[40]

In the late summer of 1757 Pitt initiated plans to take Martinique from the French for later exchange for Minorca. A battering train of artillery was supplied which included 30 pieces of heavy brass ordnance, 6 pieces of light ordnance, 4 howitzers, and 38 brass mortars together with 3,324 barrels of gunpowder, plus 5 barrels for the preparation of ammunition. The expedition failed and it was decided instead to take Guadeloupe. Martinique was eventually taken in 1761.[41]

Distribution to North America, 1758–63

Further plans were made for the capture of Louisbourg in 1758 with Amherst leading the combined military forces and Boscawen the naval squadron. Plans included not only an artillery train for the actual campaign but an increase in ordnance supplies for the combined mili-

---

[39] John Knox, *An Historical Journal of the Campaigns of North America* (1769), pp. 2–14.
[40] WO 55/357, pp. 22, 25, 30, 37, 39, 43, 8, 14, 25 July, 3, 4, 8, August 1757.
[41] Ibid., pp. 53–57, 6 September 1757.

tary forces of New York and Pennsylvania. In January a battering train of artillery was prepared for Halifax. This comprised 14 pieces of heavy brass ordnance, 2 brass howitzers, 10 brass mortars, and 1,230 barrels of gunpowder, together with 648 barrels of powder for the heavy brass guns which were to be sent from New York. A company of Artillery was sent in attendance. For New York there were 6 pieces each of heavy and light ordnance, 4 howitzers and 24 various sized mortars, for which 878 barrels of powder were supplied. Also with this were 12,000 muskets with 200 rounds of powder and shot to each, which totalled 750 additional barrels of powder. For Pennsylvania there were 10 pieces of light ordnance, 12 mortars, and 2,000 muskets with an allowance of 200 rounds of powder; this totalled 125 barrels. There were also 75 barrels of powder for shells.[42] Louisbourg was taken from the French in July. News of this reached London on 18 August and plans then began to take Quebec in 1759.

Wolfe, under Amherst's overall command and supported by a naval squadron, was to advance up the St Lawrence and capture Quebec while another force was to approach via Ticonderoga and Crown Point. Preparations continued in North America during the spring of 1759. For these expeditions a consignment of ordnance stores was sent under the command of Rear Admiral Saunders. This included 7 pieces of light ordnance, 5,000 muskets, 3 howitzers, and 7 mortars of various sizes. For these, gunpowder was supplied in the quantities of 3,232 whole, and 1,536 half barrels.[43] Quebec was taken by Wolfe in October.

In 1760 the main aim was to take Montreal and for this the colonies were asked by Amherst for as much cooperation as possible. Reaction was mixed, with the northern colonies including Massachusetts, Connecticut, and New York providing most men and those to the south providing few. For the supply of the forces in New York, for what was to prove a successful campaign in September, a consignment was sent of 144 iron ordnance pieces of various sizes, 780 barrels of gunpowder for round shot and 195 barrels for case shot. Boston was sent a large consignment of ordnance stores which included 367 barrels of powder for the troops, and 1,500 barrels of powder, 50 pieces of iron ordnance and 10 of brass, plus 8 brass mortars for the defence of the garrison at Quebec.[44] The last recorded consignment for North America was in 1761, the warrant for which bore the later date of 29 October. The order was from Bute to Ligonier, now master general, for additional stores for the artillery train already in America consisting of 14 pieces of heavy brass ordnance, 2 howitzers and 2,000 barrels of

[42] Ibid., p. 110, 5 January 1758; WO 55/358, pp. 86–109, 27 November 1758.
[43] WO 55/360, pp. 56–70, 16 November 1759.
[44] WO 55/361, pp. 70–84, 31 October 1760.

gunpowder.[45] Ordnance Office records show that for the period 1755 to 1762, at least 21,936 barrels of gunpowder were dispatched to the combined British and colonial military forces in North America. There was no delivery in 1763. The majority of ordnance equipment and stores sent to America between 1755 and 1757 was for the use of the British Army alone. It was not until the recognition by Pitt of the need for offensive action and that the colonies would, or could not provide enough supplies of their own that ordnance stores were not only increased but a larger proportion supplied to the colonists themselves.

Distribution to Germany, 1758–63

In June 1758, the government decided to send military troops, accompanied by the master and surveyor generals of the Ordnance, to join the allied army in Germany under Prince Ferdinand of Brunswick. An artillery train was ordered immediately for their use. In the long list for this consignment were included 12 pieces of light brass ordnance, ammunition waggons and 108 barrels of powder for flannel cartridges; there is no reference to other powder. Among supplies for the troops themselves were 200 muskets with bayonets, ammunition for six Battalions of Foot, consisting of 900 men each, at 200 rounds a man; for this was supplied 338 barrels of powder. For seven Regiments of Dragoons at 100 rounds a man, 59 barrels of powder were supplied. There were also 4½ barrels for one Regiment of Horse Guards, and 1½ barrels for two detachments of Artillery.[46]

Shipping was arranged on 4 July between the Ordnance Office and a private contractor and gunpowder merchant Anthony Bacon. This provided for 400 tons of shipping for the stores at £0 11s 9d a ton per month and included five vessels, together with 950 tons of shipping for the horses and forage at £0 12s. The associated shipment of horses and hay for Germany was a major undertaking; two days later this necessitated the hire of 660 tons more of shipping, and even more just prior to embarkation.[47] Messrs Warrington and Grisewood provided 368 horses and Oswald, another gunpowder merchant, the forage. All ships eventually left the Thames for Emden on 28 July and by 17 August they had returned to London, their task completed. Another artillery train was prepared in February 1759 and included 22 pieces of brass ordnance, and 6 howitzers, plus 150 barrels of powder for filling flannel cartridges,

45 WO 55/362, pp. 50–2, 29 October 1761.
46 WO 55/358, pp. 250–62, 20 November 1758.
47 WO 47/52, pp. 18, 22, 4, 6 July 1758.

together with cartridges already filled, 3 barrels of powder for filling shells and 20 lb of mealed powder.[48]

Other warrants from the secretary of state for stores for Emden concerned those of March and November 1760, March and October 1761, and October 1762. These formal warrants usually arrived well after the demand for, and actual dispatch of stores. The first included 12 additional pieces of ordnance, filled cartridges, 147 barrels of powder for filling shells and musket cartridges, and 50 lb of mealed powder which would have been for priming purposes. The second, for a company of Artillery, included filled flannel cartridges, 45 barrels of powder for six Battalions of Foot and 24 barrels for Artillery officers.[49] That of 1761, dated 4 March, concerned additional ammunition and stores including 800 barrels of corned, and 80 lb of mealed powder. The warrant of October 1761 concerned ordnance but not powder while that of 2 October 1762 pertaining to the shipment of April of that year, and the last recorded consignment to Germany of this war, included 16 pieces of ordnance, 2 howitzers and 474 barrels of gunpowder.[50]

In total, 2,046 barrels of powder were sent to Germany between July 1758 and April 1762. Whether or not the British Army in Germany had access to supplies other than those from Britain is not clear. Although it is possible that some powder for the allied forces may have been of Continental origin, there is no evidence of this in the records of the Ordnance Office. Initial action by Britain against the French in North America in 1755 was defensive, rather than offensive. As soon as this changed, when the quest for superiority between the two nations became the issue, ordnance stores were required in quantity. There was a sharp contrast between the well established routine of supply over a comparatively short route to Germany for combat in familiar terrain, and supply over the much longer route to North America for combat in more difficult and unfamiliar circumstances. Estimating needs for Germany was comparatively straightforward. In dealing with North America however, there were difficulties: uncertainty within the Cabinet about the quantity of stores to be dispatched resulted from problems of combat in unfamiliar terrain and of disagreement both within the British government, and between it and colonial governors about who should, or should not provide men and supplies. As there is no evidence of gunpowder manufacture in any of the North American colonies at this time the majority, if not all stock probably came from Britain. There is no indication that the Ordnance Office was unable to supply all that was required of it for the Army in the

---

48 WO 55/360, pp. 19–30, 16 November 1759.
49 Ibid., pp. 164–81, 18 March 1760; WO 55/361, pp. 114–21, 7 November 1760.
50 Ibid., pp. 209–19, 4 March 1761; WO 55/363, pp. 87–105, 2 October 1762.

field, although there were certainly long delays in dispatch as the result of the many requests added to a commander's original order. The fact that dispatch was frequently haphazard and inefficient was therefore not the fault of the Office alone; in many instances the problems lay entirely outside its control. Although under the influence of Pitt the political problems between Britain and North America were largely resolved, certain difficulties remained throughout, particularly those involved with communication and transportation across the Atlantic, and with storage and transportation between military headquarters and the scene of battle.

PART THREE
LEGISLATION AND TRADE

7

Private Export and Shipping

During 1755 the Ordnance Office experienced a severe shortage of gunpowder. A sudden marked increase in demand by the armed forces and their own attempts to supply the government and export trade simultaneously meant that powder makers were unable to meet the quantity agreed at contract. The demands of private trade were not of course the sole cause of poor supply but they were certainly the most significant.[1] The Ordnance Board therefore sought to safeguard its own supply of gunpowder and, as a direct result, the government introduced legislation in October 1755 to prohibit both the export of saltpetre and the coastwise movement of saltpetre, gunpowder, arms and ammunition. Export of the latter three specifically was to be prohibited by the application of an Act of 1660. This legislation had not been considered necessary at any time previously and was not employed again until 1793.[2]

The Office did not want from the mills the gunpowder intended for private trade for this was not considered to be of sufficiently high grade for the armed services. There was little difficulty in supplying merchants with powder of sufficient explosive capacity for trade. In contrast, the government required for its armed forces powder not only of good quality but consistently so. Ordnance, particularly in war, required powder with more than an explosive capability; it was essential that once large military and naval guns were positioned on a target the shot should not only be imparted with force and to the required distance but should also function consistently at each firing. This required powder of a higher quality and firing strength maintained over a longer period than that needed by most merchants. Office and trade were

---

[1] For other factors, see ch. 10.
[2] 12 Car. II c. 4, 1660, *Statutes at Large* (new edn) iii, 147–9; Ibid., 32 Geo. 3, c. 2, 1793, xvi, 289.

competing, therefore, not for the actual gunpowder but for the powder makers' time and the use of commercial plant. Although merchants did purchase powder from mills near the cities of Liverpool and Bristol too, and these were also subject to the legislation, the Office was obviously concerned primarily with mills under contract. By strict limitation of trade outlets it aimed to minimise the time they spent on work for private trade and hence maximise that spent on supply to the government. Gunpowder, together with muskets, pistols, swords, bayonets, and ammunition was in great demand for overseas trade. In Britain it was required in mines and quarries while saltpetre, its main constituent, was required for curing provisions and in North America for medicinal purposes. It was required for trade with North America, particularly towards the north, for colonial defence against the French and Indians, in connection with the fur trade, for hunting, and as gifts for Indians in forming alliances against the French. In addition gunpowder was one of the most important elements in the cargoes of slave trading vessels to Africa, and was shipped to the West Indies for defence and privateering.[3] Powder and small arms commonly formed part of a mixed cargo which could include lead bars, saltpetre, cotton, linen, woollen textiles, beads, spirits and metalware. Continually involved with the domestic and overseas gunpowder trade were the main ports of London, Bristol, and Liverpool, those of Whitehaven and Lancaster, and a number of lesser centres such as Poole.

Legislation

The gravity of the situation was soon obvious with regard to government supply. In view of the severe shortage of stock during 1755 Ligonier, then lieutenant general of the Ordnance, conveyed his concern to Holderness on 15 October on behalf of the Board. In spite of repeated orders to the powder makers to work with speed they had been so 'dilatory' that he was apprehensive about receiving enough to run the service. The Board suspected that the mills were producing for export and as this could prove detrimental to official supply he considered that all export should be prohibited.[4]

As a result, Murray, the attorney general, found provision for this purpose in the Act of 1660 which allowed the King to prohibit at any time the exportation of gunpowder, arms or ammunition.[5] Murray reported to Holderness on 17 October that in his opinion the King could

---

3 See appendix 3, tables 12–17.
4 SP 41/38, 15 October 1755; WO 47/46, p. 326, 15 October 1755.
5 WO 55/355, p. 209, 17 October 1755.

employ this prohibition for whatever period he considered necessary. As a result the King announced at a Privy Council meeting of 20 October that for a period of three months no one except the Ordnance Board could export gunpowder, or ship that intended for export, without a licence.[6] Although licences were also required immediately for overseas shipment of saltpetre, arms, and ammunition the discussion here will be confined to gunpowder for although most shipments included the latter two concern about these was very much less. When licence for gunpowder was rejected that for arms was usually permitted. The Office was not concerned with the comparatively few shipments of saltpetre. A public announcement was made about the new legislation on 21 October, and in December it was decided that the prohibition should continue for a further six months. The Act to formalise the undertaking was passed in April 1756:

> An Act to impower His Majesty to prohibit the exportation of saltpetre; and to enforce the law for impowering His Majesty to prohibit the exportation of gunpowder or any sort of arms and ammunition; and also to impower His Majesty to restrain the carrying coastwise of saltpetre, gunpowder, or any sort of arms or ammunition.[7]

By brief consultation between Privy Council and Ordnance Board the prohibition was renewed every six months throughout the war. In theory this should have successfully curtailed the trade. In practice both the national and overseas trade in gunpowder were too important to Britain to be limited and the majority of licence applications were allowed. Despite the order in Council of October 1755 such licences were issued as early as November.

Application procedure

Applications for licence were made by one or several part owners of a ship, by merchants on behalf of owners, by merchants themselves who might be part owners either of that ship or of others in this trade, by agents on their behalf or, alternatively, by the gunpowder makers themselves. Entries in the Privy Council registers detail the quantity of powder, its destination, purpose for which required, identity of merchants and ships, and of those powder makers applying for licence in

---

6   Ibid., p. 210, 20 October 1755.
7   29 Geo. 2 c. 16, 1756, *Statutes at Large* (new edn) vii, 668; PC 2/104, pp. 520, 552, 556, 20 October, 15, 18 December 1755; PC 2/105, p. 169, 29 April 1756.

their own names. The method of assessment of applications developed largely from a statement of 30 October by the Ordnance Board to the Treasury claiming that the aim of the legislation would be defeated if licences were granted without prior consultation with the Board itself. The Treasury agreed.[8] The Board obviously intended a much closer adherence to the Act than actually occurred or, for that matter, was possible. Requests from individuals or those solely for a ship's defence went direct to the Board. The Board's decision was recorded at the foot of the application before this was forwarded to the Treasury, and a certificate of 'no objection' was sent to the applicant. On receipt of both the original application signed by the Board and the Board's certificate sent by the applicant to confirm the wish to proceed, the Treasury submitted detail to the Privy Council for formal inclusion in its registers before issuing the licence. There is no evidence that the Ordnance Board's opinion on applications from individuals was ever disputed. Applications for shipment to North America were sent to the Board of Trade before the Treasury was notified that the licence could be issued.[9]

Licences to the gunpowder makers

Immediately following the introduction of the legislation the Ordnance Board faced an extraordinary situation. The aim was to restrict the export markets of its contracted powder makers but, though acting as main adviser on the subject to the Privy Council, in most cases it had no idea which applications included powder from those men, or which shipments were shared by them. From its continued concern about the time spent at the mills in supplying merchants it is obvious that considerably more powder was prepared for private trade than officially recorded. Most, if not all of the powder exported from London, some of that exported from Liverpool and Bristol, and much of that sold to British mines originated from the contracted powder makers. There are indeed many examples of this and usually the makers made no attempt at secrecy. However, it was only after some years of war and in connection with an application for a general licence from London merchants for Africa, that the Board decided to try to identify officially those mills involved. From successful applications it can be seen for example that Eade, Bridges and Wilton of Ewell shipped powder more frequently than any other, while Pyke & Edsall of Dartford, and Pryce of Chilworth did not request licences at all. The

8   T 29/32, p. 354, 5 November 1755.
9   CO 391/63, p. 34, 27 January 1756.

quantity supplied to other merchants in whose name the licence application was made would have been even greater. Gunpowder was also sold by certain of the mills to the East India Company. Included were those of Waltham Abbey and of Hounslow; in one consignment alone 500 barrels were sold to the Company.[10] No licences were recorded for the powder makers during 1762; this may have been the result of a greater effort to meet government demands, as indicated by the Waltons at Waltham Abbey. However, licences continued to be sought in the names of those responsible for purchase and export. Even the Waltons, though now intending to concentrate on government supply, still had 550 barrels of merchants' powder awaiting licence for shipment.

Licences to merchants

Among the first applications, in November 1755, was one from John Sharpe, agent for Jamaica, Barbados, and the Leeward Islands on behalf of the merchants of London who required gunpowder for ships' defence and port duty.[11] Sharpe pleaded that lack of powder would result in a total embargo on British trade to the West Indies and make inhabitants and trading ships defenceless.[12] The Ordnance Board agreed to the request immediately, and the order in Council for issue of licence was made just two weeks later. An equally pressing request was made by the merchants of Liverpool to carry powder for trade and defence to Africa for the slave trade. The Board informed the Privy Council that it was advisable to agree.[13] At the same time merchants and owners of thirteen ships bound for various destinations from the Port of London were successful with a similar request. Most of these ships were included subsequently in Sharpe's general licence for shipment to the West Indies. Individual licences were issued for purposes of defence in the following January to two others with cargoes of woollen goods for Leghorn.[14] It is significant that apart from one rejection in January an application from two London merchants to ship twenty barrels of powder to Guernsey for a privateer, resulting only from what the Board

---

[10] See appendix 3, table 17; WO 47/51, p. 179, 21 February 1758.
[11] This was one pound per ton for duty on entering port and half a pound per ton for defence. For port duty, see ch. 6.
[12] WO 47/46, pp. 473, 508, 25 November, 8 December 1755; WO 55/355, p. 240, 19 November 1755.
[13] WO 47/46, pp. 454, 546, 21 November, 19 December 1755; WO 55/355, pp. 255, 257, 19 November, 19 December 1755.
[14] PC 2/105, pp. 3, 23, 16, 29 January 1756; T 1/360.73 November 1755.

considered to be lack of storage facilities, there were no others until August 1756.

In the meantime, between January and August 1756, a combined total of almost 4,000 barrels of powder was permitted for export and defence of ships to North America, Africa, the West Indies, British mines, and for the defence of ships overseas, including privateers and trading vessels. As a large proportion of this would have been from the contracted mills the intended aims of the legislation were hardly being fulfilled.[15] Few applications were rejected throughout the war. The total quantities for which licences were issued to individuals during this war concerned only the minimum quantities exported but overall totals would have been much higher due to the 'general' licences issued in connection with Africa and North America.

General licences

Applications for 'general' export licences from certain groups of merchants were sent direct to the Privy Council. With the practice of granting general licences, issued in addition to those for individual consignments, it is impossible to calculate the total quantity of gunpowder exported during the war. These were issued to groups of merchants permitted to continue trade considered to be of national importance, without the need for application on every occasion. Notification to the Ordnance Office of the names of ships and of the total quantities involved was only required at certain intervals. In spite of the aims of the legislation such licences were permitted on several occasions with the result that the government never knew exactly how much powder was being exported at any one time. Undoubtedly, one of the main elements was the significance to the nation of the slave trade and it was early agreement for general licence with the merchants of both Liverpool and Bristol that aimed the first blow at the legislation. There is no indication that the quantities involved in such cases were ever recorded or even submitted.

The Liverpool merchants told the Privy Council in May 1756 that it was impossible to undertake trade to Africa without gunpowder and arms. As these formed a principal part of each cargo they requested that the Liverpool Customs officers be given power to inspect and permit movement of shipments without licence. The master general and Board considered initially that this would render the Act useless for other cities would follow suit. Although the application was formally refused by the Privy Council on 7 July a further request was made

---

[15] See appendix 3, tables 12–17

in August.[16] On 5 October the Privy Council reported to the Board that it had considered both the petition and the report by the master general and his Board, and as the trade to Africa was of such importance to Britain and her North American colonies the merchants of Liverpool would be permitted to export such quantities of gunpowder, arms, and ammunition as necessary for trade and the defence of ships.[17] So important was the slave trade that not only was the earlier rejection of licence reversed but agreement for general licence also given to the Society of Merchant Adventurers of Bristol. The Board considered that as trade to Africa, 'about which they never pretended to be judges', was obviously of significance, and as powder from the Bristol mills had never been purchased by the government, there was no reason to refuse its export.[18]

From the above statement by the Board, acknowledging that it was not equipped to judge the national significance of trade to Africa, it can be seen that its responsibility concerning decisions on export licences was largely beyond its normal duties and possibly even its capabilities. The fact that both applications were received at about the same time and both referred together to the Privy Council suggests, moreover, cooperation between the two cities to strengthen their case. There appears to have been little alternative but to agree in view of the significance of the trade, of certain influential personalities involved, and of the fact that at Bristol anyway much, if not all, powder was produced locally and, as already stated, was not required by the government. Clearly, if the Board had developed a method for distinguishing between powder from contracted and non contracted mills it might have been possible to apply the Act more selectively and therefore more effectively.

An indication of the scale of the trade between Liverpool and Africa is provided by the licences issued for shipments to Liverpool merchants for this purpose by Baugh, Ames & Co. from the mills near Bristol. Between June 1756 and December 1762 this involved a total of 5,200 barrels, significantly more than that indicated by individual export licences alone. The agreement with the Liverpool and Bristol merchants was followed in November 1756 by a petition from the merchants of Lancaster for general licences for shipping arms and gunpowder not only from Lancaster to Africa but also to Lancaster from Liverpool. The first was granted but the latter only with respect to arms due to the Board's concern that approval for gunpowder would

---

16 PC 2/105, pp. 191, 250, 20 May, 7 July 1756.
17 WO 47/48, p. 319, 8 October 1756; PC 2/105, p. 309, 5 October 1756.
18 PC 2/105, pp. 294, 307, 309, 1 September, 5 October 1756.

encourage supplies from other cities also.[19] Refusal of a general licence
in February 1761 for the Whitehaven merchants to ship powder and
arms from Liverpool to Whitehaven and from there to Africa, was due
to the severe powder shortage at this time. The request was only agreed
in September 1762, when government demand was decreasing, at the
same time as a general licence was granted concerning shipping from
London to Liverpool.[20] There was no application from the London
merchants for a general licence to Africa until April 1762.[21] Nevertheless, it is interesting in this connection that the Ordnance Board made
certain stipulations. When the merchants stressed that the legislation
had resulted in ships lying in the Thames with valuable assorted cargoes, manned at great expense yet unable to proceed for want of powder, the Board reported to the master general:

> The total prohibition of powder being exported may be very incon-
> venient to the Africa trade but it was thought essential towards
> obliging the powder makers to work for His Majesty that the powder
> makers have a stock by them of such sort of powder as is not fit for
> the King's service, that if leave should be granted the petitioners to
> export powder without limiting the quantity it may encourage the
> makers to neglect His Majesty's Service.[22]

The Board now suggested to the master general that it needed to
monitor the situation at the mills in terms of quantities in each of the
powder ready for trade. It considered that as long as the makers had a
certain quantity of powder ready at their mills for the Africa trade they
would have no immediate compulsion to prepare more for the purpose.
On the other hand, if licences were allowed for export of unlimited
quantities to Africa they would prepare more, and thus further neglect
the needs of the Office. It suggested that the London petitioners for
general licence be obliged to apply from time to time, stating not only
the quantity for export, name of ship and port but also the powder
makers from whom they proposed purchase, and the exact quantities
from each. It clearly realised, albeit for the first time, that to combine
information on quantities of trade powder at each mill with that currently purchased from those mills by merchants would provide detail
on quantity remaining; in turn, this would indicate the likelihood of
makers spending valuable time preparing trade powder when they
should have been honouring government contracts. The idea was to

[19] WO 47/48, pp. 508, 521, 23 November, 3 December 1756.
[20] WO 47/57, p. 182, 19 March 1761; PC 2/109, pp. 379, 405, 6 October, 10
November 1762.
[21] Possible reasons will be discussed in ch. 8.
[22] WO 47/59, p. 349, 23 April 1762.

refuse licence to merchants if the makers who were to supply them had only a small quantity of trade stock remaining. In this way neither the Africa trade nor the Office's own supplies would be threatened.[23] Although less free than for the Liverpool and Bristol merchants this method was, in reality, vague and unspecific in that no definite stipulation was made and the merchants were required only to report 'from time to time'. What is significant is that this was one of only two attempts to discover the quantity of powder prepared at the mills for trade. The first had been in December 1761 when it was compelled by shortage to consider using such stock. Little use was made of such knowledge for the only occasion on which it was put into practice concerned merchant Samuel Touchet's application in April, to export to Africa eighty barrels of powder from the Ewell mills. As this was the only trade powder then in stock at this location the application was at first refused; yet, to the traders' advantage the problem was easily solved when the Ewell partnership purchased the required quantity from an alternative source, Touchet made a further application, and the licence was issued.[24]

The decision on London merchants trading to Africa and the Office's diminishing powder requirements led to permission for a general licence for merchants trading to South Carolina and Georgia in September 1762. This was for requirements of inhabitants for defence, trade, and privateering and permitted under the same restrictions as those for Africa. Similar arrangements were made in November with the London merchants trading in furs in New England, New York, and Philadelphia and, a few weeks later, with those trading in Virginia and Maryland.[25]

Rejected Licences

It is clear, therefore, that despite the aim of the legislation surprisingly few applications for licence were rejected. There was no obvious consistency of method in selecting which licence should or should not be granted. Requests refused by the Ordnance Office during August 1756 were from the Bristol powder makers Baugh and Ames for 40 barrels of gunpowder each for Philadelphia and Jamaica, from Kilby for 72 barrels for New England, Manesty for 120 for Africa, and Knox for 30 for Virginia. Manesty was allowed to export the arms, a ruling which

[23] WO 55/362, pp. 191, 208, 8, 29 April 1762.
[24] WO 47/59, pp. 361, 369, 27, 30 April 1762.
[25] WO 55/363, pp. 1, 2, 10, 1, 30 September 1762; PC 2/109, pp. 399, 422, 3, 26 November 1762.

applied to a number of later rejections. Although these were followed by nine other, though unspecified, rejections in September and three in October for 36 barrels for Newcastle mines, 97 for Virginia, and 80 for Africa respectively, there were no others until June 1758.[26] It is surprising when considering the rejections of October 1756 that while Martin Smith's application for sixty barrels to Newcastle mines was rejected, shipments of powder were permitted to the same mines by Langstaff and Arnold just one and two weeks later.[27] In 1758 Sittwell applied unsuccessfully on behalf of the Bristol powder makers for a general licence to ship powder to mines of Wales and Cornwall and in 1759 Lewis and Jefson were equally unsuccessful in their request to ship 1,500 stand of arms and 12 barrels of powder for a storehouse in Sardinia. This was refused when the Board considered the request 'entirely new' and its own members not judges of the consequences of a magazine of arms being established in the Mediterranean.[28] There were no other rejections until November 1761, in spite of the severe shortage of government stock during 1760 when the Office took unprecedented measures to try and increase supply.[29] Not until October 1761 when the problem of stock increased further did it ask the master general to introduce a temporary restriction on all licence issue.

Anthony Bacon was refused permission to ship sixty barrels of powder for a private ship of war in November in case it might encourage others, but was permitted to ship eighty barrels and other military stores in connection with his government contract to Senegal and Goree for purchasing provisions for the garrison. The Company of Merchants trading to Africa, though allowed to export arms, was refused shipment of powder until there was more stock in the government magazines yet, in spite of continued shortage, it was permitted to ship 200 barrels to its African trading forts only six weeks later.[30] Apart from a licence for W. & J. Ewer to export powder to the Gold Coast in February no further licences were issued until April. In February and April 1762 Oswald & Co. and Hyndman & Lancaster were refused shipment when the master general decided that not even inferior quality powder should be exported.[31] However, apart from one further rejection in June, undoubtedly due to the large quantity involved (500 barrels), the issue of licences recommenced in April and there were no further refusals.

The resumption of licence issue for private shipments of gunpowder

26 WO 47/48, pp. 163, 177, 21, 24 August 1756.
27 PC 2/105, pp. 312, 323, 12, 19 October 1756.
28 WO 47/51, p. 650, 21 June 1758; WO 47/53, p. 74, 16 January 1759.
29 See ch. 4.
30 PC 2/108, p. 600, 27 November 1761; PC 2/109, p. 18, 7 January 1762.
31 WO 47/59, p. 142, 16 February 1762; PC 2/109, p. 41, 11 February 1762.

was due to the national importance of trade rather than any significant improvement in the state of government stock. Although during 1762 as a whole the powder makers delivered a higher combined total to Greenwich than in any previous year of the war, their supply during the first half of the year was particularly poor. Also, in spite of the fact that there were no further recorded shipments of gunpowder to the Army in North America after 1761, the Ordnance Board continued to be concerned about its stock until the summer of 1762. Requirements of the British Army in Germany only ceased after April of that year while the Navy not only continued to require powder until conflict ceased in the autumn but, as late as July of that year, was so short of powder at Portsmouth and Plymouth that the Admiralty had to make a formal complaint to the Ordnance Office.

The international situation and need for ordnance stores changed completely in the autumn as the result of impending peace. Although it was decided that the legislation should be applied for a further six months from 29 October, the master general announced in January that this should cease with the signing of the definitive peace treaty. The prohibition ended on 16 March.[32]

It is clear that the legislation to prohibit or severely restrict the private trade in gunpowder proved to be largely, if not entirely, ineffective. From the beginning a number of factors combined to dissuade the Privy Council or the Ordnance Board from using the full powers of the Act in a way which would have enabled government stocks to benefit. As a result the powder makers continued to supply for export throughout the war and the Ordnance Office continued to be troubled by shortage of stock in its magazines. The reasons for this were several. Means were required to boost government powder stocks, yet the bodies concerned realised the importance of the arms and powder trade in Britain and overseas. The Ordnance Board in particular was pulled in two directions: its responsibility for supplying the armed services, and its realisation of the importance of trade to the nation. Instead of fighting for supply, for which it had requested the legislation in the first place, it came gradually and inevitably to realise that it was quite impossible to prohibit trade entirely, or even partly. Thus, the only time when the issue of licences markedly decreased was in the period between November 1761 and April 1762, when government stocks were in a state of crisis.

32 WO 47/61, pp. 36, 157, 19 January, 18 March 1763; WO 55/363, p. 79, 16 March 1763.

Government versus Private Trade

There were several ways in which the Ordnance Board could attempt to encourage or compel its gunpowder makers to work more effectively: financial incentives; stipulation at contract that no powder be prepared for trade; and legislation to prohibit, or strictly limit such trade and therefore trade outlets.

Financial incentives clearly had little effect. With regard to contract, there was no stipulation that powder makers work only for the government as this would have presented difficulties for the Board. Firstly, in a volatile war situation it was impossible for the Board to judge whether it would actually need all powder produced and given its uncertain storage life surplus could not be kept indefinitely. Secondly, the Office had no use for the large quantity of powder which failed proof and it was this which formed a significant proportion of the supply for trade. Moreover, it required cooperation from its makers not acquiescence under duress: neither of the other possible suppliers was considered suitable so it was entirely dependent for British stock on those already contracted.[1] Thus the only practicable means of compelling its makers to supply more powder was by limiting trade outlets, thereby forcing more attention on work for the government. This intention resulted in the legislation of 1756 but, as has been shown, this was not implemented in the way it might have been and so proved to be virtually useless.[2]

Before looking further at the significance of private trade, consideration should be given to other aspects of the legislation's failure: whether the Act could have been intended primarily as a deterrent to the makers in their alternative trading activities; whether it was intended solely as a source of information; or whether it failed due to corruption among Ordnance staff. If intended as a deterrent the legislation certainly did not have that effect for once merchants knew that few were refused there was no problem regarding application. Neither was its purpose to provide information on the degree of involvement by its powder makers, for not until April 1762 did the Board take the opportunity to identify those supplying powder for merchants applying

---

1 See ch. 1.
2 29 Geo. II c. 16, 1756, *Statutes at Large* (new edn) vii, 668.

for licence. Although there was some corruption among certain clerks in the Ordnance department in October 1759 concerning initial examination of licence applications, those concerned were reprimanded and the occurrence is unlikely to have been of marked significance in the situation as a whole.[3]

It is obvious, therefore, that the Ordnance Board and Privy Council were in a difficult situation; the gunpowder and arms trade was so important to the nation that in terms of opportunity for use of time at the mills its needs at this time were considered largely at the expense of an adequate supply for the armed forces. Reasons for this importance and continuation of private trade require closer examination. This trade was important not only to the government and the nation as a whole but also to financial and commercial bodies in the City of London, and to certain prominent individuals. John stated that 'the gains of wartime trade were a substantial element in the financing of war expenditure'. Further, he commented on the words of Holderness: 'that we must be merchants while we are soldiers . . . and that the riches which are the true resources of this country depend upon its commerce'.[4] The obvious reluctance of the government to refuse licences for shipment suggests that John's comments could not be more true than when applied to the Seven Years War.

Africa, and the West Indies

Trade with Africa was important to the British government, to the cities of London, Bristol, and Liverpool, and to the smaller ports of Whitehaven and Lancaster. There were also close links between the gunpowder trade, government, commerce, and politics, involving many people over the wide geographical area of Britain, Africa, the West Indies and, to a lesser extent, North America.[5] Rawley shows how the wealth of the New World, including sugar, tobacco, precious metals, coffee, and cotton, was extracted by slave labour from Africa 'through the capitalistic enterprise of western Europe'. Further, this commerce was fundamental to the making of the modern world. The traffic in slaves was important not only in itself, but in the linked export from Europe of textiles, metal wares, spirits, beads, and guns; these were bartered for slaves for America and for such articles as gold

---

[3] WO 47/54, p. 356, 23 October, 1759.
[4] A. H. John, 'War and the English Economy, 1700–1763', *Economic History Review*, 2nd series 7 (1955), 339.
[5] For detailed studies of the subject see K. G. Davies, *The Royal African Company* (1957); James A. Rawley, *The Transatlantic Slave Trade* (New York 1981).

and ivory for Europe.[6] The trade in guns is well recognised but the significance of gunpowder in this connection less so; yet gunpowder formed a regular and important part of licence applications for mixed shipments to Africa.

The government had been responsible for preserving Britain's trading interests in Africa since 1730; it had granted a subsidy of £10,000 at that date to aid the Royal African Company's maintenance of its trading forts on the west coast, after which it awarded a grant annually until 1746. Further government support was given in 1750 for expansion of the trade when the Company of Merchants was formed as a regulated company open to all traders to Africa which, by 1752, had replaced the Royal African Company. The government then awarded increased annual grants with additional sums in 1753 and 1755 for building a fort at Annamaboe.[7] The strength of the link not only between that Company and the government but also with the Ordnance Office is shown by the fact that the Office supervised the construction of this fort and organised stores for its defence.[8] It would have been surprising if it had purposely refused licence for so important a part of the Company's trade.

The East India Company, one of the main subscribers to loans to the government, needed powder not only for its own ships but for the Africa trade in which it held a direct interest. Such goods as textiles, cowries, beads and corals were imported by the Company for re-export to Africa, mainly from Bristol, alongside British powder and guns. It could not afford to have shipments delayed for want of licence and, not surprisingly in view of its close government connections, this seldom occurred. The rejection of licences for Africa were few, as is shown by the grant of general licences to the merchants of Liverpool and Bristol, and later to those of Whitehaven and London. This was due not only to possible shipping links with the East India Company but also to political influence within these cities. A large number of slave traders served as mayors of Liverpool and the city's corporation constantly advanced its slave interests through politics, its representatives in Parliament being advocates of the trade.[9] This is demonstrated in the licence application of November 1755 from the Liverpool merchants concerning the trade of eleven ships, most destined for Africa and America. Among the twenty-nine merchants who signed the petition were members of the Cunliffe family, Robert, Foster, and Ellis: Ellis was

6 Ibid., pp. 4–5.
7 23 Geo. II c. 31, 1750, *Statutes at Large* (new edn) vii, 268.
8 WO 47/46, p. 119, 1 August 1755; SP 41/38, 28 February 1759.
9 Rawley, *Slave Trade*, p. 201.

currently the city's mayor, Foster Cunliffe had held that office previously:

> We represent to Your Majesty that gunpowder is an essential com-
> modity and merchandize without which we cannot possibly carry on
> the slave trade at any part of the coast of Africa and that the
> gunpowder exported for this trade is of a coarse inferior kind than
> what is used by Your Majesty's Army or Navy . . . without such
> licence the trade to Africa must be entirely stopped which will
> greatly distress the said trade and your petitioners who have many
> ships now solely detained by the said prohibition from proceeding
> on their voyages to Africa.[10]

The licence was granted, immediately weakening the aim of the legislation. The link between Liverpool politics and the Africa, and therefore gunpowder trade was supported further by the representation of
that city in Parliament by Africa merchants. John Hardman was a
member of Parliament in 1754–5, and Ellis Cunliffe in 1755 and 1761,
at the latter date with a baronetcy. Robert and Sir Ellis Cunliffe,
together with Hardman, were among the city's representatives on the
1759 official List of the Company of Merchants trading to Africa.[11]
Until 1759, when Liverpool merchants opened their own powder mills
in Thelwall, Cheshire, most of the city's powder for export was supplied
by Woolley mills near Bath.[12] The recorded shipments to Liverpool by
the Ewell makers are unlikely to respresent all powder that was sent
from the South East, and the fact that at least three partnerships, those
of Bedfont, Faversham, and Molesey mills, also rented powder magazines from the Liverpool Corporation does show definite involvement
in the Africa trade by the mills supplying the government.

The general licence awarded to the Society of Merchant Venturers
of Bristol at the same time as that awarded to Liverpool was the
outcome of a similar combination of factors. This organisation controlled the city's foreign trade and was a vehicle for securing political goals
that was largely effective until abolition of the slave trade:[13] 'In the
course of the eighteenth century mayors of Bristol, sheriffs, aldermen,
town councillors, members of Parliament, the Society of Merchant
Venturers and, indeed, men of the highest repute in the place were
engaged in this traffic.'[14] Bristol's political strength, its links with the

10 WO 55/355, pp. 255, 257, 19 November, 19 December 1755.
11 Return of Members of Parliament, 1705–1796 (1878) ii; IHR Folio BB 246, List
of the Company of Merchants trading to Africa (1759), pp. 113, 127.
12 PC 2/105–9, 1756–63.
13 Rawley, Slave Trade, p. 191.
14 C. M. MacInnes, Bristol and the Slave Trade (Bristol 1963), p. 9.

East India Company, and the representation of its powder makers, Baugh & Ames, among a large number of fellow citizens in the Company of Merchants trading to Africa must all have contributed to the general licence issued to the Society in October 1756.[15] Although Liverpool and Bristol received general licences just one year after the introduction of the Act, the majority of licences issued for shipments to Africa between October 1756 and April 1762 were the result of applications from individuals; only then did they apply as a group for a general licence. This delay may seem surprising in view of the early licences of the other two cities, but probably reflects the changing role of the capital in the slave trade. Although London merchants continued trading to Africa, and the Company of Merchants trading to Africa continued to export powder for its trading forts of Cape Coast Castle and James Fort, dominance in the trade had shifted from London to Bristol, and then to Liverpool by the 1740s. The importance of London's role in this trade did not decline but it had changed.

As far as London was concerned, increased direct trading with the West Indies had replaced the traditional triangular trade and simultaneously London had increased its role as financial and commercial centre for the trade of Bristol and Liverpool. London agents became increasingly involved in the financial arrangements concerning the contract sale of African slaves shipped by the outport merchants to the West Indies, the method now replacing sale by commission. Furthermore, as Rawley shows, London's primacy in the money market gave it another part to play in the slave trade. Londoners' insistence that indebted planters consign to them their sugar crops was an important factor in London becoming Britain's leading sugar market, thus giving it a special role in the slave trade from the mid-eighteenth century.[16] As a result, less sugar was sold in the West Indies to the outport merchants and their ships often returned in ballast which greatly altered the traditional pattern of trade. Instead of bartering slaves for sugar, merchants took bills of exchange which were drawn on London agents, thus saving time in the West Indies and becoming increasingly dependent on London in its financial role. 'It channelled London capital into the slave trade, which attained its largest proportions under London's financial auspices.'[17]

It can be seen therefore that the continuation of gunpowder exportation to both Africa and the West Indies was vital to all concerned and that, undoubtedly, success was closely linked with the connections

[15] PC 2/105, p. 307, 5 October 1756.
[16] Rawley, *Slave Trade*, pp. 221–2.
[17] Ibid., p. 222.

between trade, prominent organisations, and certain men involved with both government and politics.

North America

North America, together with the West Indies, was of importance to Britain in the conduct of very diverse trade: 'vast trades in sugar, rice, indigo, tobacco, cotton were the source of many of the fortunes, great and small, of the eighteenth century and of huge contributions to the revenues of the state'.[18] Invariably, guns and gunpowder formed a significant part of mixed cargoes from Britain. It would have been obvious to the government that when spending vast sums on the Army and Navy in the quest for supremacy in North America it was necessary to support the munitions trade on which the colonists depended. It also supported the Hudson's Bay Company which took four ships from Britain each spring carrying powder and guns for trade and defence. With few exceptions, powder export to North America, as to the West Indies, was from London. Trade with the colonies of Georgia, the Carolinas, Virginia and Maryland was mainly in cotton, rice, and tobacco respectively; trade with those from Pennsylvania northwards was mainly in timber, pitch, tar, and furs. As already shown, gunpowder was particularly important for colonists' personal protection against French and Indians, in seeking the friendship of Indians, and in connection with the fur trade, other bartering, and hunting. Evidence concerning the trade in furs is provided by the Merchants of Poole trading to Newfoundland in February 1756:

> small amounts of gunpowder are necessary for the defence and preservation of hundreds of Your Majesty's subjects there all winter to protect them from Indians . . . and for procuring them subsistence and particularly for those in that season going to the woods after furs, frequently attacked by Indians and wild beasts, from whom they cannot possibly defend themselves, get any provisions or kill those creatures whose skin they seek without gunpowder and without which the valuable branch of the fur trade from Newfoundland must inevitably cease . . . the trade is very beneficial to this kingdom in general by breeding up great numbers of seamen and consuming large quantities of our own manufactures.[19]

18 Ralph Davis, *The Rise of the English Shipping Industry* (1962), p. 393
19 WO 55/355, p. 313, 25 February 1756.

British mines and quarries

During the eighteenth century gunpowder was required in large quantities for Britain's coal, copper, tin, and lead mines and for stone and slate quarries; this meant that the Act of 1756 had little success in limiting the coastwise shipment of gunpowder at a time when there was marked national emphasis on all these extractive industries. Gunpowder was first introduced for blasting purposes from Germany in 1670 for the copper mines at Ecton in Staffordshire. From there its use spread to Somerset in 1684 and then to St Agnes in Cornwall in the early eighteenth century, by which time it was being employed in coal mining. Eighteenth century wars gave an impetus to many of the mining industries and hence to war induced investment. Government demands on the heavy metal industries and the allied manufacture of munitions had an effect on a wide range of other capital-goods industries, including coal mining. With coal being used for smelting in various metalliferous industries during the century coal production increased, as did the exploitation and enlargement of any available mines.[20] Demand for coal further arose from the increased use of the steam pumping engine for mine drainage. This applied in particular to Cornwall where there had been an upsurge in tin mining in the 1740s and, since 1748, a great wave of expansion in copper mining which was to last for nearly half a century. The number of mines producing copper more than trebled between 1740 and 1775, during which time the output exceeded that of tin, and the average annual production expanded from 11,000 to over 29,000 tons. London's interest in tin also increased because of the use of pewter and tin ware for export purposes in the African slave, and North American fur trades.[21] Increased availability of copper and tin led in turn to an expansion in the copper and brass industries and the development, from 1750, of the 'new' trades, including the manufacture of guns in Birmingham. Lead too, which was required for the expanding building industry, had growing home and overseas markets. Burt shows that the total outward trade in lead and lead products from the major primary distribution ports nearly doubled between 1725 and 1769. Bar lead was an important export to North America and Africa for preparing lead shot in the Seven Years War.[22]

An example of the need for gunpowder was a successful application

[20] George Randall Lewis, *The Stannaries; A study of the English tin mines* (Harvard 1924), p. 23; John, 'War and the English Economy', 330–4, 343.
[21] W. J. Rowe, *Cornwall in the Age of the Industrial Revolution* (Liverpool 1953), pp. 56, 58.
[22] Roger Burt, 'Lead production in England and Wales, 1700–1770', *Economic History Review*, 2nd series 22 (1969), 257; WO 47/47, p. 509, 13 May 1756.

for licence from Richard Stussey of Bristol in May 1756 to ship supplies to Truro for the Cornish mines: 'Mines in Cornwall cannot be worked without great quantities of of gunpowder and many mines must stand still and a great number of tinners be turned out of work and want bread if an immediate supply is not sent.'[23] This was the first of many licences to be issued for transportation of gunpowder for British mines at this time.[24] Only two such applications were rejected.

Gunpowder, government, and the City of London

The trade in gunpowder was important not only to the nation but also to bodies involved in financial loans to the government, certain of their directors, and certain gunpowder merchants with seats in Parliament or with positions of influence in the City. Strong links have been identified between all of these, a significant fact when considering the failure of the legislation.

Sutherland defines two main divisions in the City at this time; the 'monied interest', and the City in its wider sense of mainly 'middling men'. The former, concerned with creating and mobilising credit, particularly in war, included certain companies or individuals who invariably supported the government of the day. The middling men, including the small merchants, tradesmen and master craftsmen who dominated the Common Council and elected the four City members of Parliament, were usually in opposition to the government.[25] Of significance for the legislation was the relationship between these two groups and the various wartime administrations. The degree to which the government needed support from one group or the other determined the level of restraint it exercised on any prohibitive legislation which interfered with the groups' trading interests. Under Newcastle's administration at the start of the war the need for consultation was recognised on both sides.[26] Further links will be identified between this trade and men within each group but it is of particular interest that representing the middling, commercial group on the financing of war supplies under Newcastle was Sir John Barnard who, since 1725, had himself leased the powder mills at Bedfont from the Duke of Northumberland. The business was run by his brother-in-law Samuel Underhill

23 WO 55/356, 20 May 1756.
24 See appendix 3, table 12.
25 Lucy Sutherland, 'The City of London in Eighteenth Century Politics' in R. Pares and A. J. P. Taylor (eds.), *Essays presented to Sir Lewis Namier* (1956), pp. 49–54.
26 Sutherland, 'Devonshire-Pitt Administration', 164.

who supplied the government. Barnard's grand-daughter was Susanna Norman of Molesey mills.[27]

Unusually, Pitt was heavily dependent on the support of the commercial interest in both administrations in his direction of the war, particularly as he did not initially have the support of the King. Failure to realise the need for a close association with the City's monied interest contributed to the downfall of the first of these administrations. An 'open' subscription was introduced for loans for the government; the commercial interest liked the opportunities it offered and favoured it but the monied interest, to whom the method was a distinct disadvantage, was not interested. The government was heavily dependent on the latter group for financial support, particularly for war expenses left unpaid by Newcastle.[28] Insufficient loans thus resulted and the administration fell. The Newcastle-Pitt administration had to seek the support of both groups simultaneously. Pitt was dependent on the commercial interest but was also required to revert to the 'closed' loan in order to gain favour and financial support from the large financial bodies and prominent individuals. There could be no risk of antagonism towards either, and with each the gunpowder trade played a very definite part. Illustrative of the links between the monied interest and the gunpowder trade were those bodies which, together with the Bank of England, provided financial support to the government: the East India Company; the South Sea Company; and, to a lesser extent the Royal Exchange Assurance, and the London Assurance. Around this centre were individual operators. Discussing the links between directors of such companies and trade Namier states that there was hardly a big merchant in London between 1740 and 1800 who, if successful, did not become involved in pure finance; such men 'turned from "merchandizing" to banking and broking, they became Directors of financial companies such as the South Sea Company or various insurance companies; they dabbled in government stock'.[29] Such people and companies also had links with the gunpowder trade. The East India Company, for example, had three directors either during or just prior to the Seven Years War connected with this trade, two of whom were also powder makers under contract to the Ordnance Office: Chauncy of Oare in Kent, and Walton of Waltham Abbey, Essex.

Richard Chauncy, son of a mining adventurer of the same name and in partnership with Thomas Vigne, was under contract to the Ordnance Office in both the War of the Austrian Succession and the

[27] See appendix 1, Molesey mills.
[28] Sutherland, 'Devonshire-Pitt Administration', 164.
[29] Lewis Namier, 'Brice Fisher M.P: A mid-eighteenth century merchant and his connexions', *English Historical Review*, 42 (1927), 517.

Seven Years War. He was a linen draper of Cheapside, sold powder to the East India Company and also exported it in his own name. Most important of all, he was a director of the Company between 1737 and 1754, and chairman in 1748, 1750, and 1754. He was also one of the commissioners of the lieutenancy for the City of London, and among subscribers for the loan to the government of 1757 with an allocation of £10,000. This appears to have been made in his own right and was probably part of the list to have comprised bankers and merchants, some members of Parliament, peers, and others who had subscribed on behalf of themselves or others, which made up the greater part of the 'Treasury List'.[30] Finally, Chauncy was uncle of Chauncy Townsend, member of Parliament, and one of the commissioners for Trade and Plantations. Townsend too had lead mines in Wales from which he supplied the Ordnance Office during the Seven Years War and, at the same time, had contracts for victualling the British troops in Nova Scotia and Newfoundland. Not surprisingly, both Chauncy and his uncle received licences to ship gunpowder.[31]

Bourchier Walton, who supplied gunpowder to the Ordnance Office from his Waltham Abbey mills, was a director of the East India Company between 1760 and 1762. It is therefore hardly surprising that members of the Walton family sold openly to merchants and received licences themselves to ship gunpowder. They also supplied the East India Company for its ships and the Portuguese government on the invasion by Spain in 1762.[32] Frederick Pigou was a director of the Company between 1758 and 1774 and in partnership with his nephew Miles Andrews he ran Oare powder mills in succession to Chauncy. By 1778 he had taken over the Dartford powder mills too from Edsall and was supplying powder to the Ordnance Office. A directorship with the East India Company would have been of significance in the success of his son Frederick Pigou Jr in obtaining licences for the export of powder to Philadelphia in 1759 and 1760, and for the shipment in March 1763 of 500 barrels of powder from their mill to their magazine at Erith 'for sale to merchants'.[33]

Initially, the East India Company made regular application for licence for powder for its own ships setting sail from the Thames.

---

[30] Sutherland, 'Devonshire-Pitt Administration', 188–92.
[31] PC 2/105, p. 398, 11 January 1756; Sir Lewis Namier and John Brooke, *The House of Commons 1754–1790* (1964), iii, 536.
[32] WO 47/60, pp. 281, 351, 15 October, 18 November 1762; WO 47/61, p. 119, 28 February 1763.
[33] James Gordon Parker, 'The directors of the East India Company, 1754–90' (Unpublished Ph.D. thesis, University of Edinburgh 1977), pp. 206, 299; PC 2/107, pp. 186, 355, 9 November 1759, 30 April 1760; PC 2/109, p. 519, 9 March 1763.

Applications were recorded in detail by the Office until mid-1757 but appear subsequently only in lists for which the Office 'has no objection to licence' and, after 1758, not at all. Unlike applications from other bodies or individuals no licence for the Company was ever recorded by the Privy Council. It must be assumed therefore that its applications were either solely of a token nature so that the Board could record quantities of gunpowder, or were merely notifications of export covered by a 'general' licence as for Liverpool and Bristol merchants to Africa. Its prominent position in the City probably eliminated the need for the formality of individual licences.[34] Sutherland confirms the privileged position of the Company in eighteenth century politics and it is clear that the presence of powder makers and merchants among its directors and its loans to the government must have had an effect on the Act. At any one time several of its twenty-four directors were usually members of Parliament 'attracted like other prominent merchants by the prospects of government contracts and other profitable rewards for the support of government'. A number of other members of Parliament were also large holders of East India Company stock and therefore likely to agree with the directors on matters concerning the Company. It was also closely linked with the other main body providing loans to the government, the Bank of England, banker for the Company supplying both the short term credit necessary for its trade between sales and much of the silver bullion exported to the East.[35]

Another influential London body providing loans to the government at this time was the London Assurance. Its directors too had strong links with the gunpowder trade. Grove, Shubrick, and Aufrere have been thus identified. Silvanus Grove, Virginia Merchant of Martins Lane, Cannon Street, was a director throughout the war. He was also on a 1759 list of proprietors of the Bank of England qualified to vote at the ensuing election of its governing staff.[36] Both alone and with Messrs Russell and Anderson he received licence to export gunpowder to Maryland. It is likely that he was connected also with the many shipments to North America between 1756 and 1761 in Russell's name. Richard Shubrick, Carolina Merchant of Barge Yard, Bucklersbury, was director during the war with both Grove and Aufrere and in 1759 shipped powder, guns and ammunition for the 'India trade'. Until 1748 he had been trading in Carolina as a partner of John Nickelson, who later married his sister Sarah. Shubrick and his brother Thomas also shipped slaves during the war from Africa to South Carolina; he

---

[34] WO 47/47, p. 134, 3 February 1756.
[35] Lucy Sutherland, *The East India Company in Eighteenth Century Politics* (Oxford 1952), pp. 19–22.
[36] *List of Proprietors of the Bank of England* (1750).

would certainly not wish any limitation of such trade. As a widow, Sarah continued with her husband's Carolina trade and received licences in her own name, undoubtedly aided by her brother's position as a director.[37] George Aufrere, a London merchant of Mincing Lane, was a prominent figure in the slave trade and a member of the committee of the Company of Merchants trading to Africa. Between 1755 and 1757 he was partner of Frye and Cust of Leadenhall Street both of whom were members of the above Company, with Cust as a fellow committee member. Aufrere was also a director of the London Assurance in the latter part of the Seven Years War. Aufrere alone, and the group of Birch, Frye and Cust with whom he was associated during the early part of the war, applied for licences to export powder to Africa during 1755 and 1756. Aufrere's ten separate requests were on behalf of Bristol ship owners while the nine requests of the latter group were for ship owners in Bristol, Liverpool, and Chester. Although agreed by the Ordnance Office, these licences were not actually taken up by Aufrere. This was probably due to the fact that Bristol and Liverpool eventually received a general licence which would have made his own individual licences unnecessary.[38]

Other close connections between officials of financial bodies and trade, and between one City body and another include those of the Royal Exchange Assurance. Although it is uncertain whether there were any direct links between officials of this Corporation and the trade in gunpowder, there were certainly strong connections between officials and trade with those areas overseas for which many shipments would undoubtedly have included gunpowder. Equally important was the significant number of directors who were at the same time members of Parliament and directors of other leading City companies.[39]

Some powder merchants, though not directors of the main financial bodies important to the government, were of sufficient financial means and influence to make official loans in their own right. They were among bankers, government contractors, and other businessmen allocated places as subscribers on the list of loans to the government. For instance, Samuel Touchet, merchant of Lombard Street and exporter of gunpowder in the slave trade, appears on a list of subscribers to the loan of 1757 underwriting the sum of £30,000. In December 1759 Touchet was on a list of 'principal and most responsible men in the

---

[37] PC 2/106, p. 288, 24 November 1758; PC 2/109, p. 386, 16 October 1762; Kellock discusses roles of a number of merchants known from other sources to deal in gunpowder. Katherine A. Kellock, 'London Merchants and the pre-1776 American Debts', *Guildhall Studies in London History*, 1 (1974), 109–49.

[38] T 1/365.75, 11 October 1756; T 1/370.3, 5 February 1756.

[39] Barry E. Supple, *The Royal Exchange Assurance* (Cambridge 1970), pp. 75, 76.

City' for another loan.[40] Namier includes Touchet among twenty-two leading City men in close touch with the Treasury and deeply engaged in government finance. In 1761 he was returned as member of Parliament for Shaftesbury in Dorset and later was one of the financial advisers to the chancellor of the exchequer. He was a West India merchant and member of the Company of Merchants trading to Africa. There was little danger that so influential a figure would be refused permission to export powder to Africa. He received individual licences in 1758 and 1762 and would also have been closely involved in shipments made in the name of the above Company.[41]

Another powder merchant on the list of subscribers of 1757 and member of the Company of Merchants trading to Africa was Richard Oswald of Philpot Lane. He received licences during 1756 and 1757 to export powder to his company's trading fort on Bance Island on Africa's Windward Coast, to Boston for private ships, and to planters in Virginia. Oswald is described as an Africa and West India merchant of Glasgow and London, a prominent slave trader, and a tobacco merchant who made a fortune as a government contractor during this war; with Sir Alexander Grant he owned Bance Island, a slave trading depot, and sold to France and Holland as well as to Britain. His government contracts were for forage for horses and bread and waggons for the Hessian troops in 1756, and the same for troops in Britain in 1757 and Germany from 1758, together with horses and drivers.[42]

Political influence and the gunpowder trade

Government contracts, particularly those connected with the arming, victualling, and clothing of the Army and Navy, could be highly prestigious.[43] For some, such contracts resulted in a seat in Parliament or other position of political influence. Undoubtedly, those with government contracts who also traded in gunpowder were in a favoured position when applying for licence for its transportation. With very few exceptions such licences were issued without question. Those with government contracts during this war who successfully maintained a trade in gunpowder included Oswald, Bacon, Eade, Trecothick, Thomlinson, Hanbury, Kilby, and Barnard.

---

[40] Sutherland, 'Devonshire-Pitt Administration', 174, 189; Sir Lewis Namier, *The Structure of Politics at the Accession of George III* (1957), i, pp. 54–5.
[41] PC 2/109, pp. 223, 224, 30 April, 4 May 1762.
[42] T 1/365.88, 11 November 1756; T 1/370/89, 17 December 1756; Jacob M. Price, *France and the Chesapeake* (Michigan 1973), ii, 1049.
[43] Namier, *The Structure of Politics*, pp. 46–7.

Anthony Bacon, Africa and Virginia merchant of Copthall Court, Throgmorton Street, with land in North Carolina and Virginia received export licences for five consignments of gunpowder to Virginia between 1756 and 1760, and five to Africa between 1761 and 1762. During the Seven Years War he held several government contracts: the victualling and remittance of pay for British garrisons in Goree and Senegal, the loan of ships to the Ordnance Office and Navy for carrying troops and stores to New York, and the transportation of horses and personal baggage of the master and lieutenant generals of the Ordnance to Emden. Success with applications to export powder to Africa was closely linked with one of the above contracts. The powder was to exchange for fresh provisions in his contract for victualling the troops at the Senegal and Goree slave bases recently taken from the French.[44] Undoubtedly aided by the prestige of those contracts, he became member of Parliament for Aylesbury in 1764.[45]

Christopher Kilby, with partners Barnard and Parker, New England merchants of Budge Row, Sise Lane, received licences for a series of gunpowder shipments to North America between 1757 and 1759. He was the official London agent for the Massachusetts Assembly, and held a government contract for victualling the British troops in North America during the war. An influential link with the government was a shared contract with Sir William Baker, a prominent merchant with wide interests and land in North America, a member of Parliament, one of Newcastle's chief economic advisers, particularly concerning North America, one of those concerned in drawing up lists of subscribers to the 1757 loan to the government, and deputy governor of the Hudson's Bay Company in 1761 and 1762. Kilby also had a government contract with partner Barnard for the supply of bedding to the British forces in Nova Scotia in 1756. Kilby's brother-in-law Richard Neave was another powder merchant who successfully exported to North America and later became deputy governor of the Bank of England. Until 1757, Neave was partner of powder exporter William Neate who then went into partnership with Pigou, referred to above.[46]

John Hanbury, in partnership with cousin Capel Hanbury, was a Virginia merchant of Tower Street. He received an export licence in 1759 and as a prominent figure in the tobacco trade was probably connected also with those issued in other names at this time. He was a rich Quaker who helped the government in the Bristol election of

[44] PC 105–109, 1755–63; T 29/33, pp. 78, 105, 191, 27 July, 1 November 1758, 12 June 1759.
[45] Lewis Namier, 'Anthony Bacon M.P., An eighteenth century merchant', *Journal of Economic and Business History*, 2 (Harvard 1929), 31.
[46] Kellock, 'London Merchants', pp. 128, 136; Namier, *Structure of Politics*, pp. 51–2.

143

1754 with his financial support for Robert Nugent, and with gunpowder merchant John Thomlinson he was contractor for remittance of pay for the British Army in North America.[47] Thomlinson himself was partner of Barlow Trecothick and, as Thomlinson, Trecothick and Company, exported powder to Boston during 1757 and 1758. Termed Trecothick, Apthorp and Thomlinson of Bucklersbury, he also exported to Antigua in 1758 and to New England in 1759 and 1760 respectively. Thomlinson's father was a member of the Council of Antigua, and Apthorp, whose daughter married Thomlinson, was a wealthy government contractor. The former company had also held shipping contracts with the Ordnance Office before the war.[48] Trecothick was a London merchant also of prominence in the City, alderman of Vintry Ward in 1764, sheriff in 1766, Lord Mayor in 1766, and member of Parliament for the City in 1768.[49] Moses Franks, New England merchant of Billister Square received export licences for Virginia, Pennsylvania, New York, and Antigua in 1756 and 1757. He held a contract at this time for victualling the troops in North America in conjunction with Arnold Nesbit. The latter was also under contract for remittance of money for those troops in conjunction with Thomlinson and Hanbury. In addition, Franks was one of the subscribers to the loan to the government of 1757 submitted by Sir William Baker MP and on the list of the 'principal and most responsible men in the City' for a similar loan of 1759.[50]

Jonathan Eade of Wapping, and of Ewell mills, supplied the Ordnance Office with gunpowder with partner Alexander Bridges of Ewell and, with another partner in the powder business, William Wilton, supplied iron ordnance and shot. With the latter he also supplied iron hearths for ships of the Royal Navy. In addition, he held a government contract in 1760 for shipping members of the Artillery to Guadeloupe in the ship *Amherst* of which he was part owner, and also supplied cannon to the East India Company. He was a member of the Company of Merchants trading to Africa and by 1761 was a director of the Hand in Hand Insurance Office in the City. Not surprisingly he and Bridges were permitted powder shipments to Africa, Gibraltar, the West Indies, and to various parts of Britain.[51] Another member of the Company of

---

[47] T 1/377.85, December 1754–May 1757; T 29/32, pp. 255, 370, December 1754, 5 February 1756; A. Audrey Locke, *The Hanbury Family* (1916), p. 251; Alison G. Olson, 'The Virginia Merchants of London', *William and Mary Quarterly*, 3rd series 40 (1983), 374.

[48] WO 51/194, 11 October 1753.

[49] Kellock, 'London Merchants', p. 148.

[50] PC 2/105, pp. 259, 453, 497, 9 July 1756, 8 March, 19 May 1757.

[51] WO 47/48, pp. 355, 404, 21 October, 2 November 1756; WO 47/56, p. 170, 4 September 1760.

Merchants trading to Africa, a member of its committee, and exporter of gunpowder, was Peregrine Cust of Leadenhall Street. With partners Birch and Frye he exported powder to Africa between 1759 and 1761. He had the distinct advantage of being a member of a prominent Shropshire family, as son of Sir Richard Cust and younger brother of Sir John, Speaker of the House of Commons between 1761 and 1771. Cust himself was member of Parliament for Bishops Castle from 1761 to 1768, and a director of the East India Company from 1767 to 1769.[52]

Finally, among those merchants improving their social and financial positions and successfully trading in gunpowder were two bankers, Barclay and Coutts. David Barclay, linen draper of Cheapside, managed his father's linen business and also his banking house in Lombard Street after the latter's death in 1761. Bourne described David Barclay, who held an estate in Jamaica, as 'one of the most influential London merchants of his time'. Not surprisingly this family was successful in its licence applications to ship powder to North America during 1756 and 1757.[53] James and Thomas Coutts applied successfully for licences to export gunpowder, muskets, bayonets, and swords to North America in 1756 and 1760. The latter was also an army clothing contractor.[54] They were bankers and merchants trading as Coutts Brothers and Stephen of Jefferys Square, St Mary Axe at the beginning of the war, as Coutts and Company in 1763, and later as James and Thomas Coutts. Pitt sought financial advice at what was becoming 'the fashionable banking house of the West End'. The increasing importance of the Coutts brothers cannot have passed unnoticed and would certainly have played its part in their successful applications for export licences.[55]

Government limitations

Although the national importance of the gunpowder trade was undoubtedly paramount among possible reasons for the virtual failure of the Act, it is essential to consider other contributory factors. In theory, the government had the ability to stop or limit the trade by the Act it

---

[52] H. T. Weyman, 'Members of Parliament for Bishops Castle', *Transactions of the Shropshire Archaeological Society*, 2nd series 10 (1898), 62.

[53] PC 2/105, pp. 40, 100, 191, 12 February, 9 March, 24 May 1756; H. Bourne, *English Merchants* (1866: repr. New York 1969), ii, 131–5; D. Barclay, *Account of the Emancipation of the Slaves of Unity Valley Pen in Jamaica* (1801), p. 5.

[54] D. J. Smith, 'Army Clothing Contractors and the Textile Industries in the Eighteenth Century', *Textile History*, 14 (1983), 156.

[55] Bourne, *English Merchants*, p. 137; Anon., *Life of the late Thomas Coutts* (1822), p. 3.

had introduced in 1756. In practice, its relevant departments had little real ability to take any effective action at all due to the trade's overwhelming importance. The Ordnance Board should have acted positively concerning the legislation which it had itself sought through its important duty of advising the Privy Council on which licences should or should not be issued; yet whatever commitment it had was obviously largely suppressed almost immediately, for from the start very few applications were rejected. Even its own low gunpowder stocks were of little importance compared with the value of overseas trade. The same was true of the Privy Council which, moreover, had at least one member who stood to lose personally by enforcement of the legislation. This was the Duke of Queensbury who required powder for his lead mines in Scotland.

Baker states that war placed the heaviest demand on eighteenth century governments and led Parliament to expect most from them. Yet politicians both in government and opposition remained unwilling to extend the powers of government either positively or by default, even though aware of their inadequacy. Necessity was never stark enough to overcome deep reluctance to embark on fundamental change. The important consideration was that Britain won most of her eighteenth century wars: 'the machine creaked, but it worked'. Politicians were generally satisfied with a style of government neither over involved nor over powerful. Britain won wars and acquired colonies without sweeping new powers or curtailment of the freedom of Englishmen as conceived by those with any political influence. With this in mind it would be understandable if members of the Ordnance Board, all members of Parliament, were reluctant to employ too extensive a power in their dealings with licence applications.[56] Their loyalties were pulled in two directions. Nevertheless, the fact that they found it inappropriate to use much if any power at all is more surprising. Baker's view that prevailing methods of government appointment and promotion hardly served to stimulate full commitment to government service may well have applied to the Board. Although difficult to identify with specific Board members at this time evidence was available soon after. In 1771 it was alleged that Ordnance posts and contracts had been given to relatives and friends of surveyor general Sir Charles Frederick, including the husband of his mistress.[57] Finally, the Board itself ad-

[56] N. Baker, 'Changing Attitudes towards Government in Eighteenth-century Britain' in A. Whiteman, J. S. Bromley, and P. G. M. Dickson (eds.), *Statesmen, Scholars and Merchants* (Oxford 1973), pp. 204–5; see appendix 2, table 11.
[57] W. A. Miles, *Selim's Letters exposing the Mal-Practices of the Office of Ordnance* (1771), pp. 21, 29, 30.

mitted on certain occasions its lack of experience concerning licence applications, particularly with respect to certain overseas trade.

Although the Act of 1756 presented opportunity to the Ordnance Office and the Privy Council to limit the private trade of the gunpowder makers neither could take advantage of the situation; the trade was too important to the nation as a whole, to the government, and to certain prominent individuals and bodies either closely concerned with the government or on whom it was heavily dependent for political and financial support, particularly in time of war. The sale of gunpowder was crucial to many different branches of the trade and each, in turn, was stimulated by war. There were many links between this trade and central government, the City, and the cities of Bristol and Liverpool. For one prominent City body in particular, the East India Company, continuation of the Africa trade was vital, for its own imported goods were re-exported to Africa among mixed cargoes invariably including guns and gunpowder. As one of the main subscribers to financial loans to the government it experienced little problem with the legislation, a situation undoubtedly helped greatly by the fact that several gunpowder makers were directors of the Company and supplied powder for the Company's own ships. In such circumstances the legislation had little chance of success.

PART FOUR

THE ORDNANCE OFFICE AND
MANUFACTURE

9

Faversham Mills

The importance of Faversham mills during the Seven Years War lay in their transference from private to crown ownership in 1759, thus becoming the first gunpowder mills ever under direct government control.[1] These Kent mills, usually referred to simply as 'Faversham mills', comprised three estates located in four parishes. Water, and horse powered mills, refining and store houses, wharves and waterways, islands and gardens covered an area of some parochial complexity in Faversham, Ospringe, Preston, and Davington. Much of the later Marsh Works was in a detached portion of the parish of Luddenham. Oare mills in the north west of Davington parish were not among these for although earlier linked in business with Faversham and supplying the government during most of the remainder of the century these were, by 1750, run independently of the Faversham group.

Purchase was undertaken with the aim of increasing government stock at a time of exceptionally high demand from the armed services. This was to be achieved by reworking unserviceable gunpowder returned from naval ships and by the manufacture of new stock. The choice of established mills in preference to the construction of new, gave the advantage of a well proven site ready for immediate use with good access to Faversham Creek, the Thames Estuary, and Greenwich. The Ordnance Board considered that in order to reprocess the large quantity of unserviceable powder for the immediate use of the armed forces mills already in existence would be best suited for the purpose.[2]

---

[1] One of the closest known links between the government and any other gunpowder mill was that with Chilworth mills in the seventeenth century; Guiseppi, VCH *Surrey*, pp. 324–6.
[2] WO 47/50, p. 207, 20 September 1757.

Further additions were made to the Faversham group: between 1760 and 1790 new horse and water powered mills and magazine; and, in 1786, the new Marsh Works near Oare Creek. By the turn of the century the government had purchased much of the land it had previously rented or leased from, for example St John's College, Cambridge, the Dean and Chapter of Canterbury, the vicar of Faversham, the Chauncy family, and the Ordnance storekeeper Edward Wilks. Faversham mills, excluding the later Marsh Works, were finally sold in 1825 to powder maker John Hall.[3] There was considerable legal confusion and inefficiency involved in crown purchase of the mills because the Treasury did not fully investigate Benjamin Pryce's title to this complex land holding; this left the Ordnance Board with many problems in their subsequent administration.

Historical background and the conveyance of 1759

By 1701 both Faversham and Oare mills were run by Francis Grueber, one of five powder makers then supplying powder to the Ordnance Office.[4] Grueber died in 1730 and was succeeded by a son of the same name who by 1740 was in financial difficulties. He continued to supply powder to the Ordnance Office until October 1743, presumably from Oare mills. The family was again represented at these mills from 1768 in conjunction with makers Pigou and Andrews.[5] When, by April 1745, Grueber was bankrupt and the remainder of his twenty-one year lease of Oare mills was for sale, it was taken by the partnership of Chauncy & Vigne who entered into contract with the Office in November of that year.[6] This brought them into proximity with nearby Faversham mills with which they were soon to become more closely associated. By April 1740 the latter mills had been taken over by Thomas Pearse who ran them until 1754, at first alone and, from 1748, with his partner Stevens.

The indenture of conveyance to the Crown shows that Pearse, and Grueber before him, held Faversham mills as a combination of one freehold and two leasehold estates. One of the leasehold estates, that of Kingsmill manor which housed a large proportion of the mill buildings, had been held by Matthew Cox who had acquired it via his wife Lydia, daughter of the previous holder, John Ingham. Whether or not Cox

---

3   WO 55/1585, 16 March 1827: sale to Hall.
4   WO 51/64, p. 15, 28 February 1702 regarding contract October 1701.
5   WO 51/145, p. 64, 5 July 1740; SUPP 5/65 January 1782 (1774), p. 151.
6   CCA, U3/138/11/4, Poor Law Assessment Book, Davington 1755–68; *London Gazette*, April 1745.

himself had any direct interest in the gunpowder business is uncertain. By April 1754 he was bankrupt and the lease was for sale.[7] The sale, to the best bidder, was on 7 May when Cox was described as 'late of Ealing, mealman, dealer and chapman'. Included were horse, and water powered gunpowder mills, other buildings, and thirteen acres of land in Faversham and Preston; this was 'let on lease at the yearly rent of £110 for the life of the said bankrupt, and the remainder in fee on failure of issue of his now wife'.[8] As a result of a presumably very cursory check of Pryce's title to the Faversham estates prior to purchase in 1759, the Treasury did not realise that Kingsmill manor was no longer held by Cox. The Ordnance Board assumed that Pearse held the estate from Cox and that by 1759 Pryce had taken over Pearse's interest in the lease. However, the lease had been sold in 1754 to powder maker and late chairman of the East India Company, Richard Chauncy, who was already at Oare mills nearby with partner Thomas Vigne.[9] When warned by Chauncy prior to the sale of Faversham mills to the Crown of his own rightful claim to the manor, the Board informed the Treasury merely that it was 'ignorant how far same may affect Pryce's title'. There was no attempt to clarify the matter further.[10]

In 1753, prior to the above change in holding, Pearse had taken Benjamin Pryce into partnership; by the following January Pryce was married to Pearse's daughter Rebecca.[11] By 1754 Pearse was in financial difficulties, leaving Pryce to supply the Ordnance Office alone. In January 1759, just four months before the Faversham sale, Pearse wrote to the Ordnance Board stating that he:

had long been in possession of an estate and some powder mills near Faversham and that he, in conjunction with Benjamin Pryce, whom he had admitted into partnership in 1753, had supplied the Office with large quantities of gunpowder; that in 1754 he was prevailed on to execute to Benjamin Pryce and Edward Pryce of London some deed or instrument in writing of which he had no copy or counter-part, for assigning over to them his estate and effects in trust for paying his creditors their just demands and being informed that Benjamin Pryce is about to contract with the Board for the sale of the said estate without the knowledge of his co-trustee or the peti-tioner, and it is incumbent on him for the sake of his creditors and

[7] TS 21/874, 30 March 1748, Lease, Cox to Pearse; Hasted, *The History and Topographical Survey of the County of Kent*, pp. 338–9.
[8] *London Gazette*, April 2–6 1754.
[9] SUPP 5/64, 10, 29 April, 25 November 1766.
[10] WO 47/53, p. 394, 3 April 1759.
[11] C 11/2522/1, 31 January 1754; GMR RB704, Loseley MSS, 6 October 1759, Molyneux to Peace, Attorney of Petersfield.

for the benefit of himself and family to enquire into the nature of such contract, and that the same may not be completed and carried into execution without the knowledge of Edward Pryce and himself.[12]

No action was taken and Pearse continued until his death to proclaim Pryce's dishonesty.[13] The validity of Pearse's claim was strengthened by the fact that co-trustee Edward Pryce, powder maker of Chilworth mills in Surrey and an attorney of Grays Inn, later wrote to the Ordnance Board himself requesting financial details of the sale, about which he insisted he knew nothing.

The matter was further complicated because the Duke of Marlborough as master general of the Ordnance, although informing the Treasury officially in July 1757 of initial arrangements of purchase of the mills, undertook most of the negotiations in verbal form only. More difficulties were caused by the Duke's death prior to conveyance and Pryce's later demand for more money.[14] Also, it was later revealed that although the Board had ordered a survey of Faversham lands and buildings in January 1759, and of land boundaries for fencing in June, these had been cursory and boundaries uncertain. This is shown by storekeeper Wilks' later report to the Board: 'The engineers who planned all the estates that the Ordnance Office are in possession of were guided only by the accounts of Mr Hall. [Richard Hall, the master-worker] . . . if Chauncy's agent asks questions and we do not have a proper plan for his boundaries there could be some dispute.'[15] Not until long after purchase was the Board aware of the various pieces of land it rented which carried important access routes to certain mills, and not until November 1768 was it in possession of details of the precarious nature of their tenure. Of two access routes, one was held at will from a local farmer for £0 5s a year and the other from the Dean and Chapter of Canterbury at £0 15s. Not until 1781 did the Board order an official plan of the area.[16]

The Faversham lands comprised the two main estates, one freehold and the other leasehold, plus one smaller leasehold estate. The freehold estate comprised 'the great grist mill formerly a powder mill, mill house and lands, together with a double water powder mill, with lands and diverse utensils and materials of the gunpowder trade'. The grist mill was probably the corn mill referred to by Hasted while the double

12 WO 47/53, p. 6, 2 January 1759.
13 WO 47/53, p. 333, 16 March 1759.
14 T 29/32, pp. 174, 471, 474, 2 May, 5 July 1757.
15 SUPP 5/69, June 1768.
16 WO 47/72, p. 177, 22 November 1768; SUPP 5/69, November 1768; MPH 250 Plan of Powder Mills, Faversham, Henry Hogben Jr. 1781.

powder mill would have been Horse and Chart mill. This estate was situated to the west of Faversham town and was the centre of the three. It was sold to the Crown for £2,940. The leasehold estate of Kingsmill manor was situated to the east of the above estate and extended to the head of Faversham Creek. It comprised two water powered gunpowder mills and two horse powered mills (known as Lower Water, and Lower Horse mills), dwelling house, stove, watch, refining, corning, dusting, and store houses, brimstone and coal mills, magazine, outhouses, and utensils, plus eleven islands in the river, and meadow containing water courses and ponds, totalling thirteen acres. It also included Kings mill, a working corn mill converted for gunpowder production in 1779. This estate was sold for £1,897.[17] Added later were the New Water mills and New Horse mills, all situated near the head of the Creek.

The third, smaller estate comprised Ospringe mills and land originally leased to Pearse in 1752 by St John's College, Cambridge for twenty-one years. This was at a yearly rent of £5, renewable seven-yearly at a fine of £30, based on the price of wheat at Lady Day and Michaelmas at Cambridge market. This mill in turn was leased to Pryce at Michaelmas 1758 for a period of twenty years. When the lease was renewed by the Ordnance Office in 1779 the fine was raised to £120.[18] This holding comprised a water powered powder mill, tenement, buildings, and one acre of land. The mill is known to have worked three pairs of stones in 1768 and four pairs by 1789. Although known as Ospringe mill it was situated to the north of Watling Street and therefore north of the Ospringe parish boundary, in the parish of Faversham. The lease together with 'goods, utensils, and materials' was conveyed for £537 13s 4d.[19] Making matters complicated was the fact that the mill stones and certain other equipment, sold by Pryce for £537 were in reality still owned by St John's College. The names of the true owners were included in Pryce's original lease from St John's but, as the Treasury did not examine this lease and believed Pryce's claim to ownership, payment was made without question. The dishonesty was not discovered until 1770 when the lease was examined for the first time. Pryce was requested by the Ordnance solicitor to return the relevant money, although there is no record that he did so.[20]

Sale of the entire Faversham holding to the Crown was by Captain

---

[17] C 54/6047, 16 May 1759; Horse and Chart water mills were referred to by the Ordnance Office in the initial years of crown ownership as Horse and Cart mills and only later as Horse and Chart. They are known currently simply as Chart mills: Arthur Percival, *The Faversham Gunpowder Industry and its development* (Faversham 1967).
[18] WO 47/59, p. 102, 2 February 1762; SUPP 5/65, January 1779.
[19] C 54/6047, 16 May 1759; SUPP 5/114, November 1789.
[20] WO 47/75, p. 295, 22 May 1770.

Benjamin Pryce and his trustee Robert Drummond for £5,682. There was no reference to Edward Pryce who, according to Thomas Pearse, had been co-trustee when he, Pearse, had placed the business in their hands. On 19 June the Ordnance Board received the royal warrant, approved by the Treasury, directing that payment be made to Pryce by the Office and backdated to the original negotiations of September 1757. Pryce was to perform the duty of superintendant at the mills during his lifetime for which he was to receive 'by way of a salary a clear yearly annuity or rent charge of £600 . . . issuing out of the free and leasehold estates'. Apart from some early advice on the supply of horses there is no evidence that Pryce performed any duty whatsoever at the mills although payment was included annually by the Board in its expenses to Parliament. What was termed the 'freehold estate' was in fact conveyed for a period of 2,000 years; this was in consideration of the total fee referred to above, the annual salary to Pryce, and what was to be an annual payment of a peppercorn to the latter's executors after his death.[21]

The Treasury was mistaken in failing to investigate more fully Pryce's claim to title, particularly in view of the counter claims prior to conveyance. Neither Treasury nor Ordnance Office took notice of either Richard Chauncy's claim to Kingsmill manor or that of his son Toby which the latter insisted had been made yearly to the Office since Richard's death in December 1760. Until March 1766 the Ordnance Board continued to believe that the owner was Cox who by then had been dead for many years.[22] It was not until April 1766, when Toby Chauncy requested seven years unpaid rent for the manor, that the Office investigated the situation more fully. After the Ordnance solicitor's report on the matter in June the mistake was admitted and in November the lease was renewed until 1769 and a sum of £742 10s paid to the family based on the annual payment of £110.[23]

The remainder of the period of the leases of Kingsmill manor and the Ospringe mills and land was transferred to the Crown in 1759, and both were later sold by their rightful owners; the Chauncy family and St John's College, in 1780 and 1814 respectively.[24] Meantime, there had been other problems. In April 1760 Pryce asked for a further £2,646 from the Treasury for outstanding payment to tradesmen, for

21 C 54/6047, 16 May 1759; WO 47/53, p. 645, 19 June 1759; WO 55/359, p. 120, November 1759; WO 55/427, 11 May 1759 Newcastle, Legge & Nugent to Board.
22 WO 47/67, pp. 210, 264, 25 March, 11 April 1766.
23 WO 47/67, p. 390, 29 May 1766; SUPP 5/64 10, 29 April, 25 November 1766.
24 SUPP 5/113, 6 January 1788.

trade utensils and materials, and also for five per cent interest on the sale price of the mills for the period September 1757 to June 1759. Although disputing this, the Treasury and Ordnance Board eventually agreed, albeit reluctantly, to meet the claim.[25]

After conveyance, Thomas Pearse again denounced Pryce's claim of legal right to the mills and refused to move from his house on the Faversham land.[26] Co-trustee Edward Pryce still remained in ignorance of the financial details of the transaction eight years later, and on 27 February 1767 he asked the Ordnance Board for details of the payment made to Benjamin for the mills 'as all matters of the gunpowder trade are now settling between us'.[27] Although on ceasing business at Faversham Benjamin Pryce recommended Pryce of Chilworth mills, and there was obviously a business relationship between the two, the exact nature of either this or any family link is unclear. Correspondence with the Office by Edward and his Chilworth partner Isaac Dent in February 1770 confirmed a previous financial involvement not only between Benjamin and Edward but also with Dent, in that Benjamin still owed money to the latter two in connection with the Faversham sale. At the expiry of the partnership between Dent and himself in 1770 Edward Pryce again asked the Board for information on the sale which, he stated, concerned all three men as 'joint partners'; the purchase money had been paid by the Board into the joint partnership account but according to Edward, the former had:

brought divers sums of money, part thereof to account, but never rendered a full or exact account of the whole money received; that the terms of their partnership is now expired and as it is necessary for them to settle their partnership's accounts, they prayed the Board order an account to be made from the official books of all monies received by Benjamin Pryce as it was made out and settled between Pryce and the Board.[28]

Thomas Pearse continued to press the Board with his claims. In February 1771 he informed the Office that Pryce had died at Lisle in the previous January, 'where he had retired to screen himself from him (Pearse) and other creditors'. He now pleaded that 'the annual pension of £1,200 be made over to him who is the true and lawful proprietor of the said mills or some other allowance for the remainder of his days to

[25] WO 47/55, p. 285, 1 April 1760; T 29/33, pp. 329, 341, 10 June, 8 July 1760.
[26] WO 47/54, p. 34, 10 July 1759.
[27] WO 47/67, p. 294, April 1766; WO 47/69, p. 92, 27 February 1767.
[28] WO 47/75, p. 84, 20 February 1770; GMR 43/79/2, 9 January 1776, Lease, Edward Pryce to Anson.

prevent his becoming a burden to the parish.[29] Pryce had indeed died in Lisle on 5 January.[30]

Administration by the Ordnance Office 1759–75

Faversham mills were administered by the Ordnance Office centred in London, and managed on its behalf by Ordnance officers and staff of the Ordnance at Faversham. Immediately following conveyance the new storekeeper, Edward Wilks, took an inventory of materials and utensils and a muster of men currently employed. He was also requested to report on those mills capable of immediate work and the quantity of unserviceable powder to be reprocessed.[31] All mills were ready except Ospringe, with a decayed waterwheel. These were Horse and Chart watermill and the Lower Water, and Lower Horse mills. Kings mill was to be retained for corn milling rather than undergo conversion for powder making. Ospringe mills were set to work during the following autumn after Isaac Bull, the overseer of works, had been sent from London to organise their repair.[32] At the end of 1760 additional incorporating mills were required and the Ordnance engineer Desmaretz therefore prepared a plan for two new horse mills for the freehold estate. He based this on one of the mills at Ewell which consisted of cast iron runners and bed plates instead of stones. He informed the Board that these were believed to be 'less expensive and not so liable to accidents as stones', a point later confirmed when an explosion in one of the mills caused little damage and the machinery was returned to work soon after. His estimated cost for the two mills was £799.[33] While building went ahead discussions took place in London between the Board, Isaac Bull, and Messrs Wright & Company, iron founders, on the dimensions and weights of the necessary ironwork. In June blocks were sent for unloading the four completed runners and two bed plates, the former of which weighed 13 tons 9 cwt and the latter 5 tons 3 cwt. In order to turn the runners in the lathe at the mills, the Company had to agree a delay on its government contract for the supply of iron shot and shells.[34]

29 WO 47/77, p. 106, 8 February 1771.
30 PROB 6/147, July 1771.
31 WO 47/53, pp. 534, 604, 18 May, 7 June 1759; WO 47/54, p. 22, 6 July 1759.
32 WO 47/54, pp. 34, 336, 10 July, 18 October 1759; WO 47/56, p. 223, 26 September 1760.
33 WO 47/57, pp. 55, 133, 27 January, 27 February 1761; WO 47/60, p. 225, 21 September 1762; WO 55/2269, 23 February 1761, Ordnance Plans and Report.
34 WO 47/57, p. 247, 387, 17 April, 9 June 1761; WO 47/58, p. 291, 23 October 1761; WO 51/225, p. 131, 31 December 1763.

By May 1762 a new corning house was required 'to work off the powder at the several mills', and made even more necessary in June by the breakdown of the upper corning house where 150 barrels of powder were left uncorned. The Board approved a request for a new building with horse powered machinery designed by Desmaretz for the freehold land at an estimated cost of £392. In connection with the design of interior fitments Bull visited the corning house at Waltham Abbey; this suggests a different or more modern design at those mills. The estimate for the internal iron and brass components of the machinery for the 'horse corning engine', to be made by Canterbury millwright John Ash, was £84 16s. The parchment required for the sieves of the presses was sent from the Tower with holes punched in each through which the powder was pressed to form grains of a certain size. It was not until war had ceased that this corning house was ready for work.[35]

Following his installation as storekeeper Wilks and his son proposed their own contract with the Board to supply horses for the mills on the freehold and the Kingsmill estates, to include thirteen horses for the two new incorporating mills. On the only recorded occasion when the Board asked the opinion of Pryce, as superintendant, the latter approved the proposal provided Wilks replace immediately by purchase or hire any horses killed or disabled in case of accident in order to avoid disruption. The contract, for an initial period of eleven years, included payment for the purchase of horses at a cost of £10 each and a six-monthly payment for the purchase and maintenance of waggons, carts, and harness, plus wages for stable keepers. The latter were paid at the rate of £0 8s each a week.[36] Additional payment was made for maintenance and work of horses on Sundays, necessary at certain times during the war. Twenty-five horses were in use at any one time. This increased to twenty-seven in June 1765. The rate of payment remained the same.[37] Wilks gives some indication of the duties of the horses in correspondence in 1787. By then there were five horse mills, comprising the new double mills built in 1761 with two pairs of stones, the old double mills purchased with the estate in 1759, and the New Horse mills with one pair of stones, erected at an intervening date. The latter two were on the Kingsmill estate towards the head of Faversham Creek. The Faversham officers obviously considered that more horses were required than the four currently allowed for each mill: 'There have never been less than five horses allowed each mill working night and day, six hours on and six hours off. No horse in England will bear

[35] WO 47/60, p. 51, 20 July 1762; WO 47/61, p. 184, 31 March 1763.
[36] WO 47/53, p. 619, 12 June 1759; SUPP 5/64, 7 April 1769.
[37] WO 51/219, p. 2, 30 September 1761; WO 51/221, pp. 11, 125, 31 March, 30 September 1762.

this without help from a fifth horse to allow regular rest and to be shod. They work in pairs.'[38] This was agreed by the Board. The number of horses was as follows: 20 horses for 5 horse mills; 1 horse for the sulphur & charcoal mill; 1 horse for saltpetre; 4 horses for 2 corning houses; 4 horses for 2 powder carts.

The Faversham works were expanded by purchase of land previously rented by the Ordnance Office and also by purchase of land from Wilks in 1768. The latter consisted of an unspecified quantity of hop gardens and meadow next to the storekeeper's house which, with some foresight, Wilks had purchased in February 1761.[39] As a result of the expressed concern of the Faversham Corporation on the dangers to the town of both the existing powder magazines and of the proposed new site at the foot of Davington Hill, the Board asked the overseer of works to find a safer site. This was to be on thirty acres of land purchased from Wilks in 1776 which was to house not only the new magazine but the new Marsh Works of 1786. The magazine would be more suitably placed between Faversham and Oare Creeks for reasons of isolation, space, and ease of transport. Oare Creek, used mainly by vessels connected with Oare mills in Davington parish, had little traffic, no habitation, and easy access to the Thames estuary:

> Whereas in Faversham Creek the vessel is obliged to come so far to take powder in and the distance being near three miles from the entrance and the vessel often detained 3 or 4 days before it can get out, and at neap tides not enough water to carry the powder down to the vessel (ie in the barge) but in this place (Oare) she can in spring tides load at the magazine wharf and at the lowest neap tides the barge may come to the magazine and convey it (ie. the powder) to the vessel which has nothing to obstruct her sailing immediately with it.[40]

In Faversham Creek the powder vessel carrying powder to Greenwich had to wait well away from the town for safety reasons and because of the size of the channel. The powder barge conveying powder from the mills could sometimes be detained 'a tide or two by obstructions of other craft, on account of the narrowness of the channel'. However a barge was essential for such conveyance. The only time the master of the vessel attempted to anchor near habitation was in bad weather when the laden barge with which it was to connect could become 'ungovernable' if it went below the town.

---

[38] SUPP 5/66 September 1787; MR 909, Ordnance map of Faversham mills, 1789.
[39] WO 47/57, p. 77, 4 February 1761; SUPP 5/64 December 1768.
[40] SUPP 5/877, March, April, August 1776.

The staff at Faversham mills at the time of purchase in May 1759 totalled sixteen. It is probable that the majority continued under government administration as their experience would have been vital. Wilks is unlikely to have had any such experience as he had previously been clerk of the survey at Chatham, and storekeeper at Upnor Castle. His annual salary at Chatham had been £54 15s; his new position at Faversham mills was marked by an increase to £100.[41] He kept his own accounts and sent an annual demand of stores for the following year for the approval of the surveyor general in London. Additional finance for current service of the mills, apart from that for staff salaries and his contract for horses, had to be approved by the Board which granted the warrants of justification and finance. Such sums were then included in the next annual estimate to Parliament under the Office's extraordinary expenses. The proposed establishment of staff was submitted by the Board to the Treasury for approval in July 1759 and the relevant royal warrant received in December. This permitted the Board to insert the necessary salaries in its annual financial estimate to Parliament of ordinary expenses. The annual total of the salaries was £398 5s. Annual salaries included among the principal officers (which were new posts): storekeeper £100 0s; master worker £90 0s; clerk (previously extra clerk at Portsmouth) £54 15s; extra clerk £36 10s. Others included a saltpetre refiner, workers at the corning house, those in charge of charcoal and brimstone, and the keepers of the Lower Water Mill, and two horse mills; the salaries of each were £0 9s a week, while that of the mill keeper at Ospringe was £0 8s.[42] Others were added subsequently; these included a man to receive saltpetre from the refining house in order to grind, shift, and weigh it before taking it to the mixing house to be divided into portions, reweighed, and mixed ready for the mills. A labourer from the Royal Laboratory was appointed to the post at £0 2s a day.

By 1789 a new saltpetre refining house, a mixing house, and saltpetre and charcoal storehouses had been built in the areas immediately below Davington Hill to replace those in the Lower Water mill area near the head of the Creek. By the end of 1761 there were thirty-nine men on the staff. Certain, if not all mills worked day and night and the normal working week was of six days duration. Only in special circumstances were the mills run on Sundays, most notably between 1 October and 31 December 1761, and during the autumn of 1762 when there was severe shortage in supply to Greenwich.[43] Whether or not

41 WO 51/213, p. 38, 30 September 1759.
42 WO 47/54, pp. 62, 289, 17 July, 28 September 1759.
43 WO 47/59, p. 157, 19 February 1762; WO 47/60, pp. 40, 434, 14 July, 18 December 1762.

the Board agreed to staff pay in illness depended on the officers' character report of the men involved. When, in May 1760, William Hayes a horse mill keeper was ill for three weeks he was allowed his wages as he was 'diligent and sober'.[44] When necessary, the officers sought the services of Faversham surgeon, Jacob. In August 1761 the latter treated carpenter Paul Gibbs who fell from a beam in Ospringe mill for which, together with several visits to another injured worker, he charged £4 3s 6d. Jacob also attended two men injured in an explosion which, with the necessary medicines, cost £8 1s 6d. The fees were paid by Wilks and added to his regular accounts to the Board. After visits to mill workers injured in further explosions, Jacob proposed the care of the thirty-nine employees for an annual fee of £20 plus £0 10s. each for any additional person. This was accepted by the Board immediately.[45]

Disruption to production could be caused by factors common to any water mill. These included severe shortage of water for power, particularly in the extreme conditions of drought and frost as illustrated by the fact that Faversham employees spent extra time seeking wood for charcoal each December 'this season being unfavourable for any work at the mills'.[46] There were also difficulties caused by silting of waterways and millponds. When the stream between Lower mills and the sluice was choked with mud the entire area had to be cleared. In 1770 the pond at Ospringe mill, uncleaned for many years, was also full of mud. Wilks reported that the mill could not work for much of the time and that there was a complaint from inhabitants of Ospringe Street that by penning the water so high to get it over the mud to work the mill the meadows and houses became flooded.[47] There was opportunity for clearance when the water for Ospringe and the Horse and Chart mills had to be dammed back for five days to build a new bridge to the storekeeper's house.

Most serious was the continual risk of explosion. This was usually during either the process of incorporation or that of corning. It might be slight and cause minimal damage or, at its worst, be so great that one or more entire buildings were destroyed, men and horses killed and production severely curtailed. It was to minimise the effect that buildings were well spaced and away from habitation. For explosions and fire at the mills the staff had their own fire engine on the premises although for serious fire the official Faversham firemen were called. Six

44 WO 47/55, p. 408, 16 May 1760.
45 WO 47/ 58, pp. 111, 302, 405, 11 August, 27 October, 9 December 1761. Jacob was Edward Jacob, local historian and author of *The History of the Town and Port of Faversham* (Mr Arthur Percival, Faversham, September 1987)
46 SUPP 5/65, December 1784.
47 SUPP 5/69, August 1770.

such men attended a fire at the mills in May 1761. There was usually no warning of impending explosion, pattern of occurrence, or obvious cause. Although concern about danger of storage and carriage of gunpowder increased during the century it was not until the mid-nineteenth century that serious investigation commenced into causes of individual explosions. Among those recorded at Faversham at this time was one of December 1759 in a stove in one of the powder drying houses which, in turn, caused damage to Horse and Chart mill. It was then decided that a pallisade should be erected round such buildings to lessen effects of blast on other parts of the works. Two months later there was trouble again in a drying house when powder caught fire. On 10 June an explosion at one of the horse mills destroyed the roof.[48] Although damage from an explosion at Ospringe mill in February 1761 was not extensive, part of Horse and Chart mill was again blown up in March. In May one of the horse mills exploded, necessitating not only the services of the Faversham firemen but also the surgeon, for one man was so badly burnt that he was discharged of his duties. In September 1762 one of the new horse mills blew up. Another mill exploded in February 1764.[49] In November 1766 there was an explosion at Horse and Chart mills and in August 1769 another at the Lower Horse mills. One of the rare occasions when a cause was identified was when part of Lower Horse mills exploded again in January 1768. The mill man reported that this was caused at 5am by 'one of the horses casting his shoe upon the bedstone in going out of the mill'. In December 1770 part of the New Horse mills blew up, 'the charge having been worked but three hours and causing considerable damage'. The most serious explosion recorded at this time was in 1781 when men were killed and injured at the mills and considerable damage caused to property in the town. So serious were the effects of this explosion that Parliament ordered compensation to those affected.[50]

It is difficult to assess from contemporary reports on explosions in this and other mills the precise extent of the damage and of disruption to production. The latter was variable and dependent to a large degree not only on the extent of damage to plant and staff but on the speed with which the proprietor was able to finance necessary repair or to find a millwright. The reports to the Office on explosions at Faversham were usually brief and merely sought necessary permission to finance

[48] WO 47/54, pp. 122, 471, 2 August, 7 December 1759; WO 47/55, pp. 61, 485, 18 January, 10 June 1766.
[49] WO 47/57, pp. 87, 210, 325, 433, 10 February, 3 April, 15 May, 23 June 1761; WO 47/60, p. 225, 21 September 1762.
[50] WO 47/74, p. 52, 28 July 1769; WO 47/76, p. 303, 3 December 1770; SUPP 5/69, January 1768.

repair. This was undertaken immediately by a millwright under supervision of Ordnance engineer Desmaretz.

Output 1755–70: Faversham and other mills

Although Faversham mills were employed immediately for the preparation of new gunpowder, the Ordnance Office saw its primary function, at least initially, as the reworking or repair of the large stock of unserviceable gunpowder from Greenwich magazine. This powder had been allowed to accumulate after the Board's decision to stop its sale to the powder makers early in the war.

The account kept by the Faversham staff of reworked and new powder between 1759 and 1783 cannot be directly compared with the quantity received and proved at Greenwich. This is because the Faversham staff recorded that prepared at the mills rather than that actually dispatched; the two did not necessarily correspond for that which failed initial testing was not sent to Greenwich for official proof. Also, it is impossible to distinguish between new and repaired powder from Faversham for Greenwich officers recorded only the total quantity received. Between 1759 and 1761 there were 1,855 barrels of unserviceable powder reworked at the mills compared with the preparation of 1,780 of new. From 1762 the emphasis was on the production of new, with no further reworked powder recorded until 1772. For the entire period 1759–83, the Faversham officers recorded the reworking of 7,212 barrels and the preparation of 63,934 new. This increasing quantity of new powder illustrates the aim of the Ordnance Office to become as independent as possible of other mills.[51]

Comparisons between mills are made only on the basis of output, for the lack of relevant extant evidence makes it impossible to compare all aspects of production at each mill. Also, although it is known that the majority of men, including Pryce, prepared powder for export it is impossible to evaluate the extent of such activity, and therefore the time involved and degree to which this prevented them fulfilling government contracts. As with the majority of the other powder makers Pryce did not achieve the annual supply of 4,850 barrels originally agreed at contract. Indeed, he was well below in each year, and only in each of the years 1756 and 1757 did he achieve over 2,000 barrels. In his last complete year, 1758, his total fell dramatically to 607 barrels, undoubtedly because he planned to sell the mills. With regard to success at proof, he experienced a lower pass rate for the first year (forty-one per cent) than any other maker, although this rose during the two

[51] SUPP 5/113, p. 279, 6 January 1788, for July 1759 to December 1783.

subsequent years to eighty-seven, and eighty-six per cent respectively. The higher success rate at proof in 1758 and the first four months of 1759, of ninety-three, and ninety-seven per cent respectively are somewhat misleading as these were achieved at a time of exceptionally low supply of powder.[52]

Comparison between Pryce and the other three makers who agreed contracts in December 1754, for the four-year period to December 1758, is as shown in table A.[53]

Table A
Comparison in output: Pryce and other makers

Name	Total delivered, barrels	Total & Percentage passing proof	
Walton	13,661	10,630	(78)
Pryce	6,748	5,428	(80)
Eade & Bridges	3,099	2,481	(80)
Chauncy & Vigne	1,265	982	(78)

Although Pryce was second in order of quantity and first equal in order of quality of powder submitted his total was far short of what should, according to contract, have been 19,400 barrels for the four years in question.

There is no evidence that the Ordnance Office set a specific target for annual output for Faversham mills but the records of the Faversham officers and correspondence with the Board suggest that everything possible was done at the mills to achieve an effective service. The extent of the personal experience or knowledge of the Board in London concerning manufacture would have been minimal as these were the first such mills under its direct control. Apart from occasional references to the surveyor general travelling to Faversham to inspect the mills, the Ordnance Board did not attempt to impose marked change upon either the management or method of manufacture at this time. It had to depend on its officers at the mills. Nevertheless, there was a regular correspondence between the two locations concerning routine administration, aspects of intended expansion of buildings and output, and of the many problems involved. It was not until later in the century that considerable doubt was cast upon the efficiency of the mills, and not until the Crown owned those at Waltham Abbey too, that there was an Inspector of Royal Manufactories of Gunpowder. The

[52] See also ch. 4 and appendix 2, table 6.
[53] Compiled from all deliveries and proof sessions at Greenwich, Ordnance Minutes Books, WO 47/45–52.

main point of importance is that the Faversham staff, at mills under government control, were to experience as much difficulty with production as anyone else.

The low figure for 1759 is undoubtedly due to the time spent in establishing a new routine under entirely new management and also to the delay in organising the dispatch of the barge to Greenwich to collect unserviceable powder. The output for 1760, although higher, was still inadequate probably because one of the Faversham group, Ospringe mill, was not repaired and restored to activity until later that year. However, as the period 1759–64 should have allowed sufficient opportunity for establishing a satisfactory procedure, and as Pryce was supposed to be attending as supervisor, a higher total should have been achieved than was the case.[54] A comparison between the powder makers for the remaining complete years of war, 1760–2, is shown in table B.[55] (For annual totals see appendix 2, table 6)

Table B
Comparison in output between powder makers 1760–2

Name	Total delivered	Total & Percentage passing proof	
Walton	11,640	11,197	(96)
Underhill & Ravens	8,947	7,930	(89)
Smyth & Hill	8,661	6,072	(70)
Pyke & Edsall	7,126	6,254	(88)
Norman	5,936	5,568	(94)
Eade & Bridges	5,568	5,286	(95)
Taylor	4,674	4,441	(95)
Faversham mills	4,527	3,454	(76)
Pryce (Edward)	2,804	2,149	(77)

Apart from Edward Pryce who started at Chilworth at the same time, in 1759, Faversham delivered the lowest total quantity to Greenwich for these final three complete years of war. In terms of standard of powder Faversham was seventh in position of the nine mills supplying the government. Not until 1765 did the annual total rise above 2,000 barrels. It had, therefore, taken the Faversham staff six years to achieve approximately the same quantity as Pryce in the third year of his contract in 1757. Pryce had the benefit of experience, but even he had

---

[54] See details in this chapter on monthly totals of gunpowder submitted and percentage success at proof, for both Pryce and government.
[55] Deliveries and proof sessions at Greenwich, WO 47/55–60.

failed to reach the quantity agreed during his four years of war service. Proof results were similar.

Undoubtedly the Office's aim for Faversham was high; a large amount of money was invested in the purchase, repair, and extension of the mills and it was intended that once peace was declared dependence on the private mills would decrease. The most successful years in the first decade were those of 1766 and 1769 when annual totals were the highest of any of the mills. However, the intervening years were significantly lower and in 1767 not only was the total delivered to Greenwich the lowest at any time between 1760 and 1770 (1,153 barrels) but only half of this quantity passed proof (585). Most important, the quantities and percentages passing proof for Faversham can be seen to have been as varied as those for any other mill. For the five year period 1765–9 the total from Faversham was, at last, considerably increased in comparison with the previous five-year period. However, although the pass rate at proof in three of these years was increased, the overall success rate and uniformity of result still required improvement. The government could not rely solely on its own mills. Although there was a considerable decrease in demand in the post war period, which accounts for the marked difference in quantities delivered, that actually passing proof and going into store illustrates a continuing heavy dependence on the other mills.

Total quantities from Faversham and other mills for 1765–9 were as shown in table C.[56]

Table C
Comparison between Faversham and other mills, 1765–9

Name	Total delivered	Total & Percentage passing proof	
Faversham mills	12,182	9,399	(77)
Walton	8,355	7,186	(86)
Smyth & Hill	6,704	4,592	(68)
Eade & Bridges	5,344	5,068	(95)
Pyke & Edsall	2,942	1,771	(60)

Material on Faversham mills sheds considerable light on gunpowder supply in general at this time. If, as the Ordnance Board had supposed, the reason for unsatisfactory supply from the makers under contract was entirely due to time spent in working for export, both the quantity leaving government controlled Faversham and its quality at proof should have been much higher in comparison with other makers. It is

[56] WO 47/65–74.

of great significance, therefore, that this was not the case. With regard to proof, the only difference in the undertaking appears to have been that much of the Faversham powder which failed was retained by the Office as 'triumph' for purposes of military exercise and royal salutes. In practice, the Faversham results at proof were no more impressive or consistent than those of any other mill, or Pryce beforehand.

Expectations of output at Faversham mills could not be met, and results between 1759 and 1770, particularly those during the Seven Years War, were as unreliable as those of other mills. The manufacturing process at Faversham, at least until 1770, was no different to that elsewhere. If there had been any marked advance in method or technology at this time the Ordnance Office would, undoubtedly, have employed it. The Board, previously critical of its contracted powder makers now discovered at first hand the difficulties and limitations of production. Although it was correct in its assumption that those under contract spent valuable time in working for export it was to discover increasingly that there were other, additional, reasons for failure to achieve the quantity agreed or more regular success at proof. It was possible to improve output only on a limited basis at this time. It was later, with the combination of experience gained at Faversham mills, scientific and technological advances, and people with the appropriate organisational ability to put all of these into practice that the main areas for improvement were clearly identified and employed to advantage. Crown purchase of these mills demonstrates the problems which could result for the government from inadequate legal preparation beforehand, and attempting production in a field in which it had no previous specific experience. Even more important, the Ordnance Board discovered at first hand that there were problems in gunpowder supply other than those caused by competition from private trade.

10

Problems and Advances in Gunpowder Manufacture

At no time during the Seven Years War did the Ordnance Office receive the quantity of gunpowder agreed at contract, and much of what it did receive was not of the required standard. The legislation introduced at this time indicates that low supply caused the Ordnance Board more concern than at any other time either before or during the eighteenth century. That it was correct in connecting the problem with time spent on private trade is not in question; but equally important, and as already shown, the Ordnance staff themselves could fare no better at Faversham mills, particularly regarding the standard of powder produced. It is also probable that for much of the period under government control gunpowder produced at Faversham was of poorer standard than that at other mills, for only that which passed initial testing by eprouvette at those mills was actually submitted to Greenwich for proof.[1] Therefore, there is little doubt that a larger quantity of powder produced by the Office was of unsatisfactory standard than the official Greenwich results suggest. The quantity from Faversham increased towards the end of the first six years under government control, but the quality did not, and as a result national dependence on the private mills did not fall as had been hoped. Instead, quite the reverse occurred when Faversham mills were threatened with sale in 1783. They were saved only by the intervention of Congreve, inspector of Gunpowder Manufactories at Faversham and Waltham Abbey, who later reorganised the entire industry.

Problems of manufacture were acknowledged by both Office and makers as being among factors contributing to the disappointing supply of quality powder, but the precise reasons for unacceptable results at proof were not fully understood or even investigated. It is therefore only with hindsight that poor organisation in manufacture, absence of significant scientific or technological advance from which the industry could benefit, and inconsistencies and inaccuracies in the official method of proof can be identified as causative factors. They were,

---

[1] WO 47/71, p. 254, 20 May 1768; see also ch. 9; Faversham's variability at proof was common to most mills; for eprouvette, see below.

moreover, not new but they were greatly exacerbated by the combination of so intense a war, large demand, and lack of ability to improve, for whatever reason. Therefore, as discussed previously, poor supply in this war resulted not only from time spent on private trade but from ineffective performance in manufacture.[2]

Manufacture: development and change prior to 1750

In its research into the early development of the manufacturing process the Explosives Section of the Seventh International Congress of Applied Chemistry, of 1909, defined the various stages in the development of methods for mixing the three ingredients of saltpetre, charcoal, and sulphur: early mixing by hand with pestle and mortar; subsequent suspension of the pestle from a spring beam, and the more powerful stamp mills of the sixteenth century. Stamp mills were worked initially by hand and later by animal or water power.[3] The application of water to the process of mixing or incorporation was introduced to England in the mid-sixteenth century, at about the same time as stamp mills. It was an important stage in development within the industry in that water was a very much more effective power source. These developments took place earlier on the Continent.

Stamp mills involved the principle of the pestle and mortar but consisted of a row of depressions in a length of wood or stone with a series of uprights or pestles activated by cams to which the power was transmitted. These were later worked at the same time as, but eventually superseded by, incorporating mills consisting of a pair of vertical edge runner stones revolving on a stationary horizontal bed stone.[4] Each water wheel could power one or two individual units, each comprising one set of stones. This was the method employed in the majority of mills under study by the mid-eighteenth century. Waltham Abbey mill had both stamps and stones in 1735, and there were two water powered stamp mills on Faversham's Kingsmill estate in 1748

[2] Lack of extant business records for individual mills prevents any study of the availability of capital, nature of investment in the business, and ability to extend or modernise plant.

[3] Brayley Hodgetts, *British Explosives Industry*, pp. 15, 17, 29.

[4] A bedstone for Faversham mills from Holland in 1765 was 8ft 6ins wide and 1ft 8ins deep. Of 4 stones sent to Faversham in 1767 two weighed 8 tons each and the other two 6 tons each. Two pairs of runner stones for Faversham in 1774 cost £68 12s; WO 47/83, April 1774; SUPP 5/64, 4, 15 March 1765; the combined weight of the four cast iron runners and that of the two bed plates for Faversham's new horse mill were 13 tons 9 cwt, and 5 tons 3 cwt respectively; for illustration of stones, see Brayley Hodgetts, *British Explosives Industry*, p. 27.

although these were probably replaced by stones soon after. There is no reference to their use at either place in the Seven Years War. Each of the Faversham units was powered by a water wheel of fourteen feet in diameter, and had four troughs of fourteen feet in length, each with ten mortars with brass plates below, and twenty pestles shod with brass.[5] The only known use of stamp machinery at mills under government contract at this time was at Hounslow mills, Twickenham where this was the sole method in use. The partnership of Smyth and Hill did not consider the method outdated in June 1758 and even informed the Board that they had built three new such mills and planned two more.[6] In 1772 the government decided that such machinery had proved sufficiently dangerous, because of the greater risk of explosion, to ban its use in all but mills in the Battle area of Sussex which produced fine sporting powder. However, Hill insisted that his seven pestle mills were as efficient and safe as stones; they would work 1,350 lb of powder in twenty-four hours and it would take seven sets of stones to work that quantity in the same time, the cost of which would be £2,509 10s. He eventually received compensation when the change took place.[7]

Horse powered incorporating units continued alongside those of water in most mill complexes during the eighteenth century and in some until the early nineteenth century. In 1758 the Ordnance Office offered financial aid to makers for erecting additional horse mills to increase output, and it erected new horse mills at Faversham after its purchase by the Crown.[8] One of these, constructed in 1761, had cast iron bed and runners instead of stones. This mill, and the one at Ewell on which it had been modelled were early examples of the use of cast iron for this purpose. Horse mills were still working at Faversham in 1792, and still in evidence in 1825. At Waltham Abbey they continued until 1814 where they accounted for approximately one third of total output at the turn of the century.[9]

The main stages in manufacture were firstly, the refining, weighing and initial comparatively brief grinding of the three raw materials. This was followed by mixing and blending them to produce the charge. The charge, the intended weight of which was 36 lb, was then dampened

---

[5]   TS 21/874 1748; Brayley Hodgetts, British Explosives Industry, p. 161.

[6]   WO 47/51, pp. 267, 556, 14 March, 2 June 1758.

[7]   The cost of constructing the 7 sets of stone units necessary to equal the output of the 7 pestle mills (1,350 lb powder in 24 hrs) was £2,509 10s. Compensation given was £1,500; see appendix 1, Hounslow mills; Journals of the House of Commons, 33 (12, 13 May 1772), pp. 747, 755, 759, 769.

[8]   WO 47/51, p. 267, March 1758.

[9]   WO 52/47, p. 266, 31 March 1792; WO 55/585, 1820; W. H. Simmons, A Short History of the Royal Gunpowder Factory at Waltham Abbey (1964), p. 7; Glenys Crocker, The Gunpowder Industry (Aylesbury, Bucks 1986), p. 14.

before incorporation to reduce the risk of explosion. Incorporation, the longest stage, was followed by pressing, and by corning whereby the compressed mixture was formed into separate grains; the resulting gunpowder was then dried. Risk of explosion increased as the substance became more compact during the later stages of incorporation and during pressing.

The time agreed in Ordnance contracts for incorporation of the charge was a minimum of five hours, but as there was little scientific basis for this the Board's views on the subject were disorganised and indefinite. In 1761 the surveyor general's advice to the Bristol makers attempting contract included 'trying experiments on different compositions different times of grinding . . . by which means we may hit on the right methods as others have done'.[10] As late as 1780 the Board continued to ask its Faversham staff to experiment with the remixing of one barrel of failed powder from each maker. Tests were made with both eprouvette and mortar before and after reworking, recorning, and redrying to see if a repeat of these stages increased the powder's strength. Although representing careful experimentation this did, nevertheless, confirm a continued doubt about optimum timing for each stage in production.[11]

By the early eighteenth century there were two major innovations in gunpowder production which concerned the product itself. Firstly, there were changes in the proportions of the three ingredients. Writers on the subject have varied in the precise proportions ascribed to the constituents of earlier gunpowder. Initially the ingredients were 'mixed as fancy dictated, the amount of each being left to the whim of the powder maker concerned' but it is clear that the proportion of saltpetre gradually increased; in 1742 Robins stated that the most usual proportion in Britain and most of Europe was seventy-five per cent, with charcoal and sulphur each in the proportions of twelve and a half per cent.[12] Between that date and the Seven Years War the proportions were seventy-five, fifteen, and ten per cent respectively.

The other main change was the introduction of the process of corning. This was referred to first in Germany in 1440, and was introduced into England in the late fifteenth, or early sixteenth century.[13] The previous 'serpentine' powder was a loose, dusty mixture of the three raw materials. 'Its combustion was slow and irregular, and much gas

---

[10] Buchanan and Tucker, 'The Manufacture of Gunpowder', *Industrial Archaeology Review*, p. 198.
[11] WO 47/95, p. 183, 11 March 1780; WO 47/96, p. 837, 21 October 1780.
[12] Hogg, *English Artillery*, p. 43; Robins, *New Principles of Gunnery*, p. 120.
[13] Robert A. Howard, 'Black Powder Manufacture', *Industrial Archeology*, 1 (1975), 21.

escaped through the vent, so that a low velocity was imparted to the shot.'[14] In addition, storage and transportation were difficult as the powder tended to separate and become damp due to hygroscopic action of the saltpetre. This had meant that until the introduction of corning, gunpowder could only be prepared in small quantities with the constituents often carried separately and mixed as required. Initially, corning was by hand; the mixture was dampened, divided, compressed and placed in a sieve, where the pieces were covered by wooden balls rolled round by hand to force them through into separate grains.[15] By the eighteenth century the process was variously powered by horse or water, and machinery had been introduced to compress the mixture prior to corning. There was a press at Faversham by 1762, and Waltham Abbey had presses installed by the Ordnance Office when taken over in 1787.[16] The 'mill cake' was then broken by hand with a wooden implement before it was forced through sieves of hide bearing punched holes of specific size. Each powder maker received a pattern and punch from the Tower of London to ensure uniformity. There is no evidence on whether the Office had employed graded sizes at any time previously, but it requested only one size during the Seven Years War, to be used for both small arms and all weights of ordnance.[17] Comparatively small quantities of 'fine' powder were mainly used by the government at this time for testing small arms in the Tower. It was only later in the century that the scientific experiments of Ingenhousz confirmed the increased effect possible with graded sizes for different purposes.

After corning, any remaining moisture was removed by drying the powder on racks in a drying room. Heat was from a coal fired gloom stove set in the wall fuelled through an opening in an adjacent room. Although the exact date and place of origin is uncertain, steam drying seems to have been introduced to some mills in the 1770s; these included Worcester Park mill at Long Ditton in 1772, with a stove designed by civil engineer John Smeaton, and Oare mill by 1776.[18] This was a much safer method of drying using hot pipes in the drying

14 Brayley Hodgetts, *British Explosives Industry*, p. 28.

15 Venn, *Military and Maritime Discipline* (1672), pp. 19–20; the wooden balls were later changed to discs, (Professor Alan Crocker, December 1990)

16 WO 47/60, p. 355, 19 November 1762; although an illustration of 1735 refers to a 'corning and glazing engine' at Waltham Abbey mills, there was no reference to the process of glazing in Ordnance contracts; this involved the rotation of corned powder in wooden drums to round off and polish grains; Brayley Hodgetts, *British Explosives Industry*, p. 161.

17 WO 47/46, p. 554, December 1755.

18 Charles Seymour, *A Topographical, Historical and Commercial Survey of the cities, towns and villages of the County of Kent* (Canterbury 1776), p. 378; *A Catalogue of the Civil and Mechanical Engineering Designs of John Smeaton* (Newcomen Society 1950), p. 33.

house. Detailed experiments and comparisons continued at Faversham between 1775 and 1780 using both traditional and new methods.[19] In the latter year there were further trials between powder dried traditionally at the other mills and the same dried again by the new method. Steam drying at this time is not easy to assess as correspondence between Faversham and London on the comparative advantages of each was lengthy and indeterminate. In terms of result, it is probable that this was not among the most significant changes of the period and that the former method did not compare unfavourably; not only were the two types still run simultaneously at Faversham in 1798 but, on taking control at Waltham Abbey mills in 1787, the Office had two more traditional drying stoves installed.[20] Although Congreve later found steam ovens ideal for redrying old damp powder from ships there is no indication of dramatic advantages in the preparation of new stock, or of widespread adoption of the method at this time. The traditional method employed during the Seven Years War cannot have been a major factor in poor supply.

Raw materials

Charcoal provided carbon, saltpetre (potassium nitrate) provided the oxygen for its combustion, and sulphur or brimstone allowed immediate ignition and rapid combustion of the entire mixture. Saltpetre occurred as a natural deposit and most abundantly in certain parts of India, particularly the Patna area of Bengal. From there it was imported as grough petre by the East India Company, from whom the Ordnance Office purchased its supplies annually. It was also imported in lesser quantities from a number of other locations including Russia, Germany, and Spain, the most significant of which was Russia.[21] Samples of the East India Company saltpetre intended for the Office for the forthcoming year were taken to the Tower for inspection and weighing and for the refraction to be agreed prior to purchase; this took place in the presence of Ordnance, and Company staff, and one of the powder makers nominated by his fellows. This has been described as follows:

> if the saltpetre be heated . . . it melts and can be cast into cakes, which on breaking exhibit a crystalline fracture, which varies in

[19] WO 47/85, pp. 138, 220, 324, 21 February, 21 March, 28 April 1775.
[20] Simmons, *Waltham Abbey*, p. 27.
[21] See appendix 2, table 9; CUST 3/55–62, Importation of saltpetre and sulphur during Seven Years War.

appearance with the amount of impurity present, a property which at one time was used to roughly indicate the value of any sample of the salt, and was called the 'refraction' of the nitre. The term is to a certain extent still retained to indicate the amount of impurity present.[22]

During the Seven Years War the samples were taken from stock already in store at the Company warehouses at Rotherhithe or, if the Board required speedy agreement and purchase, they were collected direct from the Company ships arriving in port.

Saltpetre was issued from the Office stock at Rotherhithe for use at the mills, according to the quantity required for each contract. Although it had undergone filtration at source to separate it from earth it still contained many impurities, so was refined twice at the respective mills before being mixed with charcoal and sulphur. Twenty tons of saltpetre were allowed for each contract of 485 barrels of gunpowder. This was supplied by the Office on deposit of £1,200. This therefore allowed approximately 83⅓ lb of grough petre for each 100 lb barrel of powder. As indicated earlier concerning the proposal from Eade and Bridges in 1753, the quantity of the ingredients allowed for each 100 lb barrel, before mixing with other ingredients, was 80¼ lb double refined saltpetre, 15 lb charcoal, and 12¾ lb refined sulphur.[23] This therefore allowed for a loss of approximately 3 lb during refining. The total quantity of 108 lb of the three ingredients was divided into three equal parts, each of which underwent concentrated mixing and grinding by heavy edge runner stones for a period of at least five hours. From this, and Pryce's later proposal on which the other contracts were based, it can be seen that this mixing was expected to reduce the total to the required 100 lb. In turn, therefore, to obtain the required seventy-five, and ten per cent proportions for saltpetre and sulphur respectively, the total of 8 lb lost during mixing comprised respective losses of 5¼ lb and 2¾ lb.

There were a number of weaknesses in the mid-eighteenth century system. Not only was there a large quantity of saltpetre lost during refining and grinding, but there was also room for much variation at

[22] For example, WO 51/222, p. 161, 30 October 1762; WO 46/8, 8 November 1756, Ordnance Board to East India Company; the refraction in the Seven Years War was agreed at fifteen per cent; Vivian B. Lewes and J. S. S. Brame, *Service Chemistry* (1889 5th edn 1924); I am indebted to Mrs B. Timbers, Royal Artillery Library, for information on this source.
[23] Deposit of £1,200 for 20 tons of saltpetre for preparation of 485 barrels of powder meant £30 for 10 cwt for 12 barrels, £7 10s for 2½ cwt (250 lb) for 3 barrels, and £2 10s for approx: 83 lb for 1 barrel; for Eade & Bridges, see ch. 2.

the mills in the refining, and in the subsequent grinding, sifting and weighing prior to mixing.[24] The importance of the purity of the raw materials had been stressed by a number of people; these included Norton in 1628 and the surveyor general in discussion with the Bristol makers in 1761.[25] Yet, in all contracts of this period more emphasis was placed on the need for thorough mixing of the ingredients than on their individual purity, and there is no evidence of the Ordnance Board investigating the matter further. Not until later in the century were the chemical properties of saltpetre more fully understood and the refining organised more efficiently by Congreve to reduce loss of saltpetre and produce purer powder.

Sulphur was mainly imported from Italy. It was then purchased direct by the powder makers themselves or, in the case of Faversham mills, by an Ordnance messenger who arranged delivery to the Tower and subsequent shipment downstream to Faversham Creek. Refining at the individual mills was by distillation, after which the cooled sulphur was ladled into wooden tubs.

Charcoal was produced by the controlled burning of carefully selected wood. Until the more efficient cylinder method of production of the late eighteenth century this was by the traditional method of preparing stacks of wood in depressions in the ground. The wood was then charred slowly with a restricted air supply by which water and volatile compounds were extracted. Although employed for several centuries this method was, nevertheless, fraught with difficulty in bad weather. In October 1768 heavy rains flooded the charcoal pits and ruined charcoal intended for Faversham mills and this, together with shortage of timber, added significantly to difficulties in gunpowder production at this time.[26] Some powder makers grew their own timber while others purchased it either in the vicinity or further afield. Whether they selected growing wood to be taken to charcoal burners as at Faversham mills under the government, or purchased charcoal from a favoured craftsman burner at some distance as with Benjamin Pryce, depended on both tradition and force of circumstance. The main factor was the availability of suitable wood, increasingly difficult by mid-century, in spite of attempts to form new coppices near mills. Pryce of Faversham and Pearse before him had always purchased their charcoal from Smith & Son of Guildford who purchased wood throughout Surrey. Pryce's statement that 'Smith made coal for most of

[24] WO 47/55 p. 139, 15 February 1760.
[25] Buchanan, 'Black Powder', *Industrial Archeology*, 76–7.
[26] WO 47/72, p. 125, 21 October 1768.

the powder in England', implies supply for a number of other contracted powder makers also.[27]

The wood used was mainly alder, dogwood, willow, or hazel. Smith
& Son used dogwood and alder, 'chiefly the latter, the other being
scarce'. At Faversham the Ordnance staff preferred willow to alder
although the Ordnance Board found hazel best at proof. Faversham, as
other mills, experienced difficulties due to timber shortages. In order to
find suitable willow in September 1760 the master worker at Faversham was paid for horse hire and expenses at the rate of £0 10s a day for
ten days and a colleague for twenty days, while in order to find more in
November the former had to be paid for a further nineteen days. This
was supplemented by wood from crown land at Faversham and 180
sacks of charcoal purchased from Walton's charcoal maker at Waltham
Abbey. A few months later growing hazel wood was purchased elsewhere in Kent and four men employed to cut, flaw, stack and bind it
ready for charring by local charcoal burners under staff supervision.[28]
There were also problems at Waltham Abbey mills, under Ordnance
control from 1787, when wood had to be sought not only in Essex but
also in Kent, Sussex, and Surrey. In 1792 a contract was agreed for the
supply of charcoal for both crown mills from Messrs Young of Dorking
using alder, hazel, birch, and beech, while charcoal burners were sent
from Faversham to char wood at Hythe, Wye, and Charing.[29]

Each stage in the manufacturing process – the refining, weighing,
and grinding of each of the three raw materials, then mixing together,
incorporation, corning, and drying – presented opportunities for variability in the standard of the gunpowder produced. Although the ordnance Office had already stated that too much saltpetre or excessive
drying of it could be as bad as too little, it was not until Congreve's
later improvements in organisation that the significance of accurate
weighing and mixing was fully understood.[30] Weighing was found to be
crucial yet easily misjudged, not necessarily by inaccurate scales but by
insufficient drying of any or all of the three materials; this resulted in
false weight and therefore short measure. Furthermore, before Thompson's scientific experiments of 1797 it was not known that even fully
dried charcoal could re-absorb moisture according to atmospheric con-

27 GMR RB 704, Loseley MSS 1752–59, Peace to Molyneux, April 1759, Molyneux to Peace, October 1759.
28 WO47/56, pp. 182, 323, 331, 402, 5 September, 24, 28 October, 28 November
1760; WO 47/57, pp. 96, 167, 14 February, 13 March 1761; SUPP 5/64 8 May
1764.
29 SUPP 5/115, February 1792.
30 Buchanan, 'Black Powder', 77.

ditions – up to one eighth of its own weight.[31] Powder sent to the Royal Laboratory for analysis in 1770 from Waltham Abbey mills was found to contain insufficient saltpetre.[32] The Office, and subsequently Congreve, had long considered any short measure of saltpetre to be intentional and common among all the makers for deflecting into manufacture for private trade. This was obviously possible, and may have applied on this and many other occasions but given the inefficient methods of the day opportunity for deliberate activity of this sort is unlikely. The refraction had already been calculated to allow for loss of weight from impurities during refining and additional allowance made for further loss during incorporation. Even the slightest inaccuracy in refining, drying, or weighing could affect the powder produced and overall it is more likely that these were the main culprits and intentional short measure less so. Loss of strength in powder due to insufficient mixing was noted by Robins in 1742, but only under Congreve from 1780 was it fully understood that no matter how long the duration of the next stage of incorporation in the damp state, gunpowder would never be of the required standard if its constituents had not been thoroughly blended in their dry state beforehand.[33] Thus Congreve later advocated that instead of simply grinding the raw materials prior to mixing, each was to be pulverised to exactly the same degree of fineness, put in charge tubs in alternate layers, well blended, and passed through a sieve to produce 'as intimate a mixture as possible'.

Inability to achieve or sustain improvement in supply caused considerable frustration at certain of the mills. Norman of Molesey mill voiced his exasperation at a recent proof session at Greenwich to one of the Bristol makers in January 1762; he stated that the whole quantity had been returned although it was the same composition and worked the same number of hours as that which had previously passed.[34] Although this appears to have been an exaggeration, as it must have referred to his December delivery when sixty per cent of his powder failed, his annoyance was understandable as he had managed to improve the standard of his powder significantly during the previous two years; until this recent proof his rate of success for 1761 was ninety-nine per cent. Likewise, in Molyneux's correspondence of October 1759, Pryce of Faversham was stated by Charlton of the Ordnance Office to have had so much powder 'dammed' at one proof that

31 Sir Benjamin Thompson, 'Experiments to determine the Force of fired Gunpowder', *Philosophical Transactions of the Royal Society*, 87 (1797), 290.
32 WO 47/76, p. 226, 7 November 1770.
33 Robins, *New Principles of Gunnery*, pp. 120–1.
34 Buchanan, 'Black Powder', 77.

he 'quite pitied him, as thinking he did not understand it . . . it has made Mr Price very cautious of every branch of the management of it'.[35]

It must be said that during the peak demand years of 1759–62, when pressure on the mills was at its height, certain of the powder makers did manage temporarily to achieve improved results at proof. Examples were Eade & Bridges, Underhill & Ravens, Norman, Taylor and, for the specific period of March 1760 to May 1762, the Waltons. There is insufficient evidence to ascertain whether this was directly related to the overall quantity of gunpowder actually submitted; they do not appear to have either increased the quantity to reach that agreed at contract or markedly lowered it to concentrate on quality. Improvement may have resulted from coincidence, luck or, alternatively, a temporarily decreased commitment to private trade; it is more likely to have been caused by paying the strictest attention to detail at whatever expense, particularly in time. However, some makers did not achieve this temporary improvement in standard at all and none did in the period 1755–8. This suggests that any such effort was difficult or impossible to sustain and is hardly surprising when considering that, as yet, the process lacked a firm scientific basis. It is even less surprising in view of the inconsistencies later found to exist in current methods of proof.

The time for change in the industry was not yet ripe. Still to come were the contributions of science, technology, need, and reorganisation in the Ordnance department. Only then could there be significant improvement in manufacture and proof.

Post 1775 advances in manufacture and proof

A number of factors stimulated improvement in manufacture and proof of gunpowder of the late-eighteenth century. These included: the problems of supply during the Seven Years War; the fact that Faversham mills under the Ordnance Office could fare no better than independent mills; administrative reorganisation within the Ordnance Office after 1783; increased interest in scientific and technological investigation, and improvements in artillery; and the insight and organisational ability of Major William Congreve, deputy, and acting comptroller of the Royal Laboratory, Woolwich from 1783, and comptroller of the Royal Laboratory, and inspector of Gunpowder Manufactories at Faversham and Waltham Abbey from 1789. It is difficult to state with accuracy the effect of the War of American Independence on the

[35] GMR RB 704 Loseley MSS, Molyneux to Peace, October 1759.

Ordnance Office, and to assess which changes in the Office were directly due to Britain's loss and which to other factors. As Ehrman has shown the war demonstrated defects in government administration, particularly financial. Not all problems of the Ordnance Office were caused by war; many had existed already, but war was a stimulant for change even if not the direct cause of it.'[36] Further, this war came on the eve of the most rapid expansion in science and technology in British history, a fact which was to combine with administrative changes in the Ordnance Office to bring about the many advances concerning gunpowder.

In aiming for administrative reform after the war of 1775–83 Pitt considered that control of expenditure was the key. As master general, the Duke of Richmond had already planned financial reform in the Office as part of Shelburne's plan to initiate reform in the executive departments of government. The result was the Duke's proposal in the House of Commons in March 1783, which covered not only finance but also increased efficiency of administration.[37] There had long been a need, now exaggerated by national failure in war, for improved supervision of both manufacture and proof of gunpowder and ordnance. This resulted in the royal warrant of 24 January 1783 which authorised a new establishment for the Office. Among other things, this transferred the supervision of gunpowder manufacture at Faversham and after 1787 Waltham Abbey, and also the proof of powder at Purfleet magazine, from the immediate responsibility of the surveyor general and Board of Ordnance to the comptroller of the Royal Laboratory; the latter nevertheless remained responsible to the master general. Proof was also to involve the fire master and one of the Ordnance officers at Purfleet.[38] It was in this connection that Congreve was to be important in the organisational, scientific, and technological changes in the industry at this time.

Difficulties in manufacture in the mid-eighteenth century can be understood more clearly in the context of the lack of relevant scientific knowledge and efficient organisation prior to 1775. Until then the main written works on the subject were those of Norton, Venn, and Robins[39] Although these would have been of contemporary interest and are valuable in any historical study of the subject they were intended primarily for those concerned with artillery and though practi-

---

36 John Ehrman, *The Younger Pitt* (New York 1969), p. 160.

37 J. E. D. Binney, *British Public Finance and Administration 1774–92* (Oxford 1958), p. 162; J. Debrett, *The History of the Proceedings and Debates of the House of Commons* (1783), ix, p. 447.

38 Charles M. Clode, *The Military Forces of the Crown* (1869), ii, p. 230

39 Norton, *The Gunner*; Venn, *Military and Maritime Discipline*; Robins, *New Principles of Gunnery.*

cal in their advice lack a firm scientific basis. Important, though not acted upon until the late eighteenth century were the assertions made by Venn, and more particularly by Robins, that official methods of testing gunpowder were suspect. Venn merely stated that the 'common eprouvette' or 'powder trier' was 'a great fallacy, for one and the same powder in the same measure and quantities hath raised the cover to different degrees of height'.[40] The eprouvette was an implement for testing the quality and strength of powder. A small amount of gunpowder from the barrel to be tested was inserted into it and inflamed; the explosive force raised the lid to varying heights on a lever or a spring, depending on the powder's quality or strength.

Robins, as Hutton later, was not only concerned with artillery but was also a mathematician.[41] He experimented with the eprouvette, and also with a ballistic pendulum, musket and ball, in order to determine both the force of gunpowder, and a more accurate method of testing its strength. He found that even the 'improved eprouvette' which moved not a lid on a spring, but a weight, was unreliable; as the weight was activated by the instant stroke of the flame and not by its continued pressure it did not record the force of the fired powder with either the accuracy or uniformity required. The eprouvette in use at Greenwich and at Faversham, appears to have been based on the design to which he referred, and which Thompson further criticised later in the century. Robins considered the French method superior: a small mortar was used at an angle of forty-five degrees, no powder being accepted unless three ounces of it threw a solid ball of seven and a half inches in diameter a certain distance. Nevertheless, even he admitted 'a monstrous disproportion of weight of powder to ball, unconnected with conditions of real service'. The British government regarded the method as both time consuming and inaccurate as many barrels were received on the merit of a few.[42] Although Robins' results on velocity were later criticised his work was an important stage in the increased general interest in the action of fired gunpowder. Although many scientific theories of the day were later proved erroneous they were useful concepts at the time, and modern science has evolved through a series of discarded hypotheses:[43] Mathias considers that judging the

[40] Venn, *Military and Maritime Discipline*, p. 21.
[41] This supports Mathias's view that mathematicians may have played a wider role than scientists until later in the century in the endeavour to relate science to industry: Peter Mathias, 'Who Unbound Prometheus? Science and Technical Change, 1600–1800', in A. E. Musson ed., *Science, Technology, and Economic Growth in the Eighteenth Century* (1972), p. 78.
[42] Robins, *New Principles of Gunnery*, pp. 121–3.
[43] A. E. Musson and E. Robinson, 'Science and Industry in the late Eighteenth Century', *Economic History Review*, 2nd series, 13 (1960), p. 244.

effect of the contributions of science by results, rather than by endeavour greatly reduces their importance.[44]

Not until after 1775 was there intensive scientific research by such
men as Hutton, Ingenhousz, and Thompson on aspects of manufacture
and proof, and by Congreve who put the results into practice at Faversham and Waltham Abbey. The work of Charles Hutton, Professor of
Mathematics at the Military Academy, Woolwich, greatly expanded
Robins's earlier experiments on the action of fired gunpowder and was
the subject of a paper to the Royal Society in 1778. Like Robins he
employed the ballistic pendulum, but with cannon instead of musket,
to estimate the velocity of military projectiles. He announced methods
for testing the strength of different types of gunpowder and observations on different quantities of powder, types of shot, and weights and
sizes of gun. These later contributed to more accurate methods of
proof. Among other factors he found that the momentum of the shot,
when fired with the same weight of powder as employed by Robins, was
increased if the shot was proportionately heavier. Also, if the windage
was diminished by the projectile fitting more closely in the bore, only
two thirds of the original quantity of powder was required; if both
principles were applied only half the quantity was required.[45] Although
he still did not understand why some powder was ejected unfired,
which inevitably reduced the overall power, his work made an important contribution to the further understanding and improvement of
gunpowder and its manufacture.

In his paper of 1779, the scientist Ingenhousz informed the Royal
Society of the precise role of each of the three constituents of gunpowder on firing. His most important observation concerned the powder grains: 'The quickness of this propogation of fire depends in great
measure upon the interval or interstices which remain among the
grains of gunpowder.'[46] The importance of corning had indeed long
been recognised but the size of grain for the Ordnance Office, in the
mid-eighteenth century at least, had been the same for all purposes. To
date, there had been no reliable scientific evidence to prove that this
should be otherwise. Ingenhousz now stressed the importance of grains
proportionate to the size of the fire arm. This was found to be important both in the field and for more accurate proof, and was later put into
practice by Congreve.

From the lengthy scientific paper read to the Royal Society in 1781
by Benjamin Thompson (later Count Rumford), it is obvious that this
scientist had undertaken much of his own research before hearing of

[44] Mathias, 'Who Unbound Prometheus?', p. 86.
[45] Hutton, 'The Force of Fired Gunpowder', 83–5.
[46] Ingenhousz, 'An Account', 406.

Hutton's work. Commenced in 1778, his experiments provided further evidence of the uncertainties of current methods of proof. Three specific observations on factors affecting results were as follows: firstly, ramming of gunpowder in the gun increases its force; it must therefore be rammed to the same degree each time; next, the temperature of the firing piece also has a considerable effect on the force of the gunpowder; the warmer the piece through use the more readily the powder takes fire and the greater the effect on the projectile. The instrument should therefore be fired a few times initially, then allowed to cool after each test to gain uniformity of conditions. A standard interval should elapse between each firing; finally, heat and cold, dryness and moisture have a 'very sensible effect on gunpowder to increase or diminish its force'. Therefore, attention should be paid to atmospheric conditions and a different control test used each day with good powder to act as a proof mark.

Thompson stated that in each case the eprouvette was unsuitable. He used instead apparatus similar to that used by Robins and advocated it for all official testing. It comprised a gun barrel suspended twelve feet away from a pendulum of wood in an iron frame against which bullets were fired using half an ounce of powder in a cartridge for each shot. The recoil of the pendulum was measured on a ribbon suspended from it and marked with the proof mark for that day as a control. Thompson further disapproved of the eprouvette, still in common use, as neither the absolute force of powder nor the comparative force of different kinds of it could be determined in circumstances in any way representative of those in the field;

> As the force of gunpowder arises from the action of an elastic fluid generated from it in its inflammation, the quicker the charge takes fire, the more of the fluid will be generated in any given short space of time, and the greater will be its effect upon the bullet. But in the common method . . . the weight by which the powder is confined is so great in proportion to the charge, that there is time . . . for the charge to be all inflamed . . . before the body to be put in motion can be sensibly removed from its place.[47]

He considered that it was possible for the eprouvette to show powder 'better than it really is' but never 'worse than it is'. Congreve later supported this, for the reasons given by Thompson, by stating that 'nothing could be more deceptive than the former vertical eprouvette in which a soft and rotten grained powder could produce a much

[47] Thompson, 'New Experiments on Gunpowder', 298.

greater effect than hard and good serviceable powder', for the reasons given by Thompson.[48]

What is important is that although Thompson, and later Congreve, suggested that more powder was passed at proof by the eprouvette than was warranted, it cannot simply be inferred that too much passed and too little failed for, at Thompson's own admittance the eprouvette was not the only factor involved. The problem at this time was therefore less likely to have have been one of repeatedly passing inferior powder at proof, than of continual unreliability and inconsistency of result, with the continued possibility of an unknown quantity of poor powder being passed or good powder failed. This was due not only to unreliable implements but also to an overall lack of insight into the entire procedure.

Thompson's experiments over the next few years on the action of fired gunpowder confirmed the complexity of the subject. A further paper to the Royal Society in 1797 described the 'enormous and almost incredible force of gunpowder' retarded by its slow combustion rate. The inflammation of gunpowder was rapid, but combustion 'is very far from being so instantaneous as has generally been imagined'. He also answered the question raised by Hutton of why much of the powder was expelled unused from the gun by stating that slow combustibility caused it to inflame but not to burn. This observation was to have implications on the best way to prime a gun.[49] Thompson left much investigation still to be accomplished, for although he was able to account for the force exerted by fired powder he could not understand why it was not greater. The problem remained as late as 1873 when it was decided that the gas of fired gunpowder under apparently similar circumstances but at different times exerts a pressure liable to extreme variation.[50]

As a result of individual observations made by Robins and Hutton the Ordnance Office experimented with comparative methods of proof at Faversham in 1780. These used both the traditional eprouvette and a mortar, and gunpowder from the mills of Ewell and of Oare. The former sample raised the eprouvette 5 inches and the latter nearly 4 inches, while the ranges of shot from the mortar were 215, and 160 feet respectively.[51] The mortar, long recommended by many, was considered the most effective and under Congreve's subsequent administration proof was officially conducted with a mortar for large grained powder

48 Ibid., 299; Congreve, A Statement of facts, pp. 27, 28.
49 Thompson, 'Experiments to determine the Force', p. 284.
50 Francis Bashforth, A Mathematical Treatise on the Motion of Projectiles (1873), p. 12.
51 WO 47/96, p. 837, 21 October 1780.

and by 'comparative penetration' of a bullet fired from a musket barrel for that of small grain.

With regard to artillery design and manufacture, there were marked advances from the mid-1770s including Wilkinson's patent for casting and boring iron guns, and the new carronade from the Carron Company in Scotland; this was a much stronger, lighter gun than any previously.[52] As acting comptroller of the Royal Laboratory, in charge of proof of ordnance and gunpowder from 1783, Congreve recognised the considerable need for corresponding advances in the methods of manufacture and proof of gunpowder. It was, therefore, he who instigated the many changes which were to occur at the crown mills at Faversham and, after 1787, at Waltham Abbey. Further impetus was provided by Pitt's intention in 1783 to recommend to Parliament the sale of Faversham mills, because he had been informed that the powder makers elsewhere could make better and cheaper gunpowder.[53] Congreve's insight and organisational ability were being challenged. He convinced the government of the mills' potential provided they were improved; they would then make a stronger and more durable powder than any previously.[54] His subsequent action resulted in the government decisions not only to retain these mills but also to purchase those at Waltham Abbey from the Walton family. Manufacture at the two crown mills from 1783 was later seen to have made possible both the production of improved quality gunpowder and financial savings. The importance of this was twofold. It identifies the events which began to change the Office's management of manufacture in the late eighteenth century and in so doing identifies all that had been deficient in the middle of the century and before.

In 1785 Congreve experimented with the preparation of charcoal from various types of wood of approximately two inches in diameter in ovens at Faversham.[55] This stimulated detailed correspondence with the Board and also with Bishop Richard Watson, previously Professor of Chemistry at Cambridge, about alternative methods of charcoal preparation. Although the idea had previously been employed on the Continent Watson now designed his own apparatus for charcoal production using the distillation of wood in cylinders. Official experimentation with cylinders took place at Hythe in Sussex from 1787, where it was found possible to produce purer charcoal and therefore powder of greater strength, and also at Fernhurst from 1797. By 1798 Faversham

[52] Campbell, *Carron Company*, p. 91.
[53] Congreve, *A Statement of Facts*, p. 1.
[54] Congreve's work is discussed further by Simmons, *Waltham Abbey* (1963), pp. 11–15.
[55] SUPP 5/65, February 1785.

had its own cylinders for the purpose. Only when its supply ceased due to closure of the Sussex plants in the 1830's did Waltham Abbey mills acquire its own cylinders.[56] In 1785 Congreve invented and installed at Faversham a new press for extracting saltpetre from old powder, a process which had previously taken place only at Woolwich. This press made possible the extraction of more petre than previously, 71 lb instead of 65 lb, a greater financial saving.

Congreve's main contribution was the overall improvement in organisation of the two crown mills. Other improvements, some referred to above, included the use of steam drying not only for new, but for old damp powder returned from naval ships which had previously been sold to the mills after failing proof. Where necessary this was mixed with a certain proportion of new which had been prepared with the purer cylinder charcoal. He also effected greater efficiency in the royal mills by decreasing the quantity of saltpetre issued. He had found that even allowing for a refraction of fifteen per cent as previously, the petre was imperfectly refined at the mills and by refining it again before issue the refraction could be reduced to ten per cent. After the usual double refining at the mills the salptetre was found to be purer and the gunpowder of higher quality as a result. Although Congreve blamed the makers' refining methods it is probable that the grough saltpetre used had always required treble refining. He also found that gunpowder could be made more durable by increased attention to the stages of incorporation, pressing, dusting, and glazing and, obviously influenced by Ingenhousz's work described in 1779, he introduced large grained powder for cannon and small for muskets. Among Congreve's most important changes were those pertaining to proof. Acting on the results of scientific observations he made 'the most severe trials, which now correspond with the use to which the powder is applied in actual practice'.[57] The result was, therefore, the official introduction of the mortar and the musket for proof. However, although it might appear that Britain had lagged behind France in methods of proof there is no evidence that the standard of French powder was any more reliable than British, in spite of Congreve's conviction that 'British powder had been notoriously inferior to that of the enemy and a constant subject of complaint by army and navy'.

[56] SUPP 5/71 March 1797; H. W. Dickinson and E. Straker, 'Charcoal and Pyroligneous Acid Making in Sussex', *Transactions of the Newcomen Society*, 18 (1938), 62, 65; Simmons, *Waltham Abbey*, p. 24; Brayley Hodgetts, *British Explosives Industry*, pp. 20–1. Russell's reference to the method improving performance by 170% should be viewed with caution for improvements in gunpowder were based not on one factor but several, as has already been shown; C. Russell, *Science and Social Change 1700–1900* (1983), p. 124.
[57] Congreve, *A Statement of Facts*, pp. 17–21.

Coleman, a member of the Ordnance staff at Waltham Abbey, though less prominent than Congreve, also played an important part in organisational improvements in the industry. He was primarily involved with the preparation, purity and mixing of each raw material, the cylinder method of charcoal making, and the limitation of the size of each charge.[58] The gunpowder makers failed to take any initiatives themselves in improvement or innovation in manufacture at this time, no doubt because of the precarious nature of the industry.

Comparisons: Britain and France

Finally, manufacture in the eighteenth century in Britain and in France should be compared. There were definite contrasts between the two nations. Prior to the reign of Louis XIV French manufacture was in the hands of the Crown, but as this had proved unsuccessful the facilities were then leased to private entrepreneurs. Buildings included magazines in Paris and the provinces where powder was stored and saltpetre received and refined, and also the provincial mills. Until 1775 the industry underwent further decline due to lack of relevant experience; the entrepreneurs were mainly financiers who often contracted work to others.[59] Unlike Britain, France's main problem during the Seven Years War was a severe shortage of natural saltpetre and consequent heavy reliance on domestic production in sheds and warehouses outside the Paris City wall and in the provinces. This was prepared, as in England two centuries earlier, from a mixture of earth, lime, and vegetable and animal refuse. It was refined once prior to delivery, but was still in a very impure state on arrival at the magazines; it was refined once again before going to the mills. Impurities after one refining were not to be more than thirty per cent. The only natural saltpetre then available to France was that imported from Holland which, with Britain, was the main exporter of the substance from Bengal. Although this cost France twice the price of its domestic petre it continued to import supplies in peacetime. Absence of direct import in the eighteenth century was the result of Britain's increasing dominance in India. By 1774 half of the French requirements were produced at home and half imported from Holland. After this war the French industry was heavily criticised for relying on such obsolete arrangements for the supply of saltpetre. No other major power based its munitions supply on such foundations and

---

[58] R. Coleman, 'The Manufacture and constituent Parts of Gunpowder', 355–65.
[59] Charles Gillispie, *Science and Polity in France at the end of the old regime* (Princeton N.J. 1980), pp. 54–65.

no other government subjected property owners to the degradation of a saltpetre corps.[60]

Comparison between the advances of the two nations indicates that intellectual activity in France in the later eighteenth century had little real practical result in industry and that unlike England most discussion in learned societies remained theoretical in character.[61] There was more state patronage in France than in Britain and although this was to produce little obvious practical result at this time for powder manufacture, there was interest from the Academy of Science from 1775. It was then that administration was again placed in the hands of the State in an effort to improve production. The new administration was the *Régie des poudres*, a government controlled body holding a monopoly on the sale of saltpetre and manufacture of gunpowder, not fully nationalised but in the form of a privately financed commission. The four administrators, who were responsible to the controller general and included the chemist Lavoisier, provided capital and received royalties determined by production levels, while the Crown received the overall profit. With saltpetre supply the main problem the Academy sponsored a competition for scientific study of improved production methods. Lavoisier himself entered. However, by 1786 there was still no discovery worthy of award. In the field of scientific research and technological innovation in gunpowder manufacture in connection with powder manufacture Britain was, undoubtedly, more wide ranging and successful at this time. The common factor between the two nations was improved organisation. Lavoisier had the insight and ability to achieve improved staff training, increased vigilance over costs and book keeping, more efficient saltpetre production with less intrusion on the public, more accurate methods of refining and, as a result, increased production of gunpowder. In 1777 France made sufficient powder to supply North America and by 1788 had reclaimed her self-sufficiency in domestically produced saltpetre which was now said to be of far better quality than during the Seven Years War.[62]

In conclusion, attention given to private trade by the powder makers under contract to the Ordnance Office was undoubtedly the most significant cause of low supply of gunpowder to that department of government, but it was by no means the only one. The fact that Faversham mills under the government control could fare no better means that other factors were involved. Although the advances in

60 Ibid., p. 56.
61 F. Crouzet, 'England and France in the Eighteenth Century' in R. M. Hartwell, (ed.), *The causes of the Industrial Revolution in England* (1967), pp. 160–1.
62 Harold T. Parker, *The Bureau of Commerce in 1781 and its policies with respect to French industry* (Carolina 1979), pp. 156–7; Gillispie, *Science and Polity in France*, pp. 57, 65.

manufacture of the last quarter of the century should not be viewed in isloation from other industries, for they formed only one aspect of what was to be an era of considerable industrial change in Britain, they do nevertheless throw considerable light on the reasons for earlier difficulties. Significant advances in manufacture after 1775 included improved refining and drying of raw materials and their more accurate weighing, grinding and mixing prior to incorporation; the greater understanding of the importance of varying sizes of grain for small arms and large guns, and of different temperatures and therefore effects of firing pieces after varying periods of use; and, among the most important, improved and more reliable methods of proof. These were all the result of increased scientific interest in gunpowder, of certain technological innovations, and of the administration of Congreve who put the new ideas into practice and organised the industry on more efficient lines.

Conclusion

One of the main roles of the Ordnance Office, until its dissolution in 1855, was the provision of guns, ammunition, and gunpowder for the British armed forces at home and overseas. Much has been written about the events of the mid-eighteenth century, especially with regard to military, naval, political and administrative matters; the supply of gunpowder to the Ordnance Office and the role of that department as an instrument of government in the respective purchase and distribution has previously been neglected.

During the Seven Years War of 1756–63 the Ordnance Office was supplied with gunpowder by independent mills until 1759, when it purchased its own mills at Faversham, and by a combination of crown and independent mills thereafter. The number of mills supplying the Office at any one time during the war varied between eight and ten.[1] Apart from the establishment of the foundry at Woolwich for brass ordnance in 1716 this government department had been totally dependent until now on outside manufacturers for all ordnance stores. As far as gunpowder was concerned the Office remained dependent on such manufacturers even after purchase of Faversham mills, though to a lesser extent as the century progressed. For much of the period following the establishment of the first recorded watermill for the purpose in Surrey in the mid-sixteenth century individual gunpowder makers held the monopoly of supply to the Crown; by the end of the seventeenth century supply was by a number of men under contract. Apart from the Civil War period the dominant area of production was south east England because of proximity to London. There was high risk in the manufacture and transportation of this substance, and the mills needed to be within a comparatively short distance of the main government magazine at Greenwich. Although a potentially rewarding industry in wartime when demand for the product was obviously high, it was more precarious than most as demand could fluctuate greatly and with speed, and there was little or no employment in peacetime.

Negotiations between suppliers and the Ordnance Board were unlike those between other suppliers and government departments. The relationship was less formal than, for example, that between the Board

---

[1] Hounslow and Chilworth mills commenced contracts during the war. Faversham mills became crown property in 1759 but continued to supply throughout.

and the iron masters or that between the Navy Board and its suppliers. This was largely due to the nature of the product, tradition, and the limitation of the mills to the South East. The Board did not advertise for tenders for ordnance stores at this time; not until 1783 in its plans for financial saving did it propose methods for open contract, but even then it did not include gunpowder.[2] Contracts were, in part, similar to the 'standing contracts' often employed by the Navy Board, in that individual contractors were nominated as regular suppliers for indefinite periods. The Navy Board, however, usually made agreements for various quantities of materials as required, without separate contracts for each, while the Ordnance Office, although usually dealing with members of families who had supplied over a long period of time, agreed separate contracts for each clearly specified quantity.[3] Although there are indications that on certain occasions the makers combined to negotiate with the Board on such matters as payment, complaints about lack of work in peacetime, and the nomination of a representative to examine government saltpetre, most of the arrangements appear to have been conducted with individual men.[4]

There were, as previously indicated, numerous difficulties between Office and powder makers in the stark contrast between peace and war. In war there was high demand, contracts, and full employment at the mills. In peace there were few if any contracts as requirements for basic defence and military exercise and training were comparatively low. Gunpowder could not be stockpiled in anticipation of war as with other armaments as it could not be stored indefinitely. Although in 1749 the mills were kept busy with reprocessing 6,150 barrels of unserviceable government powder for return to store, and a further 1,600 barrels were later sold to the mills outright for purposes of private trade, there were no contracts for new stock between 1749 and the end of 1754.[5] Similarly, following the Seven Years War there were no contracts until the end of 1765 and then not with all mills.[6] The problem at the mills was that not only were there few or no government contracts in peacetime but, unlike some other industries, no possibility of adaptation for any other purpose. For this reason those concerned were often involved in other trades outside their mills or already had the advantage of a very definite social or commercial standing. Most important, employment at the mills in peacetime was usually concerned

[2] Debrett, *Proceedings and Debates of the House of Commons*, 452.
[3] Bernard Pool, *Navy Board contracts, 1660–1832* (1966), p. 101. Appendix, table 7.
[4] WO 47/34 27 January 1749; see also ch. 4; see also ch. 8 and appendix 1, Oare mills.
[5] See appendix 2, table 1.
[6] Ibid., table 7.

entirely with private trade and when war brought long awaited prestigious contracts with the Ordnance Office the two sources of trade were undertaken simultaneously. This was to result in severe problems during the Seven Years War.

The effective conduct of war was dependent on the adequate quantity and distribution of men, ships, ordnance equipment and stores. Distribution of gunpowder from store at Greenwich to the outports and garrisons in Britain and overseas was well established and routine by the mid-eighteenth century. Military and naval strategy in time of war, together with evaluation of the ordnance stores required for combat, were decided by the Cabinet. The Cabinet's role in this administrative process had increased since the early part of the century.[7] Administrative difficulties between the Ordnance Office, the Privy Council, and other government departments were always worse in time of war, and particularly so in this, the most demanding war yet. This put additional pressure on traditional routines and links between different government departments in serving the armed forces. Although, in general, routine communication between Privy Council, Cabinet, and Ordnance Office was well established, the main exception to this concerned supplies for North America. Considerable strain was placed on the Ordnance Office by the demand for men, ammunition, and equipment in the fight against the French. There were many problems caused by the initial political instability, uncertainty of the government in its relationship with North American governors on who should supply men and equipment, and difficulty throughout in judging the quantity of stores required in unfamiliar terrain and methods of combat, given the delays in communication over long distances. Requests were of a piecemeal nature with consequent delays in preparation and dispatch. This in turn caused problems between Office and Admiralty regarding shipping and convoy.

The expansion in the armed forces and the Ordnance Office of the late seventeenth, and early eighteenth centuries described by Tomlinson resulted in the need for improved administration and a corresponding increase in stores.[8] There does not appear, however, to have been any marked change in the basic methods of administration of the purchase, testing, storage and issue of gunpowder during the intervening period or, for that matter, any sign of obvious change in the business relationship between Office and mills. On the eve of the Seven Years War there was no reason on either side to consider that methods which had sufficed in the basic needs of previous wars would not do so again.

[7] Tomlinson, *Guns and Government*, pp. 18–19.
[8] Ibid., p. 219.

What neither the Ordnance Board nor its suppliers could possibly have foreseen was the scale of the Seven Years War, to be the most severe, extensive and demanding to date. This war was to result in the need for more ordnance stores than ever before and what must have entailed the greatest test yet for supplier and administrator. From a total absence in demand between 1750 and 1754 mounting Anglo-American conflict brought a sudden and immediate need for an increase in stock in December of that year. With respect to gunpowder in particular, there were immense problems on both sides throughout the war. The Office experienced low stock due to inadequate supply from the mills. Although it met the needs of the Army, albeit with frequent delays, it could not supply certain ships of the Royal Navy at the height of the war and, equally serious, it was prevented from running an efficient service throughout. The powder makers tried, with extreme difficulty, to satisfy their two markets simultaneously, with serious consequences for the Office. Among the more interesting aspects to emerge from this study is how the Board tried to deal with the situation.

It is important not to view this shortage of powder as being the result solely of a scale of demand too great for the mills to meet. The mills could, and did, produce large quantities. The problem was that although many hundreds of barrels of powder were submitted to Greenwich for testing many of these failed and were returned; also, much of the production was intended for private trade, in connection with which it is impossible to calculate the total.[9] How much failed powder was the result of the general lack of scientific and technological knowledge of the period regarding manufacture and proof, and how much it was the result of concentrating on private trade is difficult to assess. It is likely to have been a combination of these. As private trade was an essential source of employment in peacetime it could not be allowed to lapse in war; also, merchants paid more and were satisfied with stock of lower quality. Peace offered little employment, yet war too much. The mills could not satisfy both markets simultaneously. Although the Office was not competing for the same powder, as it required stock of higher quality, it was competing for the makers' use of time. The Board also feared that saltpetre intended for government powder would be employed for trade. There were, therefore, problems for the Ordnance Office which had low stock throughout and was unsuccessful in its attempts to correct the situation, and also for the mills where, although total output was large, the fact that both markets had to be supplied simultaneously, made it impossible to provide the government with the quantity or quality agreed. Even worse, for both

[9] Some idea of the minimum quantity can be gained from appendix 3, table 17.

sides, were the fluctuation and unpredictability of proof results. The Board recognised the problem of private trade at an early stage of the conflict. This was not a new situation, but because of the greatly expanded scale of demand of both war and trade it was now very much more serious.[10] It was impossible for the Board to impose any penalty for, apart from imported Dutch powder at the beginning of the war, they were totally dependent on this source of supply. For various reasons there were no other suitable mills available at this time.

With increased British commitment in North America, the dispatch of troops to Germany from July 1758, and continuing low stock, the Office responded in three main ways in an attempt to improve supply: by financial incentives; by organising crown purchase of Faversham mills; and by use of the legislation to limit private trade. The latter two were unprecedented. None of these was effective. Financial incentives were concerned with the Board's desire for expansion of buildings at the mills and with improved output; no one was tempted by the first and the second produced an insignificant response. Faversham mills fared no better under direct government administration than under private ownership, no better than other mills and, in this war at least, brought more problems than relief.

The aim of the legislation, introduced in October 1755, was to limit the powder makers' trade outlets, and therefore minimise time spent at the mills on private trade and compel concentration on government contracts. No non-government arms or powder were to be shipped without licence. Although arms were included there was much less concern about these.[11] In theory, such legislation was the answer to all problems; in practice it proved to be almost entirely meaningless. As far as gunpowder was concerned few applications for licence were refused, trade continued throughout the war, and the legislation was ineffective.

Why was this so? From the very beginning the Ordnance Office and Privy Council were powerless to effect the full powers of the legislation. Investigation of the reasons for this has produced considerable detail of close links between the gunpowder trade, the financing of war, government contracts, City companies, members of parliament and prominent individuals, many of whom were essential to the secretaries of state for their own political support. The war was popular in the City where Pitt's successful strategy resulted in a marked accession of trade which, in turn was a substantial element in meeting the expense of the

---

[10] There had been provision for the prohibition of the trade in gunpowder in previous legislation; see ch. 7.
[11] On the few occasions when licences for powder were rejected, the arms and ammunition were usually allowed.

war.[12] This was dilemma indeed. Although supportive of the legislation initially, neither the Privy Council which administered it, nor the Ordnance Board as advisers, had any chance of improving supplies for the armed forces by putting it into full effect because of the very widespread opposition to such a move. Merchant strength in this case was similar to that concerning the search for crew for trading ships at the expense of naval manning.[13] Although greatly detrimental to the efficient performance of government contracts the trade was too important to be prohibited.

The way in which the legislation might have been applied more effectively and with less likelihood of restriction to trade would have been to identify immediately which applicants purchased stock from the contracted mills and which from those mills further afield which posed no direct problem; at least some degree of limitation could then have been achieved. No such enquiry was made until much later in the war and even then not with any sense of purpose and certainly no positive result. Meantime, many hundreds of barrels left the mills for export not only in the names of merchants to whom they were sold but also in the names of the contracted powder makers themselves.

The government's decision to purchase mills of its own was intended as an additional source of national supply and, as already stated, for possible eventual decrease of dependence on other mills. What the Ordnance Board did not realise was that the problem of supply was not caused solely by private trade; it was caused also by technological limitations both in production and proof. Not only did it suffer for many years from legal complications concerning purchase, but its staff managed no better at Faversham mills than powder makers at other mills. Most of its staff lacked the experience which other men or families had accumulated over many years. Considerable administrative organisation was required before the mills could contribute effectively to national supply.

It was not generally recognised in the mid-eighteenth century that in the current level of scientific and technological knowledge, and organisation of manufacture it was virtually impossible for the quantity or quality of gunpowder to be improved to any significant degree. Although the Board seriously questioned the application and intent of its powder makers, there is evidence that the latter continually tried to meet the required standard and were perplexed by the very varied results at proof. Although long criticised by certain artillerists, official proof methods were not yet critically examined by the Office. Not

[12] D. M. Joslin, 'London Bankers in Wartime 1739–84' in L. S. Pressnell (ed.), *Studies in the Industrial Revolution* (1960), pp. 171–2.
[13] Gradish, *British Navy*, p. 203.

until later was the entire procedure changed. Information from firstly, papers read to the Royal Society from 1775, and from the statements of Congreve, supervisor at the crown mills, on his reorganisation of the industry and, secondly, from late eighteenth century advances in science, technology, and organisation of manufacture makes it possible to identify and analyse certain mid-century problems.[14] Although unsuccessful in producing an immediate increase in supply in the Seven Years War it can be seen that crown ownership of Faversham mills was of later value in this context in demonstrating to the Board that manufacturing methods and organisation needed investigation and that improvements could be made within the industry itself. Among the main advances towards the end of the century were improved refining and drying of the raw materials, more accurate weighing and mixing prior to incorporation, variation in the size of grain, increased understanding of the chemical properties and action of fired gunpowder, and more reliable methods of proof. When comparing eighteenth century manufacture and standard of product between Britain and France it is apparent that the former had no more problems or weaknesses than France at this time, and probably many less.[15]

Ordnance records show that for the years 1755–7 only about half the quantity of gunpowder agreed was actually supplied. Even the more realistic target of the following year was not met.[16] How, in spite of the unprecedented severity and geographical extent of conflict, could Britain have fought and even won the Seven Years War with what must appear to have been inadequate stock? Was the Ordnance Office trying to obtain more from the mills than was actually required and, if so, was it not really as short of stock as it suggested? Firstly, it is impossible to define the meaning of 'too much', for it was not a question of ordering more from the mills than the armed forces would require but rather that of needing more than might actually be used. More was needed in store and in the field than the minimum requirements. The quantity the Office actually issued to the armed forces was based on the respective orders from the secretaries of state and the Admiralty. Its own responsibility, with regard to the quantity it sought from the mills, was in connection with its magazines at home and overseas; it was from these that the powder was issued. There was certainly a severe shortage at this time but it is likely that it was the Office and its magazines rather than the armed forces which took most strain at this time. British powder was supplemented by Dutch until the beginning of 1759, which partially removed the burden of the disappointing output

14 Congreve, A *Statement of facts*.
15 See ch. 10.
16 See appendix 2, tables 1, 5.

from the mills. It was only subsequently, with British forces in Germany from mid-1758, Pitt's decision to make a greater contribution of powder to the colonists in North America, increased conflict, and increasing demands from bases in other parts of the world, that more pressure was put on the Office. It was continually running out of stock in one magazine and having to ship in stock from another which was expensive and time consuming. Ordnance staff did what they could to run the service as well as they were able; there were problems in North America with delays in receipt of stores for certain campaigns but these were usually due to delays in dispatch beyond the Board's control rather than inability to supply the correct quantity. The fact that large quantities of stock could be on the high seas for weeks at a time did nothing to improve the situation but, in spite of delays, often considerable, it would appear that the majority of orders were eventually met. The main exception to this was when certain ships of the Royal Navy at Portsmouth and Plymouth could not be supplied at the height of the war. In short, therefore, the Office did not seek more powder than was necessary, but it certainly received much less than it sought.

It has been possible to identify the many problems of both Ordnance Office and gunpowder makers in the manufacture, supply, and distribution of powder in the mid-eighteenth century, and to understand more clearly their respective causes. As far as apparent inefficiencies in the system were concerned it has to be recognised that it was usually the firm, traditional, and unchanging methods to it was accustomed which enabled the Office to function as effectively as it did within the very great demands that it faced. Any change in administrative methods in this government department would have necessitated simultaneous change within others too. War was not the best time for that sort of change, while peace usually eliminated the immediate need for it. To suggest that the Ordnance Office, its gunpowder suppliers, or other departments with which it liaised should, or could have functioned any more effectively during this period underestimates the very complex circumstances and restrictions of the day.

APPENDIXES

APPENDIX 1

Gunpowder mills supplying the Ordnance office in the mid-eighteenth century

The mills supplying the Ordnance Office over the longest, continuous period during the century were those of Bedfont, Faversham, and Waltham Abbey. All but two of the mills of the Seven Years War supplied also in the War of the Austrian Succession; the exceptions were those of Chilworth and of Hounslow. Chilworth mills were established in the early seventeenth century but do not appear to have been in production during the earlier war; those of Hounslow were only established in 1757. The individual descriptions that follow link closely with both the discussion in the main text concerning the Ordnance Office, supply, trade, and problems of production, and with the tables in the appendix of contracts, deliveries, prices, trade, and proof. Precise dates of powder makers' commencement at the mills are given where known. Names are those known to have been at the mills between the dates given. This does not necessarily mean that they supplied the government continuously in the intervening period; in peacetime it was difficult to gain government contracts and in time of mill disrepair, especially as a consequence of an explosion, production often had to be interrupted.

Bedfont mills, Middlesex

Located on the Duke of Northumberland's River in the parish of East Bedfont.

Eighteenth century gunpowder makers: Capt. John Richardson, 1700–4; Henry Bosseville, 1704–11; Jonathan Fogg, by 1720–1725; Catherine Fogg, 1725–7; Samuel Underhill, 1727–55; Samuel Underhill & Thomas Ravens, April 1755 – October 1762; Thomas Ravens & John Taylor, October 1762–5; Mark Nesfield, January 1766–7; Mark

Nesfield & Richard Taylor, 1767–89; Richard Taylor & Heneage Legg, from 1789.[1]

The upper and lower mills were on individual sites to the north west of Baber Bridge. By 1755 a large area was covered by the many mill buildings, set among orchards and avenues of trees. Included were incorporating mills, saltpetre and brimstone refining houses, powder drying houses, offices, and Samuel Underhill's house and gardens. The Upper site had both horse and water powered mills while the Lower site, converted from a paper mill in about 1690, was powered by water alone. Another powder mill, to the south of Baber Bridge was leased with these; it functioned until 1750.[2] During the century all three mills were leased from the Duke of Somerset and, subsequently, from the Earl and Countess, and Duke and Duchess, of Northumberland respectively.

Until 1704 the lessee and gunpowder maker was John Richardson; his widow Elizabeth took over the lease in 1705 and the business was then run by Bosseville, who appears to have been Richardson's son-in-law; he was followed by Fogg.[3] The next lease, from 1725 and again for a period of twenty-one years, was held not by the powder maker, as with Richardson, but by Fogg's brothers-in-law John Barnard of Clapham and Nicholas Godschall of East Sheen.[4] Sir John Barnard, knighted in 1732 and Lord Mayor in 1737, was the brother of Catherine Fogg, Jonathan's widow. He was also grandfather of Susanna Norman and Jane Sutton (nee Hankey) of Molesey mills.[5] Godschall, described as an ironmonger, owned property in London and East Sheen; he inherited the manor of Weston in Albury, Surrey from his brother Robert who was Lord Mayor in 1741 and MP for the City of London.[6] From 1746 the lessees were Barnard, and James Underhill, the latter a wine merchant of Albemarle Street, London. The annual rent at this time was £45 together with 50 lb of gunpowder.[7] With the new lease of 1767 to Richard Taylor, the annual rent was increased to £200 and 100 lb of gunpowder.[8] Until approximately 1750 the lessees also held another powder mill to the south of Baber Bridge although it

[1] Taylor sometimes spelt Tayler.
[2] SH Northumberland Papers BXIII 7a, Map East Bedfont mills 1755; MXIV 21 1751; Philo and Mills, 'Bedfont Gunpowder Mills', 97.
[3] SH MXIV 2h, 1705; WO 47/23, p. 123, 4 February 1706.
[4] SH MXIV 2i, 1725; PROB 11 594, 1723.
[5] See ch. 8 for Sir John Barnard's position in the City.
[6] Manning and Bray, *History and Antiquities of the County of Surrey*, ii, p. 127; PROB 11 762, 1748.
[7] SH MXIV 2k, 1746; MXIV 21, 1751.
[8] SH MXIV 2m, 1767.

is unclear whether this played a part in supply to the government in conjunction with the Bedfont mills.

Fogg owned land and a magazine at Barking Creek in Essex in partnership with the powder makers of Waltham Abbey, Molesey, Faversham and Oare mills.[9] Fogg's widow Catherine continued the gunpowder business at her husband's death in 1725 and was joined by Samuel Underhill in 1727 after their marriage. Underhill, grandson of Sir William Underhill, inherited Idlicote Manor in Warwickshire; he had an office in Threadneedle Street in the City and, apart from his position as gunpowder maker and merchant, he was a governor of the Foundling Hospital, and of St Bartholemew's Hospital. Underhill continued the business until his death in 1762. He left approximately £1,400; the remainder of his estate was unspecified.[10] Simultaneously he used the magazine at Barking Creek and managed the site there on behalf of Catherine's two daughters.[11] Bethia Fogg married John Taylor, who replaced Underhill at the mills; her marriage settlement of £12,000 in 1740 was arranged by her two uncles, Barnard and Godschall, who were also guardians, and trustees.[12] Bethia's sister Catherine married Heneage Legge, son of the Earl and Countess of Dartmouth, who purchased Idlicote manor from Underhill in 1754, and joined his nephew Richard Taylor, son of John, in the business in about 1789.[13] In addition to shared land at Barking Creek, proprietors of these mills were joint lessees of a powder magazine at Liverpool; in 1737 this was shared with Faversham and Molesey mills. This would have been in connection with the African slave trade.[14]

Chilworth mills, Surrey

Located on the Tillingbourne, a tributary of the River Wey, in the parish of St Martha near Guildford.

Eighteenth century gunpowder makers: Francis Grueber, for an unknown period from 1728; Edward Pryce, by May 1759; Edward Pryce & Isaac Dent, by April 1766; Isaac Dent, by 1770–90; William Tinkler, from 1790, joined by Edmund Hill in 1796.

---

9 SH DXXII 5g (1), June 1720; see Molesey mills.
10 BL Add MS 37827, W. Underhill, 'Underhill family connections' (1898); PRO PROB 11 880, 1762; J. H. Morrison, *The Underhills of Warwickshire* (Cambridge 1932), pp. 166–7.
11 SH DXXII 5g (2), 1738.
12 GLRO Acc. 606/61b, 1740.
13 Underhill, 'Underhill family collections'.
14 Ibid; see also ch. 8.

The mills were established in the 1620s and a contract was agreed to supply the Crown in November 1635.[15] To what extent they were productive during the early eighteenth century is uncertain. Francis Grueber leased the mills in 1728 although it is unlikely that they were working at that date.[16] This may have been the powder maker of the same name then at Oare and Faversham mills who was followed at his death in 1730 by a son of the same name; whether either supplied from all three sites simultaneously is not clear.[17]

The first definite agreement for supply from the mills during this period was with Edward Pryce on 26 May 1759.[18] Pryce, an attorney of Gray's Inn, was recommended to the Office by Captain Benjamin Pryce of Faversham mills when the latter withdrew from business and sold his mills to the Crown.[19] Although not known if the two were related there was certainly a business link; both men were trustees of Faversham mills which were later purchased by the Crown.[20] Most correspondence with the Board concerning Faversham and Chilworth mills was conducted by a William Stevens, firstly on behalf of Benjamin and, on the latter's retirement, of Edward. It would seem that Stevens was in daily charge of each mill in turn. An individual of the same name in partnership with Pearse at Faversham was supplying the Office at an earlier date.[21] They may have been the same person.

Edward Pryce supplied powder during the remainder of the Seven Years War. One of his main problems was the distance from London and delays in carriage by barge down the Thames. On more than one occasion he missed an increased payment for delivery for this reason. One example was in October 1761, when 200 barrels of powder were delayed at Guildford while waiting for a vessel.[22] There may have been problems at the mills at the end of the war for not until November 1763 did he complete his last contract dated September 1762 for 242½ barrels of powder.[23] By October 1765 the mills were in disrepair.[24] Once they were active again, by now under Pryce and partner Dent, the Office had ceased to require further stock and a request by the partnership for a contract was refused. By 1770 Dent was working

[15] Giuseppi, VCH Surrey, pp. 318–19; Crocker, Chilworth Gunpowder, p. 3; with reference to the Civil War period see Roy, 'Royalist Ordnance Papers', 43, 49.
[16] Crocker, Chilworth Gunpowder, pp. 5, 6.
[17] See Oare mills.
[18] PRO WO 51/206, p. 57, 26 May 1759; WO 47/54, p. 138, 10 May 1759.
[19] WO 47/53, p. 473, 28 April 1759.
[20] See ch. 9.
[21] WO 47/48, p. 84, 27 July 1756; WO 47/60, p. 198, 11 September 1762.
[22] WO 47/58, p. 371, 24 November 1761; WO 47/66, p. 172, 25 October 1765.
[23] WO 47/62, p. 264, 25 November 1763.
[24] WO 47/66, p. 172, 25 October 1765.

the mills alone. At his death in 1790 he left the business and lease to a close friend, William Tinkler.[25]

Edward Pryce was involved in a legal battle concerning not only Faversham mills, but also seven acres of land at Chilworth for which he paid £640 in 1765. Ten years later he mortgaged the land to his sister Judith Pryce of St John's, Westminster. However, attorney William Anson claimed subsequently that Pryce, owing him £1,300 transferred the land to him as part payment of his debt but with no reference to the mortgage. Both Pryce and his sister eventually lost both land and money, Pryce became bankrupt, and was later arrested and held in Fleet prison where he claimed dishonest treatment by Anson.[26]

The mills were owned from 1720 as part of the Chilworth estate by Sarah, Duchess of Marlborough, and subsequently by the Earls Spencer. The estate was sold in 1796 to Edmund Hill of Hounslow powder mills. Hill left Chilworth mills and most of his lands there and elsewhere to colleagues John Fish and John Hambrough.[27]

Dartford mills, Kent

Located on the River Darent in the parish of Wilmington.

Eighteenth century gunpowder makers: Edward Pyke & Thomas Edsall, 1732–48; Edward Pyke & Thomas Edsall Sr & Jr, by April 1755 until June 1757; Thomas Edsall Sr & Jr, June 1757–69; Thomas Edsall Jr, by 1775–8; Pigou & Andrews, from 1778.

Pyke and Edsall, powder makers and merchants of Tooley Street, Southwark started the business in 1732.[28] This was the first recorded use of the site for gunpowder production. In 1740 when Pyke described himself also as a 'grocer' they insured buildings near their mills with the Sun Insurance Office. These included a dwelling house, stable, barn, cowhouse, and saltpetre refining house, together with goods and stock, valued at £1,200; any loss caused by fire at the powder works was to be excluded.[29] Obviously due to the risk involved this is one of only a few insurance records pertaining to buildings near such a mill; there is no evidence of any gunpowder maker being able to insure his mill during

[25] PROB 11 1189, March 1790, Isaac Dent.
[26] GMR 43/78, 16 December 1775, 10 January 1776; 43/79, 9 January 1776; 43/82, April 1786.
[27] Giuseppi, VCH Surrey, p. 327.
[28] S. K. Keyes, Dartford: further historical notes (Dartford 1938), p. 132.
[29] GL Sun Insurance 11936.56, p. 562 No. 86503, 8 January 1740; GL Hand in Hand Insurance 8674.59, p. 185 No. 8841, 26 August 1740.

the century.[30] The partnership of Pyke & Edsall was that most favoured by the Ordnance Board during the Seven Years War.[31]

In 1778 Thomas Edsall Jr was bankrupt, although there is no evidence that this was directly connected with his powder business.[32] The mills were then purchased by Pigou and his nephew Miles Andrews, who were already running the business at Oare mills. The partnership had a gunpowder magazine for storage purposes at Erith. During 1759 and 1760 Frederick Pigou Jr exported powder to Philadelphia. Frederick Pigou Sr was a director of the East India Company between 1758 and 1774.[33]

Ewell mills, Surrey

Located on the Hogsmill River in the parish of Ewell.

Eighteenth century gunpowder makers: Jonathan Eade, from October 1745; Jonathan Eade & Alexander Bridges, by 1751–81; Alexander Bridges Jr & Robert Bridges, 1781–98.

The precise date of commencement of business is unknown. Reference has been made to powder mill buildings at this site in 1720.[34] However, there is no mention in Ordnance Office records of a contract with any person likely to have been at this location before 1745, the date of the first contract with Eade.[35] The first mention of Bridges at the site concerns changes made by him to the river 'the stream which Alexander Bridges turned in 1751 out of its ancient course . . . for the use of the mills erected by him'.[36] It is possible that either Eade commenced here alone and Bridges joined him in 1751, or that the contracts of the War of the Austrian Succession, although only in the name of Eade, included both men.

Eade and Bridges were joined in the gunpowder business by William Wilton in March 1763, although Wilton is not named in Ordnance records pertaining to gunpowder.[37] Wilton was also in a separate partnership with Eade throughout the Seven Years War for supplying the

[30] See ch. 1.
[31] See ch. 4.
[32] Keyes, *Dartford*, p. 132.
[33] See ch. 8.
[34] James Thorne, *Handbook to the Environs of London* (1876, 2nd edn Bath 1970), p. 213.
[35] See appendix 2, Gunpowder and the Ordnance Office, table 1.
[36] SRO 2238/10/8, Map of Ewell River, 1753; 2238/10/114 Lease, Northey to Bridges, 25 January 1780.
[37] WO 47/61, p. 137, 11 March 1763.

Ordnance Office and East India Company with cannon and shot; both men were ship chandlers, in connection with which Eade held warehouses in Wapping near King Edward's Stairs. This was also the location of their offices.[38] Eade was a director of the Hand in Hand Fire Insurance office from 1761.[39]

In Surrey, Bridges held freehold, leasehold, and copyhold land in Ewell and the freehold estate of Langshot Manor in Horley, together with land in Chipstead.[40] In addition to the land he inherited, Alexander Bridges Jr owned estates in Banstead and Charlwood. The Ewell land on which the mills were located was owned by the Duke of Bedford, and subsequently by William Northey.

The Ewell business consisted of a co-partnership of Bridges with Eade and Wilton. The former had one half share, and the latter one quarter share each of mill buildings, utensils, stock in trade, profits and losses, all of which were quoted in Alexander Bridge's will and valued at £17,680 15s in 1778.[41] The co-partnership was due to expire on 25 March 1781. Bridges planned that unless all should agree to continue at that date, or if he should die beforehand, his eldest son Alexander would inherit his half, and another son Robert would have Wilton's quarter share. If Eade did not wish to continue, then Robert would have his share also. By 1 March 1781 both Alexander Sr and Wilton had died; Eade appears to have withdrawn and the business was continued by Alexander Jr and Robert until 1798.[42] On Alexander's death at this date the business was left in trust to his son Henry (later Sir Henry) and run temporarily by Robert and another brother John. The business stayed in the Bridges family until 1861. Apart from his Surrey estates and the powder business left to his eldest son, Alexander Sr left £3,000 to each of his nine younger children.

Ewell mills possessed one of the earliest examples of a horse mill with cast iron bed and runners instead of stones.[43] This was used as a model for a new horse mill at Faversham mills.

Hounslow mills, Middlesex

Located on the River Crane in the parish of Twickenham.

Eighteenth century gunpowder makers were brothers Edmund and John Smyth, June 1757–February 1758; Edmund and John Smyth, &

[38] GL Hand in Hand Insurance 8674.73, p. 57 No. 39657, 25 October 1748.
[39] See ch. 8.
[40] PROB 11 1075, March 1781.
[41] Ibid.
[42] WO 47/97, p. 248, 13 March 1781.
[43] WO55/2269 23 February 1761.

Edmund Hill, February 1758–February 1760; John Smyth & Edmund Hill, February 1760–November 1764; Edmund Hill, from November 1764.

John and Edmund Smyth, of Whitton and Hounslow respectively, were termed 'breeches makers' of Hounslow when purchasing a freehold corn mill in Isleworth in 1746, and merchants of Bankside in Southwark ten years later.[44]

The gunpowder mills, situated at Milford Stakes, had been built by the Smyth brothers by mid-1757. Whether or not the entire mills, or part, were designed originally for corn grinding is unclear, but the lease from the owners, the Earl and Countess of Northumberland, dated November 1757, clearly states that the Smyths had expended £1,000 in erecting a corn mill. This was for 'grinding corn only' and, if the mills should be used for making gunpowder without written consent, the property would be repossessed.[45]

Consent for powder making at these mills was not given until February 1768 when the lease was renewed.[46] Yet, the brothers had already proposed contract with the Ordnance Office in June 1757.[47] The answer to the mystery appears to lie in a promise made by the Earl to local inhabitants before the mill was built that there would be no gunpowder production at the site.[48] It is obvious that once constructed the mills were soon thus used and it is most unlikely that the Earl would have been unaware of the fact. The new twenty-one year lease of 1768 was delayed as a result of John Smyth's death which left Hill in sole possession of the mills. This included permission for gunpowder production. At the same time the annual rent was increased from £30 to £50 together with one barrel of gunpowder to be delivered to Syon House.[49]

The Smyths were joined by their nephew Edmund Hill in February 1758. The mills suffered serious damage from explosion in the following year as a result of which financial assistance was sought from the Ordnance Office for rebuilding.[50] The mills were worked entirely by pestles rather than stones, which caused a problem in 1772 when the government banned the use of such machinery in all but certain mills in Sussex due to increased risk of explosion. Hill was awarded compen-

---

[44] GLRO Acc. 1319/27A, 20 October 1746;
[45] SH Northumberland Papers MXIII 11e, November 1757; the mill should not be confused with the brothers' freehold corn mill in Isleworth.
[46] SH MXIII 11e & f, February 1768.
[47] WO 47/49, p. 634, 24 June 1757; WO 47/50, p. 8, 5 July 1757.
[48] W. S. Lewis (ed.), *Horace Walpole's Correspondence* (Oxford 1967), p. 365.
[49] SH MXIII 11e & f, February 1768.
[50] This is discussed more fully in ch. 4.

sation of £1,500 towards the cost of replacing his seven pestle mills with sufficient stones to produce the same quantity. The pestles worked 1,350 lb of powder in 24 hours. The cost of the sets of stones, brick-work and millwright's work was estimated at £2,509.[51]

Edmund Smyth's departure from the business in February 1760 and John's death in November 1764, left Hill supplying the Ordnance Office alone. John Smyth left £3,300 to his sister, £500 to his niece Mary, and his half part in both the freehold corn mills at Isleworth, and the lease, business and stock in trade at the powder mills to Hill.[52] At his death in 1774, Edmund Smyth left all his freehold and leasehold property to his sister and to Hill.[53]

With the help of property left by his uncles Hill gradually increased his land holding. This eventually included 1,000 acres and a powder mill in Stanwell in Middlesex, the Isleworth property, the Chilworth estate and powder mills purchased in 1796, and lands at Woking. The latter, including a corn mill, were purchased towards the end of Hill's life from William Ashby, miller of Bermondsey.[54] When he later lost his sight Hill was helped in the business by colleagues John Fish and John Hambrough. He left over £67,000 together with a considerable amount of land, most of which was left to Fish and Hambrough. Fish had married Hill's cousin Mary, the daughter of Edmund Smyth. Hill also left a yearly sum of £250 to the widow of William Godin, formerly the manager at the mills.[55]

Molesey mills, Surrey

Located on the River Mole in the parish of East Molesey.

Eighteenth century gunpowder makers: Robert Stiles, by 1720–8; Robert Norman, 1728–54; Robert & James Norman, by 1754–7; James Norman, 1757–62; Susanna Norman, January–March 1763; Susanna Norman & Thomas Sutton, 1763–7; Thomas Sutton & Beaumont Hotham, 1767–80.

This, the Upper mill, was one of two powder mills in the locality; the other, Lower mill, had ceased production in the 1660s.[56] The mills were

---

51 *Journals of the House of Commons*, 33, pp. 747, 755, 759, 769, 12–18 May 1772.
52 PROB 11 904, November 1764.
53 PROB 11 994, January 1774.
54 PROB 11 1505, November 1809; See also Chilworth mills.
55 Ibid.
56 Crocker, *Gunpowder Mills Gazetteer*, p. 21.

part of the manor of East Molesey later held by the Clarke family.[57] The powder maker and lessee of the mills by 1720 was Robert Stiles of Molesey and Lambeth. In June of that year Stiles, Grueber of Oare and Faversham, Walton of Waltham Abbey, and Fogg of East Bedfont, formed a co-partnership to purchase four acres of ground at Barking Creek from John Weldale for a total of £170.[58] This was for the construction of a powder magazine as the result of an Act of 1718, which made it unlawful from the following year to keep more than 600 lb of gunpowder within the Cities of London and Westminster or their suburbs, or within three miles of the Tower or St James's Palace.[59]

Robert Norman, also of Molesey and Lambeth, took over the business in about 1728. Stiles died five years later.[60] Robert had married Stiles' daughter and been given £1,713 as part of a marriage portion of £2,800, and received Stiles's share in the Barking ground in lieu of the remainder.[61] This share passed subsequently to James Norman and was later leased by Norman's two sisters to Thomas Sutton and Beaumont Hotham.[62] Although the other powder makers involved in the Barking purchase held government contracts for supply during the 1720s and 1730s there was no contract recorded for Molesey mills at this time. Norman's first contract was in December 1739 after which he supplied during the War of the Austrian Succession. His son James, not yet twenty-one years of age, had joined the business by 1754. Prior to this he had been a 'timber merchant' of Blackfriars and in 1756 was dealing in hemp with a stock at Southwark valued for insurance purposes at £1,800.[63]

Robert Norman died in 1757, leaving to James the remainder of the mill lease, two-thirds of his stock in trade, £4,000 with which to continue the business, the share in the freehold land at Barking, and a lease on a powder magazine near Liverpool held from the City Corporation. This had been held jointly with Underhill of Bedfont and Pearse of Faversham. The other third of the stock was for his wife and two daughters. Stock included mill stones belonging to the horse mills, while the horses, harness, waggons, carts, ploughs, hay and corn were to be counted as part of his residuary estate. He also left £50 to Thomas

---

[57] VCH *Surrey*, iii (1910), p. 454
[58] SH Northumberland Papers, DXXII 5g (1), 23, 24 June 1720.
[59] 5 George II, c. XXVI, 1718, *Statutes at Large*, v, p. 233.
[60] PROB 11 656, January 1733.
[61] SH DXXII 5g (3), 26, 27 June 1728.
[62] SH DXXII 5a (4), April 1771.
[63] GL Hand in Hand Insurance 8674.75, p. 159, No. 43623, 9 February 1749; HIHI 8674.86, p. 123, No. 76576, 15 April 1756; Sun Fire Insurance 11936.117, p. 228, No. 153802, 14 September 1756.

Stevens, his clerk of works at the mill, who continued in the post under James Norman.[64]

James's wife Susanna was a grand daughter of Sir John Barnard, who had held the lease at Bedfont mills earlier in the century; her father, Sir Thomas Hankey, was married to Sir John's daughter Sarah.[65] At his death in December 1762, James left the business to Susanna, with provision to be made for his mother from the annual profits, either from the overall profit after deduction of costs and expenses or, if Susanna should be in partnership, from her share. It was to be £200 if the clear profit was £1,000, £150 if between £900 and £1,000, £100 if between £800 and £900, but nil if less than £800.[66] Initially, contracts were in Susanna Norman's name alone but from March 1763 until 1770 she was in partnership with her brother-in-law Thomas Sutton. Sutton, an attorney of Basinghall Street in London, was married to Jane Hankey, Susanna's sister.[67] In 1767, Susanna married Beaumont Hotham, later the MP for Wigan and one of the Barons of the Court of Exchequer; he was knighted in 1775.[68] After his marriage Hotham became Sutton's partner at the mills. James Norman's sisters and their husbands, by now owners of the share in the Barking land, leased and then sold it in 1771, and 1792 respectively to the current partners.[69]

Oare mills, Kent

Located to the south west of Oare Creek in the parish of Davington.

Eighteenth century gunpowder makers: Francis Grueber Sr & Jr, by 1719–30; Francis Grueber Jr, 1730–43; Richard Chauncy & Thomas Vigne, June 1745–December 1760; Toby Chauncy, January 1761–October 1762; Stephen Grueber, January–June 1768; Grueber, Pigou & Andrews, June 1768–98; Pigou & Andrews, from 1798.

The Grueber family supplied the Ordnance Office from the end of the seventeenth century to 1743.[70] Francis Sr ran both the Oare mills, established by 1719, and nearby Faversham mills.[71] A Francis Grueber is also known to have leased Chilworth mills in 1728.[72] After his

---

64 PROB 11 829, March 1757.
65 *The Complete Peerage*, vi (London 1926), p. 578.
66 PROB 11 882, December 1762.
67 *Burke's Extinct and Dormant Baronetcies* (1844), p. 513; see Bedfont mills.
68 *Complete Peerage*, p. 578.
69 SH DXXII 5g (3), May 1771; DXXII 5f (1), March 1792.
70 WO 51/62, p. 36, 26 June 1701, contract 23 April 1696; see ch. 9.
71 Percival, *The Faversham Gunpowder Industry*, pp. 4, 5.
72 See Chilworth mills.

father's death in 1730 Francis Jr continued at Faversham until 1733, when replaced by Pearse, and at Oare until 1743. He was in financial difficulties by 1740 and declared bankrupt in 1745.[73]

The remainder of the twenty-one year lease of Oare mills was taken by Chauncy & Vigne, who agreed contract with the Office in November of that year.[74] The two had difficulty in maintaining a regular supply of gunpowder during the Seven Years War; both men died in 1760, Chauncy at seventy years of age.[75] The partnership of Pigou & Andrews, who joined Stephen Grueber, was later at Dartford mills also.[76] Grueber termed himself 'agent' of the partnership when he requested purchase of unserviceable powder from the Office in 1771. This was later followed by contract for the supply of new.[77] In 1776, Oare mills had one of the earliest examples of equipment for the steam drying of gunpowder.[78]

The co-partnership between Chauncy & Vigne, both merchants of Walbrook, commenced on 24 June 1745. It was agreed that at his death Chauncy's share in the business should go to his second son Toby provided he settle for the full value with his father's executors. If Toby then survived Vigne he would take over the latter's share too and pay the solicitors the appropriate sum.[79] As both partners died in 1760, Toby took over the entire business which he ran until the mill lease expired in October 1762.[80]

Richard Chauncy held the 1,340-acre Edgcote Manor in Northamptonshire, inherited from his father of the same name, together with £5,000.[81] He also held the freehold of Kingsmill Manor, part of the Faversham estate.[82] He was a director of the East India Company between 1737 and 1754, and chairman in 1748, 1750, and 1753.[83] As a linen draper he also held a three-storeyed house in Walbrook valued for insurance purposes at £2,000.[84] Vigne was also in partnership with Robert Myer, his brother-in-law and Peter Luard. This had ended by 1754, at which time the entire business stock was held by Vigne and

[73] See ch. 9; *London Gazette*, April 1745.
[74] See appendix 2, table 1; CCA U3/138/11/4, Poor Law Assessment Book, Davington, 1755–68.
[75] PROB 11 861, December 1760; George Baker, *The History and Antiquities of the County of Northampton* (1822), pp. 494–5.
[76] CCA U3/138/11/4
[77] WO 47/77, p. 103, 8 February 1771.
[78] See ch. 10.
[79] PROB 11 861, December 1760.
[80] WO 47/60, pp. 245, 292, 6, 22 October 1762.
[81] Baker, *County of Northampton*, pp. 494–5.
[82] See ch. 9.
[83] See ch. 8.
[84] GL Hand in Hand Insurance 8674.89, p. 225 No. 34163, 1 February 1758.

valued for insurance purposes at £10,000. The nature of the stock is unspecified but may have been linen, the subject of insurance a few years later.[85]

Waltham Abbey mills, Essex

Located on the River Lea in the parish of Waltham Holy Cross.

Eighteenth century gunpowder makers were William Walton, 1702–March 1711; Philippa Walton, 1711–33; Philippa & John Walton, 1733–49; John Walton 1749–August 1757; Thomas & Bourchier Walton, August 1757–78; Bourchier Walton, by January 1779; James Walton, June 1779–87.

These were established as gunpowder mills in 1665 by the Hudson family.[86] Most members of the Walton family who followed held property in London from where their trade in gunpowder was conducted. William Walton's first contract was dated February 1702.[87] He also manufactured gunpowder, probably by horse power, at Balham House, Tooting Bec in Surrey during the same period.[88] Philippa Walton his widow, left with nine young children, continued the business after him. Originally of Balham in Surrey, and subsequently of Ongar in Essex, she was a daughter of John Bourchier MD, of the same county.[89] In 1718, the powder mills and lands were sold by Samuel Bluck to Alexander Cleeve and Jane Bourchier, Philippa's brother-in-law and sister respectively. The mills were to be for the use of Philippa and her heirs during her lifetime.[90] In May 1732 they were sold to Philippa and to her son John.[91]

Philippa Walton also owned a quarter share of four acres of freehold land and a powder magazine at Barking Creek, land purchased in 1720 in conjunction with the powder makers of Molesey, East Bedfont, Faversham, and Oare mills.[92] The Waltons' share was later sold to the

[85] GL Royal Exchange Assurance 7252.1, p. 221 No. 27139, September 1754; REA 7252.2, p. 40 No. 30384, December 1754; REA 7252.7, p. 216 No. 33308, July 1759.
[86] Fairclough, 'Early Gunpowder', 15.
[87] WO 51/65, p. 8, 30 June 1702.
[88] Keith Fairclough, 'Gunpowder production at Balham House', *London's Industrial Archaeology*, 4 (1989), 32.
[89] Memorial to Philippa Walton in parish church of Mickleham, Surrey.
[90] PROB 11/766, December 1748; PROB 11/775, December 1749; SH Northumberland Papers DXXII 5a (4) 3, p. 7 Abstract of title to land at Barking, 1846.
[91] Ibid.
[92] SH DXXII 5g (1), 23 June 1720.

government. In 1833 it was sold by the government to William Tinkler of Chilworth mills.[93] Philippa was accompanied in the business by her second son John from 1733. Although Ordnance contracts continued to bear both names during the War of the Austrian Succession, and she continued to be involved until her death at the age of seventy-four in 1749, Philippa Walton spent her final years in Mickleham in Surrey. Undoubtedly, John had been in charge at the mill for some time.[94] At his death he left the mills to Thomas Walton, who was then joined by another brother, Bourchier.[95] The latter was a director of the East India Company from 1760 until 1762.[96]

Although Philippa's eldest son William of Yarmouth in Norfolk was not involved with the business his son James acquired the property in June 1779 in the apparent absence of any direct heir of the uncles who had run the business before him.[97] The mills eventually became the property of John Walton, nephew and heir of James. It was this John who sold the mills, together with the land at Barking Creek, to the Crown. Negotiations commenced in 1787 but, undoubtedly more careful after the confusion surrounding the sale of Faversham mills, the Ordnance officers expressed doubts about title to certain lands, as the result of claims by Sir William Wake of Waltham. There was no immediate conveyance. The Ordnance Office took possession but the sale price of £10,000 was invested by its treasurer in January 1789 in the purchase of three per cent reduced annuities to the value of £13,688 12s 6d. These were in the joint names of Walton, William Smith the Ordnance treasurer, and Augustus Rogers its secretary, with the dividends to be received by Walton. Final settlement was not achieved until 1795.[98]

Worcester Park mills, Surrey

Located on the river Hogsmill in the hamlet of Tolworth in the parish of Long Ditton. Also known as Long Ditton, Malden, or Tolworth mills.

Eighteenth century gunpowder makers: William Taylor, 1720–March 1764; Taylor's executors John Bland, Thomas Gasson, and Isabella

[93] SH DXXII 5a (4), Abstract of title, 1846.
[94] ERO D/P 75/11/8, 23 August 1733 Poor Rate book; PROB 11/775, March 1749.
[95] PROB 11/832, July 1757.
[96] See ch. 8.
[97] SUPP 5 682/5 14 August 1795; SUPP 5 682/38 14 August 1795.
[98] SUPP 5 682/38, 14 August 1795; KAO U145 27/2, 17 December 1787, agreement for purchase of mills.

Wood on behalf of William Taylor Jr, March 1764–74; William Taylor, son of William Taylor, from 1774.

The mills were at, or near the site of those which supplied the Crown in the sixteenth and early seventeenth centuries. Those mills were run by the Evelyn family from 1589; members of the family also ran powder mills in other parts of Surrey; they eventually lost the monopoly of supply in 1636.[99] For a short period, 1607–17, the patent was in the name of the Earl of Worcester, keeper of the Great Park of Nonsuch in which the mills were situated, and it was obviously from him that the area and the later mills gained their name.[100] Part of the original Great Park was purchased by William Taylor in 1752, including the mills and approximately 300 acres of farmland for a sum of £7,300.[101] It is likely that Taylor was first at the site in 1720, although this may have been a time when the mills were in disrepair and prior to the actual establishment of the business.[102] The first recorded contract between Taylor and the Ordnance Office was not until December 1740 and first delivery in June 1741.[103] He lived in Putney and in 1748 was termed 'merchant of Fish Street Hill, with a warehouse at St John, Wapping.[104] The estate, by now termed Worcester Park, was held previously by the Walter family.

At Taylor's death in March 1764, the mills and lands were left in trust for his son William, aged 11, until his coming of age. The trustees were John Bland, banker of Lombard Street in London, Thomas Gasson, nephew of Taylor, and Isabella Wood of St Mary, Newington. Gasson, who appears to have been managing the mills recently on Taylor's behalf, was the main trustee and, as such, was to make an inventory of mill stock, assess any debts due, or owing from the business and also the sum required to continue production. Taylor estimated that he himself had undertaken management of the mills and mill lands with a fund of £4,000; he now directed by his will that if Gasson employ the same he was to be at liberty to take half of the annual profits and, on young William's coming of age, £1,000 of the capital sum, leaving the latter the remainder.[105] The latter ran the business from May 1774 until 1852.

99 Giuseppi, VCH Surrey, pp. 314–17; see ch. 1.
100 Dent, The Quest for Nonsuch, p. 218.
101 C 54 5887, Close Rolls 25–29 G II Part 3, 26 February 1752.
102 G. F. Prosser, Select Illustrations of the County of Surrey (1828).
103 WO 51/146, p. 134, 16 June 1741.
104 GL Hand in Hand Insurance 8674.72, p. 186 No. 38700, June 1748.
105 PROB 11 897, March 1764; WO 51/228 p. 247, 8 March 1766.

Gunpowder and the Ordnance Office

Table 1
The supply of gunpowder to the Ordnance Office 1740–9

The total supplied is that which passed proof; this includes both new and reworked powder. Quantities in barrels.

Supply during the War of the Austrian Succession, 1740–8

Powder makers	Period under contract	Total supplied	Percentage, new
Pearse & Stevens	Apr 1740 – Oct 1748	35,301	76
Walton	Apr 1740 – Dec 1748	24,679	80
Underhill	Apr 1740 – Dec 1748	21,764	84
Pyke & Edsall	Dec 1740 – Dec 1748	12,055	78
Norman	Feb 1740 – Dec 1748	11,809	78
Taylor	Dec 1740 – Dec 1748	11,069	72
Eade	Oct 1745 – Nov 1748	2,620	74
Chauncy & Vigne	Nov 1745 – Nov 1748	2,098	81
Grueber	Dec 1741 – Oct 1743	585	83
Combined total of new and reworked powder		121,980	
Percentage, new			78

Supply of reworked powder in first year of peace 1749 (no new powder)

Pearse & Stevens	1,382
Walton	760
Pyke & Edsall	755
Underhill	713
Chauncy & Vigne	661
Eade	659
Norman	615
Taylor	605
Combined total	6,150

Comparison with the Seven Years War

Combined total of new and reworked powder supplied during Seven Years War and preceding year: complete years 1755–62	115,948	
Percentage of total which was new powder		99.47
Mean annual supply for the nine-year period of the War of the Austrian Succession	13,553	
Mean annual supply for the eight-year period of the Seven Years War (complete years 1755–62)	14,493	

(For reworked powder (1757) see table 3. From analysis of consignments of gunpowder received 1740–62: WO 51 Ordnance Bill Books)

Table 2
Prices paid by the Ordnance Office
for new and reworked gunpowder 1740–9

Prices paid per barrel of new gunpowder 1740–8

Mid-February 1740 – mid-February 1741	£0 14s
Mid-February 1741 – mid-December 1748	£1 0s

Prices paid for reworked powder October 1740 – December 1748

The price fluctuated between £0 14s, £0 16s 6d, and £1 0s.

Fluctuation in price may have been due to government incentives connected with the reworking of unserviceable powder similar to those for the preparation of new powder during the Seven Years War. This cannot be confirmed due to the absence of extant Ordnance minutes for the period.

Prices paid for reworked powder in first year of peace 1749

(No new powder was prepared at this time.)

6 December 1748 – 10 March 1749	£1 0s
15 April 1749 – 16 December 1749	£0 14s

The method of payment chosen by the makers was in the form of saltpetre. The quantity per barrel of powder is not specified, but is likely to have been between that specified as an alternative payment in the contracts of December 1754 and that proposed by the makers in December 1749; these were the quantity of grough petre equal to 25 and 30 lb respectively of double refined petre.

(WO 51 Ordnance Bill Books 1740–49)

Table 3
Prices paid by the Ordnance Office
for new and reworked gunpowder 1755–66

(See also chapters 2 and 4)

Price per barrel of new powder 1755–1763

December 1754– April 1755
Grough saltpetre equivalent to 25 lb double refined petre, or 31¼ lb unserviceable powder (at the option of the Board). No money payment involved.

April 1755– November 1756
£0 17s 6d or 36 lb unserviceable powder or grough saltpetre equivalent to 28 lb refined saltpetre (saltpetre was preferred by the makers).

November 1756 – January 1757
£0 17s 6d. Payment now solely in money; no further choice of method of payment until December 1761.

January 1757– March 1763
Payment according to results of certain money incentives made by the Office for improved supply.

7 January 1757
Additional £0 2s 6d per barrel (ie. £1 0s per barrel) if a minimum of 80 barrels pass proof of each minimum consignment of 100 submitted.

11 March 1757
£1 0s per barrel if 80% pass proof of whatever quantity submitted.

23 October 1761
Additional £0 5s per barrel (£1 5s) for every 100 passing proof providing 80% pass of whatever quantity submitted.

December 1761
Return to choice of payment either in money (as above) or of 36 lb. of unserviceable powder.

Price per barrel of new powder in peacetime 1765–6

£1 2s 6d (No powder, new or reworked was purchased during 1764)

Price per barrel of reworked powder

The only powder reworked for the Office and returned to store was in 1757, (combined total of 620 barrels) for which each maker was paid at the same rate as for new.

(From analysis of contracts, warrants, and consignments 1755–66: WO 47; WO 51 Ordnance Minute Books and Bill Books)

Table 4
Unserviceable government gunpowder sold to the powder makers

This was for private use, by direct sale, or as makers' chosen method of payment. Quantities in barrels. DS – Direct Sale: PNP – Payment for new powder. It should be noted that the price of old powder purchased by the makers included the value of the saltpetre content; new powder sold by them to the Office did not. Saltpetre for new powder was supplied by the Office.

1755

Name	Total	Month	Price per barrel
Eade & Bridges	800 (DS)	Jan Feb Mar Apr (200 each)	£2 10s
Pryce	700 (DS)	Mar (200 & 300) Aug (200)	£2 10s
Walton	600 (DS)	June (100) Aug (200)	£2 10s
		Sept (300)	£3 0s
Pyke & Edsall	400 (DS)	May & Aug (200 each)	£2 10s
Underhill & Ravens	400 (DS)	May & Aug (200 each)	£2 10s
Taylor	200 (DS)	July	£2 10s
Chauncy & Vigne	200 (DS)	Apr	£2 10s

Requests refused: Eade & Bridges (May & June) Walton (May)
Chauncy & Vigne (July)

1758

Name	Total	Month	Price per barrel
Pryce	300 (DS)	Mar (200) July (100)	£3 5s
Walton	600 (DS)	Mar & Apr (300 each)	£3 5s
Eade & Bridges	200 (DS)	June	£3 5s

(Office stated that sale to latter partnership to be in proportion
to quantity of new powder passing proof; proportion not specified)

1761

Name	Total	Month	Price per barrel
Eade & Bridges	225 (PNP)	Dec	£2 15s

(This is stated to have been payment for new powder at the rate of
36 lb per barrel, as per contract of Dec 1754 (table 3). In practice
this appears to have been at the rate of 46 lb).

1762

Name	Total	Month	Price per barrel
Eade & Bridges	223 (PNP)	Feb	£2 15s
Eade & Bridges	223 (PNP)	Mar	£2 15s
Eade & Bridges	223 (PNP)	June	£2 15s
Eade & Bridges	223 (PNP)	Aug	£2 15s

Name	Total	Month	Price per barrel
Eade & Bridges	223 (PNP)	Nov	£2 15s
Eade & Bridges	203 (DS)	Oct	£2 15s

1763 (until March only)

Eade & Bridges	110 (PNP)	Jan	£2 15s
Eade & Bridges	200 (DS)	Mar	£2 15s
Norman	223 (PNP)	Mar	£2 15s
Norman	300 (DS)	Mar	£2 15s

(From analysis of Ordnance Office transactions pertaining to unserviceable gunpowder 1755–63: WO 47/45–61 Ordnance Minute Books)

Table 5
Annual totals of gunpowder agreed at contract 1755–8

There was no agreed annual total specified by the Office after 1758 other than individual agreements, usually as the result of incentive. Only the combined annual total agreed is given. For combined annual totals actually delivered and those passing proof see table 7. Quantities in barrels.

1755

Contracts of December 1754

Agreement for each man or partnership, 485 per month or 4,850 per year
Combined annual total expected, 19,400
(Contract with Pryce on which contracts of Chauncy & Vigne, Eade & Bridges, and Walton were based)

Contracts of April 1755: individual agreements

Powder maker	April	barrels per week thereafter	annual total
Norman	50	40	1,450
Pyke & Edsall	30	50	1,780
Underhill & Ravens	50	50	1,800
Taylor	50	50	1,800
Therefore, annual total expected from April contract			6,830
Combined annual total expected for 1755 from both groups			26,230

1756 and 1757

Annual total expected for each of these years is based on the agreements for
1755: i.e.   December contract 4,850 for each maker   19,400
            April contract 2,600 for each of three makers   7,800
            and for the fourth maker   2,080

1757 included the agreement for 10 barrels per week from 5 July for the
remainder of the year for Smith & Hill: i.e. 25 weeks (250)

Therefore, total expected for 1756   29,280
Total expected for 1757   29,530

1758

Ordnance Board compelled to lower agreements due to supply far short of
above expectations. Makers now asked to state own individual annual targets.
No evidence of agreement with either Chauncy & Vigne, or Pryce; it must be
assumed that Pryce continued with original agreement of 4850/yr

Underhill & Ravens	3,500	Walton	3,000	Pyke & Edsall	2,500
Norman	2,000	Taylor	1,500	Smith & Hill	1,300
Eade & Bridges	800				

Therefore, expected combined annual total 1758   19,450

(From analysis of Ordnance Office contracts 1754–63: WO 47 & WO
51)

Table 6
Gunpowder submitted to the Ordnance Office
and percentage passing proof 1755–65

All gunpowder listed below is new powder as opposed to old, reworked. Only that passing proof went into store (% passing proof in brackets). No new contracts in 1764. Certain makers changed during the period (See mills) Ordnance records refer to powder makers rather than mills.

	1755	1756	1757	1758	1759	1760	1761	1762	1763	1764	1765
B.Pryce	1,018	2,624	2,499	607	396	Mills sold to Crown May 1759					
	(41)	(87)	(86)	(93)	(97)						
Faversham mills under Crown					637	1,370	1,319	1,838	1,809	1,183	2,378
					(07)	(63)	(79)	(84)	(86)	(73)	(91)
Chauncy & Vigne	733	532	–	–	150	342	250	273	–	–	–
	(69)	(89)			(00)	(80)	(76)	(07)			
Eade & Bridges	289	856	332	1,622	2,115	1,606	1,253	2,709	150	–	247
	(87)	(81)	(51)	(84)	(73)	(95)	(93)	(96)	(91)		(99)
Norman	451	1,326	881	1,515	1,808	1,513	1,159	3,264	111	–	–
	(79)	(77)	(88)	(88)	(70)	(96)	(94)	(93)	(93)		
Pyke & Edsall	1,366	2,745	1,804	2,592	2,934	2,646	2,154	2,326	572	–	323
	(93)	(91)	(99)	(97)	(87)	(94)	(87)	(82)	(06)		(80)
E.Pryce	Commenced May 1759				570	952	831	1,021	114	–	–
					(91)	(69)	(85)	(77)	(20)		
Smyth & Hill	Commenced	61	1,393	2,669	2,366	2,489	3,806	861	136	695	
	mid-1757		(62)	(67)	(65)	(74)	(75)	(64)	(54)	(82)	(81)
Taylor	822	1,357	1,685	1,602	1,457	1,104	1,393	2,177	264	–	56
	(84)	(82)	(81)	(89)	(91)	(99)	(95)	(93)	(39)		(82)
Underhill & Ravens	1,730	4,541	3,365	3,217	3,033	2,797	2,023	4,127	317	–	110
	(92)	(82)	(76)	(81)	(91)	(91)	(89)	(87)	(99)		(96)
Walton	2,341	3,994	3,676	3,650	3,926	3,826	3,572	4,242	1,213	–	370
	(64)	(78)	(82)	(82)	(81)	(96)	(99)	(94)	(94)		(100)

(From analysis of gunpowder deliveries and proof results 1755–65: WO 47/45–64)

Table 7(a)
Supply of gunpowder to the Ordnance Office 1755–62

Quantities in barrels; all new powder. See also tables on supplies agreed at contract, and supplies from individual powder makers.

1755	1756	1757	1758	1759	1760	1761	1762
Combined annual total expected according to agreements in individual contracts. (No specific agreement after 1758)							
26,230	29,280	29,530	19,450				
Combined annual total delivered for proof							
8,750	17,975	14,303	16,198	19,695	18,522	16,443	25,783
Combined annual total successful at proof							
6,582	14,941	11,849	13,758	15,363	16,302	14,631	21,902
Total successful as percentage of total delivered							
75	83	83	85	78	88	89	85
Number of mills supplying gunpowder, including Faversham under Crown							
8	8	8/9	9	9	10	10	10

Table 7(b)
Supply of gunpowder to the Ordnance Office 1763–70

1763	1764	1765	1766	1767	1768	1769	1770
Combined annual total delivered for proof							
5,411	1,319	4,179	10,982	9,859	9,312	7,338	3,066
Combined annual total successful at proof							
3,903	973	3,759	9,558	7,292	6,734	6,402	1,719
Total successful as percentage of total delivered							
72	74	90	87	74	72	87	56
Number of mills supplying gunpowder, including Faversham under Crown							
9	0	7	7	8	8	8	3
		from October					

(Tables 7(a) and 7(b) from analysis of all deliveries, contracts, and results at proof 1755–70: WO 47/45–76 Ordnance Minute Books, Surveyor General; WO 51/144–234 Ordnance Bill Books)

Table 8
English and Dutch stock November 1756 – August 1759

Returns from Ordnance officers at the magazines of Greenwich, Upnor, Gravesend and Tilbury, Plymouth, Portsmouth, and Sheerness. This includes powder 'under order for issue'. Quantities in barrels.

Date	Total English	Total Dutch	Combined total	% English	% Dutch
1756					
November	6,800	6,105	12,905	53	47
December	8,016	5,980	13,996	57	43
1757					
January	8,426	5,768	14,194	59	41
February	6,095	4,587	10,682	57	43
March	5,694	4,289	9,983	57	43
April	4,715	10,008	14,723	32	68
May	6,400	10,570	16,970	38	62
June	6,250	10,636	16,886	37	63
July	4,857	10,126	14,983	32	68
August	3,172	9,157	12,329	26	74
September	3,569	12,369	15,965	22	78
October	3,290	11,670	14,960	22	78
November	3,307	11,535	14,842	22	78
December	unrecorded				
1758					
January	2,841	14,473	17,314	16	84
February	2,280	14,116	16,396	14	86
March	4,464	13,833	18,297	24	76
April	4,387	10,173	14,560	30	70
May	3,506	9,950	13,456	26	74
June	4,470	8,284	12,754	35	65
July	5,348	7,156	12,504	43	57
August	6,636	6,744	13,380	50	50
September	6,721	5,722	12,443	54	46
October	5,499	4,884	10,383	53	47
November	5,041	4,818	9,859	51	49
December	6,421	4,313	10,734	60	40
1759					
January	6,110	788	6,898	89	11
February	5,736	766	6,502	88	12
March	6,834	886	7,720	89	11
April	4,541	716	5,257	86	14
May	6,140	680	6,820	90	10
June	5,690	675	6,365	89	11
July	4,593	675	5,268	87	13
August	3,822	625	4,447	86	14

(1756–9: WO 47/48–54; returns were only made for the above period)

Table 9
Prices and quantities of saltpetre 1754–63

Quantities supplied by, and prices paid to the East India Company

Year of supply	Quantity (tons)	Price per ton	Total price
1754	200	£45 0s (£2 5s cwt)	£ 9,000
1755	200	£45 0s	£ 9,000
1756	400	£45 0s	£18,000
1757	500	£53 0s (£2 13s cwt)	£26,500
1758	500	£53 0s	£26,500
1759	500	£53 0s	£26,500
1760	500	£53 0s	£26,500
1761	500	£53 0s	£26,500
1762	500	£53 0s	£26,500
1763	500	£53 0s	£26,500

Price increase for 1757 was according to standing agreement between Ordnance Board and East India Company for such increase in time of war.

From February 1763 there was agreement for some of the Company's stock to be stored at the Tower and for the Company to sell any quantity from that store provided it retained sufficient for the Ordnance Board's order for each following year (i.e. equal to quantity purchased the previous year). Until required by the Board all stock in peacetime was to remain on the Company's accounts.

(WO 47/61 p. 78. 11 Feb 1763)

Price of saltpetre at the East India Company open sales at India House
(as reported by the Ordnance storekeeper of saltpetre to the Board, 1758–63)

March	1758	£5 3s per cwt
August	1759	£5 0s
August	1760	£4 10s 6d
October	1760	£4 0s 6d
March	1761	£3 10s
June	1761	£3 11s – £3 18s
September	1761	£3 15s 6d
July	1762	£4 1s – £4 4s
September	1762	£4 3s
March	1763	£4 6s

APPENDIX 2

Deposits to the Ordnance Office by powder makers for receipt of saltpetre

Deposits made at rate of £60 per ton (£3 per cwt). For each contract for either 485 or 242 1/2 barrels of powder the deposit was £1,200 or £600 for 20 tons or 10 tons respectively. Deposits in the form of East India Bonds, Victualling Bills, South Sea Annuities, Ordnance Debentures, or Navy Bills. The Office received petre in grough format 15% refraction.

(From orders, deliveries, and payments 1754–63: WO 51 & WO 47 Ordnance Minute Books and Bill Books)

Table 10
Main locations receiving gunpowder

Locations in Britain & Ireland

Outports, for Royal Naval ships: Portsmouth, Plymouth, Woolwich, Chatham, Sheerness, Upnor, Gravesend & Tilbury

Port with small store – Kinsale

Ports supplied for specific naval ships: Hull, Leith, Aberdeen, Milford Haven

The ten main garrisons: Berwick, Hull, Chester, Pendennis, Jersey, Guernsey, Edinburgh, Stirling, Fort William, Carlisle

Smaller forts & castles supplied from outport divisional land service stock

Army regiments in the field, incl. encampments in SE England. Supplied either direct or from nearest garrison or outport

Cinque Ports: Deal, Dover, Walmer, & Sandown Castles, Sandgate, & Archcliffe Forts

Beacons and Batteries on S. Coast

Royal Artillery Regiment at Woolwich under direct administration of Ordnance Office

Woolwich, for preparing ammunition & testing ordnance

Tower of London, for testing small arms. Some storage of Dutch powder

Marines

Militia, from mid-1759

Dublin, to supplement powder made in Ireland

Locations overseas

Ordnance bases in Colonies for supply of garrisons & Royal Naval ships. N. America, W. Indies, & Mediterranean

North America, for military action concerning British & Colonial troops

Germany, for British troops from July 1758

Royal Artillery Regiment accompanying East India Co. to India

Africa, for official defence of West coast trading posts

222

Table 11
Master General and Ordnance Board in the mid-eighteenth century

Position	Name	Other
Master General		
1755–8	Duke of Marlborough	
from 1759	Sir John Ligonier MP	Also Commander in Chief HM Forces 1757–66
Lieutenant General		
1749–57	Ligonier	
1758–60	Lord George Sackville MP	
from 1760	Marquis of Granby MP	
Surveyor General	Charles Frederick MP	Previously Clerk of Deliveries 1746–9
Clerk of the Ordnance		Previously Clerk of
1740–72	William Rawlinson Earle MP	of Deliveries 1732–40
Storekeeper		Previously Clerk
1746–62, 1765–78	Andrew Wilkinson MP	of Deliveries 1741–6
Clerk of Deliveries		
1751–8	Job Staunton Charlton MP	
from 1759	Charles Cocks MP	
Treasurer	Francis Gashry	South Sea Director
& Paymaster		1756–7
1751–62		

(WO 54/113 Quarter Book 1755; *Return of Members of Parliament, 1705–1796*, 11 (London 1878); Namier, Sir Lewis & John Brooke, *The House of Commons, 1754–90* (History of Parliament, London 1964)

223

Licences issued for shipment of gunpowder

The many licences issued during the Seven Years War are scattered individually among the varied entries of the Privy Council Registers. These include names of applicant, destination, ship, quantity of powder and, occasionally, intended use. Emphasis here is on scale of annual shipment and main areas involved. Port of embarkation is London unless otherwise stated. Quantity of powder (barrels) is followed by the number of licences involved (in brackets) if other than single. Locations are as given in the Registers. Tables should be studied in conjunction with text. (From analysis of all applications 1756–63: PC2 104–9 Privy Council Registers).

Table 12
Licences issued for shipment to British mines and quarries 1756–63

The entry 'Mines' indicates type unspecified. Destination is the centre for distribution; precise locations of mines are seldom given. Ten of the licences concerned embarkation from Bristol.

Destination	1756	1757	1758	1759	1760	1761	1762	1763
Aberystwyth, mines & lead mines	50	140	–	–	–	600	–	
Caernarvon, lead mines	–	–	–	–	–	–	150	–
Exeter, rock quarries & mines	–	86 (2)	–	–	50	–	–	–
Falmouth &/or Truro, tin mines	1,351 (6)	190 (2)	200 (2)	400	490	–	150	100
Falmouth & Penzance, tin mines	–	900 (3)	225 (3)	590	50 (2)	–	–	
Glasgow, lead & copper mines	–	150	–	–	–	–	–	100
Hull and/or Gainsborough, mines & lead mines	–	–	100	95	320 (3)	220 (2)	180 (2)	
Lancaster, mines	–	–	–	–	–	–	–	400

Destination	1756	1757	1758	1759	1760	1761	1762	1763
Leith,	25	220	360	426	440	313	170	–
lead & coal mines,	(3)	(7)	(7)	(5)	(5)	(2)		
& stone quarries								
Montrose,	–	–	–	–	40	–	–	–
Strontian lead mines								
Newcastle,	326	491	433	450	550	460	450	150
lead & coal mines,	(8)	(8)	(6)	(5)	(5)	(4)	(5)	
lime/ millstone quarries								
Padstow & Boscastle,	–	–	–	–	500	–	–	–
mines of Cornwall								
St Ives, mines	–	200	–	–	–	–	–	–
Scotland,	–	116	–	–	–	–	–	–
Duke of Queensbury's		(2)						
mines at Wanlockhead,								
& coal mines								
Whitehaven, mines	–	–	100	–	–	–	300	–
Annual totals	1,702	1,928	2,233	1,596	2,980	1,043	2,000	750

Table 13
Licences issued for shipment to Africa 1755–63

The majority of applications refer to slaves and/or onward route to the West Indies from Africa. These are minimum quantities only; excluded in the Privy Council registers are the large number of unspecified quantities exported by general licence (see text). Ten of the licences concerned embarkation from Whitehaven, five from Liverpool, two each from Portsmouth and Glasgow, and one from Poole.

One licence only issued for 1755, for 430 barrels from Liverpool.

Destination	1756	1757	1758	1759	1760	1761	1762	1763
Africa (unspecified)	69 (3)	20	338 (7)	477 (10)	889 (11)	1,336 (15)	604 (8)	40
Angola	342 (2)	–	200	–	17	20	80	–
Annamaboe	–	–	–	–	–	64	–	–
Bance Island	–	250 (2)	–	350 (2)	–	50	–	20
Bonny	102	–	–	–	–	–	–	–
Cape Coast Castle	–	170 (2)	–	–	224	–	552 (2)	–
Cape Coast Castle & James Fort	130	–	260	–	–	–	–	–
Gambia & River Gambia	37 (2)	60	–	–	–	–	–	–
Gold Coast	–	–	–	–	–	–	160 (2)	–
Guinea, Coast of	–	–	–	60	25	–	–	–
James Fort	–	45	–	–	40	110	95 (3)	–
Senegal	–	–	–	–	–	4	90	–
Senegal & Goree	–	–	–	–	20	140 (2)	90	–
Windward Coast	–	–	–	–	50	–	–	–
Windward Coast & Gold Coast	175 (3)	–	–	–	–	–	–	–
Windward Coast & River Gambia	45	–	–	–	–	–	–	–
Annual total	900	545	798	887	1,265	1,760	1,671	60

Table 14
Licences issued for shipment to North America 1756–63

Eight licences involved embarkation from Bristol, five from Poole, and two from Gosport.

Destination	1756	1757	1758	1759	1760	1761	1762	1763
North America (unspecified)	90	–	–	–	–	–	–	220
Boston	50	860 (7)	298 (5)	140 (2)	200	–	–	–
Georgia	40	–	15	–	–	–	–	80
Halifax	–	–	–	–	–	12	–	–
Hudsons Bay	112	108	116	141	120	124	148	–
Maryland	203 (4)	360 (6)	80 (2)	52	445 (6)	100	–	–
Massachusetts	–	40	–	–	–	–	–	–
New England	144	550 (4)	450 (3)	300 (2)	400 (2)	600 (3)	–	400 (2)
New York	20	780 (8)	490 (6)	170 (3)	120 (2)	–	–	160 (2)
Newfoundland	57	46 (2)	200 (2)	40	60	–	–	–
North Carolina	–	15	–	–	30	–	–	–
Nova Scotia	–	–	–	–	–	–	–	30
Pennsylvania	467 (5)	280 (2)	200	–	–	100	–	–
Philadelphia	20	990 (6)	200 (7)	653 (6)	1,305	50	–	200
Philadelphia & New York	–	–	200 (2)	15	–	–	–	–
Quebec	–	–	–	–	–	160 (5)	–	155 (2)
South Carolina	–	717 (6)	663 (9)	490 (8)	948 (7)	300 (3)	184 (4)	350 (3)
S. Carolina & Georgia	111	41	–	140 (3)	60	420 (3)	555 (2)	–
Virginia	744 (10)	372 (6)	490 (6)	860 (12)	910 (7)	500 (3)	160 (2)	200
Virginia & Maryland	–	150	–	100	160 (2)	150	–	150
Annual totals	2,058	5,309	3,402	3,141	4,758	2,516	1,047	1,945

Table 15
Licences issued for shipment to the West Indies 1756–63

Seven licences were for embarkation from Bristol. One licence only issued for 1755, of unspecified quantity, for defence & port duty for trading ships to the West Indies.

Destination	1756	1757	1758	1759	1760	1761	1762	1763
West Indies (unspecified)	–	20	–	–	–	–	–	–
Antigua	80 (2)	112 (2)	290 (5)	10	–	60	–	–
Antigua & Barbados	60	–	–	–	–	–	–	–
Barbados	70 (2)	210 (4)	–	50	–	40	–	–
Guadeloupe	–	–	–	–	25	20	–	–
Jamaica	286 (5)	250 (5)	300 (2)	–	86	30	–	–
Martinique	–	–	–	–	–	–	–	200
Montserrat	–	15	–	–	–	–	–	–
St Christopher	22 (2)	154 (4)	–	–	75 (3)	–	–	–
St Christopher & Antigua	–	–	–	–	200	–	–	–
Annual totals	518	761	590	60	386	150	–	200

Table 16
Other licences issued

Destination	Year	Quantity
Leith, for dealers in Scotland	1757	60
Hull	1758	50
Jersey, for defence		40
Bermuda	1760	30
Exeter, for Guinea trade		40
Island of Tayal		50
Bermuda, for inhabitants	1761	12
Canaries, for trade		20
Liverpool, for Africa trade		300

Table 17
Licences issued to the powder makers under contract

The number of licences in which makers were directly involved, but in which issue was in the names of others, is unknown. Most of the entries below already appear in the preceding tables.

Applicant	Destination	Quantity
1756		
Walton, Norman, Taylor	Falmouth, for tin mines of Cornwall	146
1757 none		
1758		
Eade & Wilton	Greenock, ships fitting for West Indies	30
Eade & Wilton	Folkestone, a privateer	16
Eade & Wilton	Scarborough, two new ships	12
1759		
Chauncy & Vigne	Philadelphia, inhabitants	56
Eade & Wilton	Whitby, three ships	22
Eade & Wilton	Hull, two ships	10
Smyth & Hill	New York, planters	50
Eade & Bridges	Barrowstoness, mines	30
Underhill & Ravens	Hull & Gainsborough, lead mines	95
Eade & Bridges	Barrowstoness, lead mines of Earl of Hopton	60
1760		
Underhill & Ravens	Maryland, inhabitants	25
Eade & Bridges	Montrose, lead mines	40
Eade & Bridges	Leith, lead & coal mines	50
Eade & Wilton	Whitby, ships for coal	unknown
Eade & Wilton	Guinea Coast & West Indies	25
Eade & Bridges	Guadeloupe, privateers	25
Underhill & Ravens	Hull & Gainsborough, lead mines	120
Eade & Bridges	St Christopher	30
T. & B. Walton	Portsmouth-London for reworking	450
Eade & Bridges	Leith, lead mines at Strontian	40
Taylor	Hull & Gainsborough, lead mines	100
Eade & Wilton	Africa trade	60
Eade & Bridges	Leith, lead & coal mines	100
1761		
Eade & Bridges	Liverpool, for Guinea Coast	150
Eade & Bridges	Barbados, private ships	40
Eade & Wilton	Jamaica, private ships	30
B. Pryce	Quebec, Indian trade	50
Eade & Bridges	Leith, coal mines	60

Applicant	Destination	Quantity
Eade & Bridges	Gibraltar, private ships	60
Underhill & Ravens	Hull & Gainsborough, lead mines	120
Taylor	Falmouth & Penzance, tin mines	50
Eade & Bridges	Leith, coal & lead mines	50
Underhill & Ravens	Newcastle, for mines	unknown

1762   none

Bibliography

Primary sources

The major manuscript sources for this study are certain classes of the War Office Series which contain the wide range of Ordnance Office records. These are held at the Public Record Office. At its abolition in 1855 the Office was merged with the War Office. Other important classes include those of the Admiralty, Chancery, Colonial Office, Customs, Ministry of Supply, Privy Council, Probate, State Papers, and Treasury. All sources in the text are to be found at the Public Record unless otherwise stated. Other sources are as listed.

Public Record Office
Piece numbers are given with class number to correspond with precise pieces and dates in the text.

War Office (all refer to the Ordnance Office)

WO 46/8	Ordnance Board out-letters/general correspondence, 1756–8
WO 47/34–96	Minutes, Surveyor General, 1749–80
WO 51/62, 65,	Bill Books, Series 2, 1701, 1702,
WO 51/144–234	1739–67
WO 52/47	Bill Books, Series 3, 1792
WO 54/113	Quarter Books: staff and salaries, 1755

Ordnance miscellanea (WO 55) holds a wide range of records, several sections of which are among the most important regarding the Ordnance Office:

WO 55/2, 3	Ordnance Reports, 1758 and 1762
WO 55/354–63	Entry Books of Orders in Council, and Warrants, 1753–62; majority concern artillery trains and additional ordnance
WO 55/427	Original warrants, 1759
WO 55/585	Return of Ordnance Buildings, 1820
WO 55/1585	Lands, rents, and buildings: Faversham mills, 1827
WO 55/2269	Plans of lands and buildings: Faversham mills, 1761
WO 55/1739	Receipts, issues, stores, including those to the Royal Navy: Ship Establishment Book, 1716
WO 55/1743	Ship Establishment Book, 1743

Admiralty

Adm. 1/4010–12	In-letters, Ordnance Board to Admiralty,	1755–62
Adm. 2/531	Out-letters, Admiralty to Ordnance Board,	1761

Chancery

C 11/2522/1   Chancery Proceedings, 1754
C 54/6047   Close Rolls, 1759

Colonial Office/Board of Trade

CO 5/1129, 1067   Reports, correspondence, America and West Indies, 1755, 1756
CO 326/28   Registers, Colonies General, 1756
CO 391/63   Minutes, Board of Trade, 1756

Customs

CUST 3/55–62   Imports and Exports, 1755–62

Ministry of supply

SUPP 5/64–115, 877   Royal Ordnance Factories, 1766–92

Privy Council

PC 2/104–5   Registers, 1755–6

Probate

PROB 6   Administrations
PROB 11   Registered Copy Wills

State Papers

SP 41/38   Military, 1755–60

Treasury

T 1/360–77   Treasury Papers, 1755–7
T 29/32,33   Minute Books,   1755–9
TS 21/874   Treasury Solicitor, deeds, 1748

Maps

MPH 250   Faversham mills, 1781 (WO 78/1212)
MR 909   Faversham mills, 1789 (WO 78/1517)

British Library, Department of Manuscripts

Add MS 32996, 33046   Additional Manuscripts: Newcastle Papers, Memoranda and papers relating to the Army and Navy
Add MS 37827   Additional Manuscripts: Underhill Collections

Canterbury Cathedral Archives
U3/138/11/4   Poor Law Assessment Book, Davington, Kent

Essex Record Office
D/P 75/11/8   Poor Rate Book, Waltham Holy Cross, Essex

Greater London Record Office
Acc 1319/27a   Lease, Hounslow mills
Acc 606/61b   Marriage settlement, Fogg of Bedfont

Guildford Muniment Room
RB 704   Loseley Manuscripts, correspondence
43/78–82   Deeds, Godwin-Austen Estates

Guildhall Library
8674 Hand in Hand Insurance
7252 Royal Exchange Assurance
11936 Sun Fire Insurance

Institute of Historical Research
List of Merchants trading to Africa, 1759

Kent Archives Office
U145 27/2 Purchase Agreement, Waltham Abbey Mills

Surrey Record Office
Northey Muniments, 2238/10/8,14 Ewell, Surrey

Syon House, Muniment Room
Northumberland Papers, BXIII, DXII, DXXII, MXIII, MXIV, NXII

Secondary sources

Place of publication, London, unless otherwise stated.

Books and journal articles
Anon., *Life of the late Thomas Coutts* (1822)
Atthill, R., 'The gunpowder mills of north Somerset', *The Countryman* (1971)
Baker, G., *The History and Antiquities of the County of Northampton* (1822)
Barclay, D., *Account of the Emancipation of the Slaves of Unity Valley Pen in Jamaica* (1801)
Bashforth, F., *A Mathematical Treatise on the Motion of Projectiles* (1873)
Batchelder, R. W. and Freudenberger, H., 'On the Rational Origins of the Modern Centralised State', *Explorations in Economic History*, 20 (1983)
Binney, J. E. D., *British Public Finance and Administration 1774–92* (Oxford 1958)
Blackman, H., 'The Story of the Old Gunpowder Works at Battle', *Sussex Archaeological Collections*, 64 (1923)
Bourne, H., *English Merchants* (1866; repr. New York 1969)
Bovill, E. W., 'Queen Elizabeth's Gunpowder', *Mariners' Mirror*, 33 (1947)
Brayley Hodgetts, E. A. (ed.), *The Rise and Progress of the British Explosives Industry* (1909)
Buchanan, B. J., 'A Comment on the Manufacture of Black Powder', *Industrial Archeology*, 2 (Washington 1976)

————— and Tucker, M. T., 'The Manufacture of Gunpowder: a study of the documentary and physical evidence relating to the Woolley Powder Works near Bath', *Industrial Archaeology Review*, 5 (1981)

Burke's Extinct and Dormant Baronetcies (1844)

Burt, R., 'Lead Production in England and Wales, 1700–1770', *Economic History Review*, 22 (1969)

Calendar of State Papers Domestic, 1603–34 (1857–63)

Campbell, R. H., *Carron Company* (Edinburgh 1961)

Carter, A. C., *Getting, spending and investing in early modern times* (Assen, Netherlands 1975)

Catalogue of the Civil and Mechanical Engineering Designs of John Smeaton (Newcomen Society 1950)

Chaudhuri, K. N., *The Trading World of Asia and the English East India Company, 1660–1760* (Cambridge 1978)

Christie, I. R., *Wars and Revolutions: Britain 1760–1815* (1982)

Clode, C. M., *The Military Forces of the Crown*, ii (1869)

Cobbett, W., *The Parliamentary History of England 1753–65*, xv (1813)

Coleman, R., 'The Manufacture and constituent Parts of Gunpowder', *Philosophical Magazine*, 9 (1801)

Complete Guide to London (1755, 1758, 1763)

Congreve, W., *A Statement of facts relating to the savings which have arisen from manufacturing gunpowder at the Royal Powder Mills and of improvements made in its strength and durability since 1783* (1811)

Corbett, J. S., *England in the Seven Years War* (2 vols., 1907)

The Court and City Register (1750–63)

Crocker, G., *Chilworth Gunpowder* (Guildford 1984)

————— *Gunpowder Mills Gazetteer* (Guildford 1988)

————— *The Gunpowder Industry* (Aylesbury, Bucks 1986)

Davies, K. G., *The Royal African Company* (1957)

Davis, R., *The Rise of the English Shipping Industry* (1962)

Debrett, J., *The History, Debates and Proceedings of both Houses of Parliament*, iii (1792)

————— *The History of the Proceedings and Debates of the House of Commons*, ix (1783)

Dent, J., *The Quest for Nonsuch* (1962, 2nd edn 1970)

Dickinson, H. W. and Straker, E., 'Charcoal and Pyroligneous Acid Making in Sussex', *Transactions of the Newcomen Society*, 18 (1938)

Ehrman, J., *The Younger Pitt* (1969)

Fairclough, K., 'Early Gunpowder Production at Waltham', *Essex Journal*, 20 (1985)

————— 'Gunpowder production at Balham House', *London's Industrial Archaeology*, 4 (1989)

Flinn, M., *Men of Iron, The Crowleys in the Early Iron Industry* (Edinburgh 1962)

The Gentleman's Magazine, 25–30 (1755–63)

Gillispie, C., *Science and Polity in France at the end of the old regime* (Princeton N. J. 1980).

Gordon, H., *The War Office* (1935)

Gradish, S. F., *The Manning of the British Navy during the Seven Years' War* (1980)

Hale, J. R., *Renaissance War Studies* (1983)

Hamilton, M., *Sir William Johnson: Colonial American, 1715–1763* (New York 1976)

Hartwell, R. M. (ed.), *The Causes of the Industrial Revolution in England* (1967)

Hart, W. H., *A Short Account of the Early Manufacture of Gunpowder in England* (1855)

Hasted, E., *The History and Topographical Survey of the County of Kent*, vi (Canterbury 1798)

Hime, H. W. L., *Gunpowder and Ammunition* (1904)

Hogg, O. F. G., *Artillery: Its origin, heyday and decline* (1970)

——— *English Artillery, 1326–1716* (1963)

——— *The Royal Arsenal* (2 vols., 1963)

Houlding, J. A., *Fit for Service: The training of the British Army 1715–1795* (Oxford 1981)

House of Commons Sessional Papers, xvii (1819)

Hutton, C., 'The Force of Fired Gunpowder and the initial Velocities of Cannon Balls', *Philosophical Transactions of the Royal Society*, 68 (1778)

Ingenhousz, J., 'An Account of a new kind of inflammable air or gas and a new theory on gunpowder', *Philosophical Transactions of the Royal Society*, 69 (1779)

John, A. H., 'War and the English Economy, 1700–1763', *Economic History Review*, 2nd series 7 (1955)

Journals of the House of Commons, xxvii–xxxiv (1754–72)

Judd, G. P., *Members of Parliament, 1734–1832* (New Haven 1955)

Kellock, K. A., 'London Merchants and the pre-1776 American Debts' *Guildhall Studies in London History*, 1 (1974)

Kennedy, P. M., *The Rise and Fall of British Naval Mastery* (1976, 2nd. edn 1983)

Keyes, S. K., *Dartford: further historical notes* (Dartford 1938)

Knox, J., *An Historical Journal of the Campaigns of North America* (1769)

Labaree, L. W. (ed.), *Royal Instructions to British Colonial Governors, 1670–1776*, i (New York 1935, repr. 1967)

Lewes, V. B. and Brame, J. S. S., *Service Chemistry* (1889 5th edn 1924)

Lewis, G. R., *The Stannaries; A Study of the English tin mines* (Harvard 1924)

Lewis, W. S. (ed.), *Horace Walpole's Correspondence* (Oxford 1967)

Lincoln, C. H. (ed.), *The Correspondence of William Shirley*, ii (New York 1912)

List of Proprietors of the Bank of England (1750)

Locke, A., *The Hanbury Family* (1916)

The London Gazette (1754–63)

MacInnes, C.M., *Bristol and the Slave Trade* (Bristol 1963).

Manning, O. and Bray, W., *The History and Antiquities of the County of Surrey* (3 vols., 1804–19)

'Memorial of the Gunpowder Merchants to the Lords of the Treasury in November 1818', *House of Commons Sessional Papers*, xvii (1819)

Middleton, C. R., 'A Reinforcement for North America, Summer 1757', *Bulletin of the Institute of Historical Research*, 41 (1968)

Miles, W. A., *Selim's Letters exposing the Mal-Practices of the Office of Ordnance* (1771)

Mockridge, A H., 'The proving of ordnance and propellants', *Journal of Royal Artillery*, 67 (1950)

Morrison, J. H., *The Underhills of Warwickshire* (Cambridge 1932).

Mortimer, *The Universal Director* (1763)

Munro, J. (ed.), *Acts of Privy Council of England, Colonial Series, 1745–66*, iv (1911)

Musson, A. E. (ed.), *Science, Technology, and Economic Growth in the Eighteenth Century* (1772)

—— and Robinson, E., 'Science and Industry in the late Eighteenth Century', *Economic History Review*, 2nd series 13 (1960)

Namier, L., 'Anthony Bacon, M.P., An Eighteenth Century Merchant', *Journal of Economic and Business History*, 2 (Harvard 1929)

—— 'Brice Fisher M.P., A mid-eighteenth century merchant and his connexions', *English Historical Review*, 42 (1927)

Namier, Sir Lewis., *The Structure of Politics at the Accession of George III* (1957)

—— and Brooke, J., *The House of Commons 1754–1790* (1964)

Needham, J., 'The Guns of Khaifeng-fu', *Times Literary Supplement* (11 January 1980)

Nef, J. U., 'The Progress of Technology and the Growth of Large Scale Industry in Great Britain 1540–1640', *Economic History Review*, 1st series 5 (1934)

Norton, R., *The Gunner, showing the whole Practise of Artillerie* (1628)

O'Callaghan, E. B. (ed.), *The Documentary History of the State of New York*, ii (Albany 1849)

Olson, A. G., 'The Virginia Merchants of London', *William and Mary Quarterly*, 3rd series 40 (1983)

Pares, R. and Taylor, A. J. P. (eds.), *Essays presented to Sir Lewis Namier* (1956)

Pargellis, S. (ed.), *Military Affairs in North America, 1748–1765* (New York 1936)

Parker, H. T., *The Bureau of Commerce in 1781 and its policies with respect to French industry* (Durham, N. C. 1979)

Partington, J. R., *A History of Greek Fire and Gunpowder* (Cambridge 1960)

Pennsylvania Archives, 1st. series 2 (Philadelphia 1853)

Percival, A. J., *The Faversham Gunpowder Industry and its development* (Faversham 1967)

Peters, M., *Pitt and Popularity* (Oxford 1980)

Philo, P. and Mills J., 'The Bedfont Gunpowder Mills', *London Archaeologist*, 5 (1985)

Pool, B., *Navy Board Contracts, 1660–1832* (1966)

Pressnell, L. S. ed., *Studies in the Industrial Revolution* (1960)

Price, J. M., *France and the Chesapeake* (Michigan 1973)

Prosser, G. F., *Select Illustrations of the County of Surrey* (1828)

Rawley, J. A., *The Transatlantic Slave Trade* (New York 1981)

Return of Members of Parliament, 1705–1796, ii (1878)

Riker, T. V., 'The Politics behind Braddock's Expedition', *American Historical Review*, 13 (1908)

Robins, B., *New Principles of Gunnery* (1742; new edn with notes by Charles Hutton 1805)

Rogers, H. C. B., *The British Army of the Eighteenth Century* (1977)

Rowe, W. J., *Cornwall in the Age of the Industrial Revolution* (Liverpool 1953)

Roy, I. (ed.), 'The Royalist Ordnance Papers 1642–1646', *Oxfordshire Record Society*, 43, 49 (1964–75)

Russell, C., *Science and Social Change 1700–1900* (1983)

Savory, Sir Reginald A., *His Britannic Majesty's army in Germany during the Seven Years War* (Oxford 1966)

Schomberg, I., *Naval Chronology* (1802)

Seymour, C., *A Topographical, Historical and Commercial Survey of the cities, towns and villages of the County of Kent* (Canterbury 1776)

Simmons, R. C., *The American Colonies* (1976)

Simmons, R. C. and Thomas, P. D. G. (eds.), *Proceedings and Debates of the British Parliaments respecting North America, 1754–1764*, i (New York 1982)

Simmons, W. H., *A Short History of the Royal Gunpowder Factory at Waltham Abbey* (1964)

Singer, C., Holmyard, E. J., Hall, A. R., Williams, T. I. (eds.), *A History of Technology*, iii (Oxford 1957)

Smith, D. J., 'Army Clothing Contractors and the Textile Industries in the Eighteenth Century', *Textile History*, 14 (1983)

Spain, R. J., 'The Loose Watermills', *Archaeologia Cantiana*, 88 (1973)

Statutes at Large, iii–xvi (new edn 1660–1793)

Stephenson, O. W., 'The Supply of Gunpowder in 1776', *American Historical Review*, 30 (1925)

Supple, B. *The Royal Exchange Assurance* (Cambridge 1970)

Sutherland, L. S., 'The City of London and the Devonshire-Pitt Administration 1756–1757', *Proceedings of the British Academy*, 46 (1961)

—— *The East India Company in Eighteenth Century Politics* (Oxford 1952)

Thayer, T., 'The Army Contractors for the Niagara Campaign', *William and Mary Quarterly*, 3rd series 14 (1957)

Thompson, Benjamin., 'New Experiments on Gunpowder', *Philosophical Transactions of the Royal Society*, 71 (1781)

Thompson, Sir Benjamin., 'Experiments to determine the Force of fired Gunpowder', *Philosophical Transactions of the Royal Society*, 87 (1797)

Thorne, J., *Handbook to the Environs of London* (1876, 2nd. edn Bath 1970)

Tomlinson, H. C., *Guns and Government* (1979)

Venn, T., *Military and Maritime Discipline* (1672)

Victoria County History of Essex, ii (1907)

Victoria County History of Kent, iii (1932)

Victoria County History of Middlesex, ii, iii (1911, 1962)

Victoria County History of Surrey, ii, iii (1905, 1910)

Ward, H. M., *Unite or Die* (Washington 1971)

Weyman, H. T., 'Members of Parliament for Bishops Castle', *Transactions of the Shropshire Archaeological Society*, 2nd series 10 (1898)

Whiteman, A., Bromley, J. S., and Dickson, P. G. M. (eds.), *Statesmen, Scholars and Merchants* (Oxford 1973)

Whitworth, R., *Field Marshal Lord Ligonier* (Oxford 1950)

Williams, L. J., 'A Carmarthenshire Ironmaster in the Seven Years' War', *Business History*, 2 (1959)

Unpublished Theses

Ashley, R., 'The organisation and administration of the Tudor office of ordnance' (B. Litt. thesis, University of Oxford, 1973).

Fraser, E. J. S., 'The Pitt-Newcastle coalition and the conduct of the Seven Years War, 1757–60' (D. Phil. thesis, University of Oxford 1976)

Lewis, D. E., 'The Office of Ordnance and the parliamentarian land forces 1642–8' (Ph. D thesis, Loughborough University of Technology 1976)

Middleton, C. R., 'The Administration of Newcastle and Pitt: the departments of state and the conduct of the war, 1754–60' (Ph. D thesis, University of Exeter 1969)

Parker, J. G., 'The directors of the East India Company, 1754–90' (Ph. D thesis, University of Edinburgh 1977)

Index

239